Human Chromosome Methodology

Contributors to This Volume

MURRAY L. BARR

SHEILA BRUNTON

LEROY P. CHRISTENSON

D. G. HARNDEN

WILLIAM J. MELLMAN

SUSUMU OHNO

KLAUS PATAU

WALTER J. RUNGE

WERNER SCHMID

J. H. TJIO

J. WHANG

JORGE J. YUNIS

Human Chromosome Methodology

Edited by

JORGE J. YUNIS

MEDICAL GENETICS LABORATORY
DEPARTMENT OF LABORATORY MEDICINE
UNIVERSITY OF MINNESOTA
MINNEAPOLIS, MINNESOTA

1965

ACADEMIC PRESS   New York and London

ACADEMIC PRESS INC.
111 Fifth Avenue, New York, New York 10003

United Kingdom Edition published by
ACADEMIC PRESS INC. (LONDON) LTD.
Berkeley Square House, London W.1

LIBRARY OF CONGRESS CATALOG CARD NUMBER 65-18443

PRINTED IN THE UNITED STATES OF AMERICA

List of Contributors

Numbers in parentheses indicate the pages on which the authors' contributions begin.

MURRAY L. BARR, Department of Anatomy, Faculty of Medicine, University of Western Ontario, London, Ontario, Canada (1)

SHEILA BRUNTON, Medical Research Council, Clinical Effects of Radiation Research Unit, Western General Hospital, Edinburgh, Scotland (57)

LEROY P. CHRISTENSON, School of Dentistry, Dental Illustration Laboratory, University of Minnesota, Minneapolis, Minnesota (129)

D. G. HARNDEN, Medical Research Council, Clinical Effects of Radiation Research Unit, Western General Hospital, Edinburgh, Scotland (57)

WILLIAM J. MELLMAN, Department of Pediatrics, University of Pennsylvania, Philadelphia, Pennsylvania (21)

SUSUMU OHNO, Department of Biology, City of Hope Medical Center, Duarte, California (75)

KLAUS PATAU, Department of Medical Genetics, University of Wisconsin, Madison, Wisconsin (155)

WALTER J. RUNGE, Department of Medicine, University of Minnesota, Minneapolis, Minnesota (111)

WERNER SCHMID, Section of Cytology, Department of Biology, The University of Texas M. D. Anderson Hospital and Tumor Institute, Houston, Texas (91)

J. H. TJIO, National Institute of Arthritis and Metabolic Diseases, Bethesda, Maryland (51)

J. WHANG, National Cancer Institute, Bethesda, Maryland (51)

JORGE J. YUNIS, Medical Genetics Laboratory, Department of Laboratory Medicine, University of Minnesota, Minneapolis, Minnesota (187)

Preface

Recent advances in human cytogenetics have stimulated widespread interest among many investigators in the medical and biological sciences. As a direct result of this interest, a genuine need has been felt for an authoritative and up-to-date treatise which would serve as a text and reference. Readily comprehensible chapters are offered covering each phase of laboratory investigation from the preparation of materials for sex chromatin and chromosome techniques for bone marrow, blood, skin, and gonadal specimens to the subject of autoradiography and chromosome identification. Included also are guides to microscopy and photomicrography as well as an up-to-date treatment of chromosomes in disease. It is hoped that this volume will serve as an adequate guide to laboratory techniques and their applications for research workers, students of genetics, and members of the medical profession involved in setting up a laboratory of cytogenetics.

JORGE J. YUNIS

Minneapolis, Minnesota
March, 1965

Contents

PREFACE vii

INTRODUCTION xiii

Sex Chromatin Techniques

Murray L. Barr

I.	Introduction	1
II.	Historical Sketch	2
III.	Morphological Characteristics of the Sex Chromatin	3
IV.	Sex Chromatin Techniques	5
V.	Origin of the Sex Chromatin	13
VI.	Sex Chromatin Patterns and Sex Chromosome Complexes	14
	References	16

Human Peripheral Blood Leucocyte Cultures

William J. Mellman

I.	General	22
II.	The Mononuclear Leucocyte as the Mitotic Cell in Culture	23
III.	Collection of Peripheral Blood Leucocytes and Preparation of Cell Inoculum	26
IV.	Initiation of Mitosis in Blood Cultures: The Role of Phytohemagglutinin and Other Potentially Mitogenic Agents	33
V.	Influence of Culture Conditions on Cell Proliferation	36
VI.	Preparation of Metaphase Spreads for Cytogenic Studies	38
VII.	Life Span of PHA Initiated Cultures: Evidence for Secondary Mitoses in Culture	40
VIII.	Further Application of the Leucocyte Culture System	41
IX.	Methods for Culturing Human Peripheral Blood Leucocytes	42
	References	46

Direct Chromosome Preparations of Bone Marrow Cells

J. H. Tjio and J. Whang

I.	Introduction	51
II.	Procedures	52
III.	Discussion	53
	References	56

The Skin Culture Technique

D. G. Harnden and Sheila Brunton

I.	Introduction	57
II.	Media and Materials	58
III.	Step by Step Procedure	63
IV.	General Discussion of Method	66
	Appendix	72
	References	73

Direct Handling of Germ Cells

Susumu Ohno

I.	Introduction	75
II.	Fixing, Squashing, and Staining Gonadal Material	76
III.	Various Methods of Pretreatment	77
IV.	Interpreting the Findings	85
V.	Summary	90
	References	90

Autoradiography of Human Chromosomes

Werner Schmid

I.	Introduction	91
II.	Methodology	94
III.	Synopsis and Sequence of Technical Procedures for	
	Autoradiography of Human Chromosomes	97
IV.	Techniques	98
	Appendix	108
	References	109

Bright Field, Phase Contrast, and Fluorescence Microscopy

Walter J. Runge

I.	Introduction	111
II.	Theory of Light Microscopes	112
III.	Properties of Microscopic Lens Systems: Bright Field Microscopy	117
IV.	Phase Contrast Microscopy	123
V.	Fluorescence Microscopic Technique	125
	References	127

Applied Photography in Chromosome Studies

Leroy P. Christenson

I. Introduction 129
II. Photomicrography 131
III. Photosensitive Materials and Processing 142
Appendix 152
References 152

Identification of Chromosomes

Klaus Patau

I. Morphological Identification in the Absence of Special Markers 155
II. Markers and Other Aids to Chromosome Identification 166
III. Nomenclature 173
IV. The Human Complement 177
References 185

Human Chromosomes in Disease

Jorge J. Yunis

I. Introduction 187
II. Sex Chromosomal Abnormalities 189
III. Autosomal Chromosome Abnormalities 209
IV. Chromosomes in Malignant Diseases 230
V. Diseases with a Normal Chromosome Complement 234
VI. Conclusion 234
References 235

AUTHOR INDEX 243

SUBJECT INDEX 252

Introduction

T. C. HSU

Section of Cytology, Department of Biology,
The University of Texas M. D. Anderson Hospital and Tumor Institute,
Houston, Texas

In the history of scientific research, whenever a new idea, a new material, or a new method was discovered, heavy research activities followed for a period of time. The field of cytogenetics has been no exception. When the genetic importance of polytene chromosomes of Diptera was rediscovered in the early thirties, practically every *Drosophila* geneticist played with salivary glands. Similarly, when the effects of colchicine on mitosis was described in the late thirties, all plant cytogeneticists used colchicine, at least for getting good preparations. However, scientific research, like any other activity, may follow the law of diminishing returns. When a new method or a new idea is extensively explored, progress is retarded or even stops completely. This is what happened to cytogenetics at the beginning of the last decade.

One of the dark alleys of cytogenetics was mammalian karyology. Before the invention of modern technological devices, even determining the diploid number of a mammalian species was considered a difficult accomplishment. The chromosomes were hopelessly crowded in metaphase. An experienced cytologist would have to spend days or months to find a figure that was slightly favorable for a count. No one used photographs because all one could see from a photograph was a cluster of chromosomes, one on top of the other. Drawings were the only sensible way of presenting a figure because one could use lines to indicate overlaps. However, since there were so many overlaps, those pictures rarely meant very much.

Technological improvements during the past 10 years include:

1. Tissue culture. Cells *in vitro* (or in ascites) are either suspended or form a monolayer instead of a tissue block. This allows the full effects of pretreatments as well as fixation.

2. The colchicine pretreatment. Colchicine, or its derivative, Colcemid, interferes with the mitotic spindle so that dividing cells are blocked at metaphase. It also allows the chromosomes to contract further in the blocked metaphase stage. With proper concentration of colchicine and duration of treatment, large numbers of excellent metaphases can be accumulated to facilitate observation and analysis.

3. The hypotonic solution pretreatment. The osmotic pressure causes the cells to expand and the chromosomes to scatter.

4. The squash or air-dried method. Even though the chromosomes are spread apart by the hypotonic solution treatment, they are distributed over the entire expanded cell. The squash or air-dried method forces the chromosomes to lie in one plane of focus, so that errors in chromosome characterization can be minimized.

Because of these technical advances, mammalian cytology suddenly became an important part of medical research. The discovery of the correct diploid number for man and aneuploidy in some congenital syndromes set the foundation of human cytogenetics which has invaded practically every branch of medicine. The demand for qualified cytogeneticists during recent years has been so high that it is possible to fill only a fraction of the positions available. There has been no training center or enrichment course of this type. Those who desire to learn the techniques could not find a pertinent manual or handbook to follow. Therefore, a book describing all the modern procedures used by active investigators in this field is indeed most timely and appropriate.

I must mention at this point a fallacious notion held by noncytogeneticists concerning chromosome study: Who can't count to 46? Indeed, anyone, after learning in a cytogenetic laboratory for a week or two, is able to make leucocyte cultures and good chromosome preparations. But cytogenetics does not mean just "chromosome counts." Mastering techniques alone does not make one a competent cytologist, although a competent cytologist must master as many techniques as possible. A vast background in genetics and cytogenetics, in cell biology, and in molecular biology is necessary for carrying out a good project as well as extending research frontiers.

Sex Chromatin Techniques

MURRAY L. BARR

Department of Anatomy, Faculty of Medicine, University of Western Ontario,
London, Ontario, Canada

I. Introduction 1
II. Historical Sketch 2
III. Morphological Characteristics of the Sex Chromatin 3
IV. Sex Chromatin Techniques 5
   A. Buccal Smears 5
   B. Sections of Tissues 8
   C. Peripheral Blood Neutrophiles 11
V. Origin of the Sex Chromatin 13
VI. Sex Chromatin Patterns and Sex Chromosome Complexes 14
   References 16

I. INTRODUCTION

The sex chromatin of interphase nuclei has proved a useful marker, in spite of its diminutive size, in several practical and theoretical problems of biology and medicine. It is widely used as a diagnostic aid in errors of sex development, especially in hermaphroditism, Turner's syndrome, and Klinefelter's syndrome. As a companion technique to chromosome analysis, study of the sex chromatin pattern allows one to determine the number of X chromosomes in the complement, according to the rule that the maximum number of sex chromatin masses is one less than the number of X chromosomes. This is a helpful, indeed a crucial, rule in certain chromosome abnormalities, because the X chromosome is almost identical, in size and the more obvious structural characteristics, with autosomes 6 and 7. The sex chomatin test has also been used in a number of studies where an indication of the cells' sex chromosome complex was needed. To cite a few examples, the sex chromatin has been a useful marker in determining the success of homologous tissue transplants when donor and recipient were of unlike sex (Peer, 1958; Woodruff and Lennox, 1959);

1

using the neutrophiles' drumstick as a marker, the same principle was applied in studying the results of bone marrow replacement (Davidson *et al.,* 1958). Attempts have been made to study the sex factor in spontaneous abortions (Bohle *et al.,* 1957; Schultze, 1958; Wagner, 1958; Serr *et al.,* 1959; Moore and Hyrniuk, 1960), and there have been provocative findings, whose significance is not yet understood, in teratomas in males (Hunter and Lennox, 1954; Tavares, 1955; Myers, 1959; Theiss *et al.,* 1960). In more recent work, evidence for genetic inertness of the X chromosome that forms the sex chromatin, and the probability of an X chromosome mosaicism in females, have opened new avenues in research that are likely to have an important influence on genetic theory (Ohno, 1961; Lyon, 1961, 1962; Beutler *et al.,* 1962; Grumbach and Morishima, 1962).

The sex chromatin principle is thus basic to a rather wide range of studies. This chapter deals, however, with sex chromatin tests that are useful as a diagnostic aid in developmental anomalies caused by an abnormality of the sex chromosome complex.

II. HISTORICAL SKETCH

A brief account of the development of the sex chromatin tests will perhaps be of interest to those who use them as a diagnostic aid.

Cytologists studying insect material have known for some time that the X chromosome may have the property of heteropycnosis in interphase nuclei and form a distinctive chromatin mass or chromocenter (Geitler, 1937). The first intimation that the same principle applies in mammals came with the demonstration of a female-specific chromocenter in nerve cells of the cat (Barr and Bertram, 1949). This initial disclosure was followed by nuclear studies on a variety of mammals, including man (Moore and Barr, 1954), which showed that sex chromatin could usually be demonstrated, in the various tissues of animals examined, in females but not in males. The possibility that nuclear sexual dimorphism might be useful diagnostically was first explored in hermaphroditism, by use of skin biopsy specimens (Moore *et al.,* 1953). Davidson and Robertson Smith (1954) showed that neutrophiles had a sex characteristic, in the form of a drumstick-shaped nuclear lobule, in a small proportion of neutrophiles of females. A search for a simpler technique for demonstration of the sex chromatin pattern resulted in the buccal smear test, which is now in general use (Marberger *et al.,* 1955; Moore and Barr, 1955). The tests were applied promptly to patients with puzzling anomalies of sex development, and it was found that most females with gonadal agenesis or Turner's syndrome had chromatin-negative nuclei (Polani *et al.,* 1954; Grumbach *et al.,* 1955), whereas the majority of males with seminiferous tubule dysgenesis or Klinefelter's syndrome had chromatin-positive nuclei (Bradbury *et al.,* 1956; Plunkett and Barr, 1956). The chromosomes of similar patients were studied soon after the appropriate techniques became available, resulting in the crucial demonstration of an XO sex chromosome complex in patients with Turner's syndrome and chromatin-negative nuclei (Ford *et al.,* 1959a) and an XXY sex chromosome complex in patients with Klinefelter's syndrome and chromatin-positive nuclei (Ford *et al.,* 1959b; Jacobs and Strong, 1959). The relationship between sex chromatin and the sex chromosome complex (the derivation of the sex chromatin from a single X chromosome) was established largely through the work of Ohno and his collaborators (e.g., Ohno and Hauschka, 1960; Ohno and Makino, 1961). The most recent notable development concerns the genetic inertness of the heteropycnotic X chromosome that forms the sex chromatin and the possibility of a mosaicism in mammalian females, the paternal X being active in some cells and the maternal X in others (Lyon, 1961, 1962). The foregoing items are only a few of a long series of developments, during a period of a little over a decade, that saw hundreds of papers published dealing, in one way or another, with the sex chromatin.

III. MORPHOLOGICAL CHARACTERISTICS OF THE SEX CHROMATIN

With the exception of the opossum, where a sex chromatin mass occurs in the cell nuclei of both sexes (Graham and Barr, 1959), this chromocenter is normally a female characteristic, and the following description applies to cells of females. There seem to be no important differences in the intrinsic morphology of the sex chromatin from one mammalian species to another or in different tissues, although the position of the sex chromatin in the nucleus does vary to some extent with the species and cell type. Nuclei of representatives of the orders Rodentia and Lagomorpha, except in embryonic material and a few mature cells such as those of mesothelium, are unsuitable for sex chromatin studies because of the coarse chromatin pattern and multiple large chromocenters.

For reasons of intranuclear dynamics that are not clear, the sex chromatin is usually situated against the inner surface of the nuclear membrane

(Fig. 1). Exceptions to this generalization are found in nerve cells. For example, the sex chromatin is usually adjacent to the large nucleolus in neurons of carnivores (Moore and Barr, 1953) and free from any nuclear surface in neurons of the opossum (Graham and Barr, 1959). The proportion of nuclei in which sex chromatin can be seen varies with the type

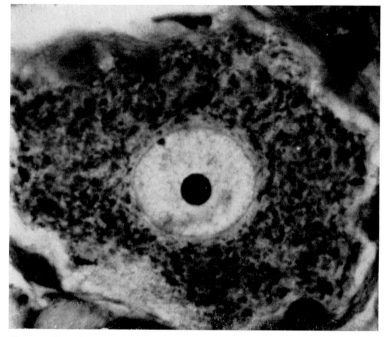

FIG. 1. Dorsal root ganglion cell, with typical sex chromatin at the nuclear membrane (Barr *et al.,* 1950).

of preparation and the tissue being studied. Counts approaching 100% are obtained in whole mounts of amniotic membrane and in relatively thick sections of nervous tissue. But the count is usually of the order of 60%, and often lower in buccal smears, in which many nuclei are not suitable for the study of fine, intrinsic detail. The frequency of sex chromatin in a preparation may be influenced by the mitotic activity in the cell population being studied, because the sex chromatin probably disappears during the period of replication of deoxyribonucleic acid (DNA) and chromosomes in preparation for the next mitotic division.

The sex chromatin is of the order of 1 μ in diameter; measurements of large numbers of sex chromatin masses in human tissues give a mean value of 0.7 μ × 1.2 μ. Its shape is variable, but a planoconvex or triangular outline is seen most frequently because one surface adheres to the nuclear membrane. Except for an occasional bipartite appearance, little structural detail can be made out in the usual preparations. But the bipartite appearance is enhanced, regions of differing density are seen, and there may be a suggestion of strands intertwining in a complicated manner in preparations from which ribonucleic acid (RNA) has been removed by mild acid hydrolysis (Klinger and Ludwig, 1957) or if the sex chromatin of living cells growing *in vitro* is examined with phase contrast. As is to be expected, fixation tends to condense the sex chromatin and obscure its structural detail.

The reaction of the sex chromatin to stains is that of chromatin, chromocenters, and chromosomes generally. It has an affinity for basic dyes such as cresylecht violet, fuchsin, gallocyanin, hematoxylin, pinacyanole, and thionine, and is stained well by orcein, a dye much favored by chromosome cytologists. Because of the sex chromatin's DNA content, it is Feulgen-positive, has an affinity for methyl green in the methyl green-pyronine staining procedure, and persists after mild acid hydrolysis or treatment with ribonuclease.

IV. SEX CHROMATIN TECHNIQUES

A. BUCCAL SMEARS

The study of a smear preparation from the buccal mucosa is by far the most convenient method of applying the sex chromatin test in clinical investigation. Certainly no other form of the test is as applicable to surveys (of newborns or institutionalized retardates, for example) or as simple to do in a hospital laboratory. From the strictly cytological point of view, buccal smears are inferior to carefully prepared sections of some tissues, to monolayers of cells growing *in vitro*, or even to smears taken from the vulva or the urethral orifice. But cytological disadvantages are outweighed by the universal availability of buccal smears, and errors of interpretation should not occur if the necessary precautions are taken. The procedure is as follows.

Obtain epithelial cells by drawing the edge of a metal spatula firmly over the buccal mucosa. The long narrow spatula used for analytical weighing is recommended and is superior to the wooden tongue depressor that was recommended when the test was introduced. Discard the material first obtained, since gentle scraping of the mucosa a second time secures deeper and healthier epithelial cells. Spread the material over a small area of an albuminized slide; a common mistake is to make a smear that is too thin. Fix the smear promptly, i.e., with no opportunity for drying, for 15–30 minutes in 95% ethyl alcohol. Longer fixation, although unnecessary, does no harm up to 24 hours. Immerse the slide in absolute alcohol for 3 minutes, followed by 2 minutes in a 0.2% solution of Parlodion in equal parts of absolute alcohol and ether. (The last step attaches the cells firmly to the slide.) Dry in air for 15 seconds, pass through 70% alcohol for 5 minutes and two changes of distilled water for 5 minutes each. The preparation is now ready for staining.

A variety of staining methods are in use. All of them give satisfactory results and the choice is usually made on the basis of previous experience. Suitable dyes are, among others, cresylecht violet, thionine, acetoorcein, and carbolfuchsin. Feulgen staining of buccal smears has been advocated but is perhaps inadvisable as a routine method. Acetoorcein squash preparations, a technique that has been popular for many years with chromosome cytologists, give good detail of the nuclear chromatin, and the method is rapid (Sanderson, 1960). Guard (1959) introduced a staining method that is potentially very useful because a large chromocenter, such as the sex chromatin, is stained differently from small chromatin particles. In the Guard method, biebrich scarlet in the presence of phosphotungstic acid has a strong affinity for nuclear chomatin generally. Fast green has a slow differentiating action and can be made to replace the biebrich scarlet in the general chromatin while the sex chromatin retains the dye. Thus, in successful preparations, the sex chromatin is red against a green background. The method needs refinement because it is difficult to obtain consistently good results.

We have used carbolfuchsin as a routine stain for buccal smears for several years in our laboratory. Our attention was attracted to this dye by illustrations in a paper by Eskelund (1956), and it was found later that carbolfuchsin is also an excellent stain for human chromosomes (Carr and Walker, 1961). It is simple to apply in the staining of mucosal smears, the results are uniform, there is no objectionable staining of bacteria, and the preparations are permanent.

The staining solution is prepared as follows:

Stock solution
    Basic fuchsin (CF-41, Coleman & Bell)   3 gm
    70% Ethyl alcohol   100 ml
        (Solution will keep indefinitely.)
Working solution
    Stock solution   10 ml
    5% Carbolic acid in distilled water   90 ml
    Glacial acetic acid   10 ml
    37% Formaldehyde   10 ml
        (Let stand for 24 hours before using. The solution should be freshly prepared monthly, or more frequently if many smears are being stained.)

Stain for 5–10 minutes in the working solution of carbolfuchsin, followed by differentiation for about 1 minute in 95% alcohol and about 1 minute in absolute alcohol. The exact time for differentiation varies a little, depending mainly on the thickness of the smear. Clear in xylol and mount in a neutral medium.

The smear should be examined with the oil immersion objective of a good binocular microscope and, to obtain maximum contrast, a green filter should be used when studying preparations stained with carbolfuchsin. If the chromatin is not finely particulate in a substantial number of nuclei, the test should be repeated to obtain deeper and healthier cells. It is good practice to examine 100 healthy looking nuclei and record the number containing sex chromatin. The number of chromatin-positive nuclei with sex chromatin is often lower in buccal smears than in other kinds of preparations and there is a wide range (from 30% to 80%). However, this is compensated for by the virtual absence, in chromatin-negative smears, of a chromatin mass simulating sex chromatin. One must be on the alert for nuclei that have more than one mass of sex chromatin, which indicates the presence of more than two X chromosomes (*vide infra*).

In the main, the sex chromatin of buccal smears conforms to the general description that has been outlined (Fig. 2). It is probably always at the nuclear membrane, but whether this is obvious depends on the orientation of the nucleus. The sex chromatin is often more flattened against the nuclear membrane than it is in tissue sections and other preparations. In some buccal smears, the nuclei of both sexes contain a chromocenter that is not in contact with the membrane. This is probably nucleolar-associated chromatin and, because of its position, need not be confused with sex chromatin. Any error that occurs in the interpretation of a buccal smear will probably be in the direction of reading as chromatin-negative a smear that is really chromatin-positive. Such an error can be avoided by refraining from trying to interpret a preparation of inferior technical quality.

The possibility that certain factors may alter the sex chromatin in buccal smears should be borne in mind when using this test. Smith *et al.* (1962)

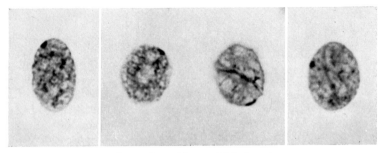

FIG. 2. Chromatin-positive nuclei in buccal smears.

and Taylor (1963) found that the incidence of nuclei with sex chromatin may be very low in newborn females, the normal value being reached by the fourth day of life. Sohval and Casselman (1961) reported a reversible reduction in the size of sex chromatin in buccal smears after oral administration of the antibiotics: chlortetracycline, chloramphenicol, benzylpenicillin potassium, and sulfafurazole.

B. SECTIONS OF TISSUES

Although the skin biopsy method is seldom used now, it has a place occasionally when buccal smears are of consistently poor quality or when confirmation of an unusual sex chromatin pattern in a buccal smear is desired. But there are frequent opportunities for studying the sex chromatin pattern in tissues obtained at operation or post mortem.

Tissues that have been processed routinely in a pathology laboratory are not as a rule suitable for the study of fine nuclear detail. Special handling of the specimen is needed if the nuclei are to be free from shrinkage artifact and to achieve optimal definition of the nuclear chromatin. The procedure outlined below has been shown to result in satisfactory sections for the study of sex chromatin.

1. *Fixation*

The chromatin particles tend to be indistinct if the specimen is fixed in formalin alone. While the addition of acetic acid perhaps accentuates the size of chromatin particles as an artifact, in practice use of the formalin–alcohol–acetic acid mixture given in the accompanying tabulation gives good chromatin detail without excessive clumping of the chromatin. The blocks should be not more than 1/2 cm in thickness.

Formalin (analytical reagent, 37%)	20%
95% Ethyl alcohol	35%
Glacial acetic acid	10%
Distilled water	35%

Transfer the tissue blocks to 70% alcohol after 24 hours (not longer) in this fixative.

2. Dehydration, Embedding, and Related Procedures

Harsh treatment of the specimen during this phase will cause nuclear shrinkage and pycnotic changes. The times shown in the accompanying tabulation for the various steps are shorter than those usually used for routine histological purposes.

95% Alcohol	3 hours
Absolute alcohol	1½ hours
Absolute alcohol and xylol (equal parts)	30 minutes
Xylol until clear	5–15 minutes
Xylol and paraffin (equal parts), 56°C	30 minutes
Paraffin, 56°C, three changes	30 minutes,
	30 minutes, and
	1 hour

Embed and cool quickly. Section at 5 μ.

3. Staining

A good hematoxylin-eosin stain is satisfactory for most sex chromatin studies. The hematoxylin should be prepared by the method of Harris (Gatenby and Beams, 1950). It is advisable to stain the sections rather vigorously with hematoyxlin and to use a light counterstain of eosin.

For material of special interest, one may wish to use, in addition to hematoxylin-eosin, staining methods that are specific for DNA or that give a superior picture of nuclear chromatin. This is especially important when studying a tissue whose nuclei have nucleoli that are peripherally placed as occurs, for example, in hyperplastic prostatic epithelium. For these purposes, the Feulgen procedure (Gurr, 1953), staining with thionine after mild acid hydrolysis (Klinger and Ludwig, 1957) or staining with gallocyanin after treatment of the sections with ribonuclease (Lennox, 1956) is recommended.

For the central nervous system and peripheral ganglia, fixation should be in 10% formalin and 10-μ sections should be stained with either cresylecht violet or thionine.

The incidence of sex chromatin in sections of tissues from normal females varies between 60% and 80%. In normal males, up to 10% of nuclei contain a chromocenter that simulates sex chromatin. The spinous layer of the epidermis is the most favorable region for study in skin biopsy specimens (Fig. 3). In other tissues, any nuclei that are reasonably vesicular are suitable for study. The sex chromatin is well defined in fibroblasts, smooth muscle cells, cartilage cells, and cells of adrenal cortex,

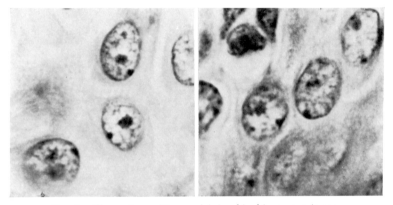

FIG. 3.   Chromatin-positive nuclei in skin biopsy specimens.

among many others (Moore and Barr, 1954). Leydig cells are suitable for the study of chromatin detail; this is a useful point in connection with testis biopsy specimens from patients with Klinefelter's syndrome.

It is not proposed to deal here with methods of making preparations from cell cultures for nuclear studies. It might be emphasized, however, that the chromatin pattern, including the sex chromatin, is especially clear in a monolayer of cells growing *in vitro* (Miles, 1959) (Fig. 4), and that such preparations are adaptable to the examination of sex chromatin in living cells by phase contrast (DeMars, 1962).

It is occasionally desirable to examine, for sex chromatin, interphase nuclei in a chromosome preparation from a leucocyte culture, a culture of embryonic material, a skin biopsy specimen, etc. A preparation for chromosome analysis is usually unsatisfactory for sex chromatin because of the effect of treatment in a hypotonic medium on interphase nuclei.

But nuclei can be examined for their sex chromatin pattern if another preparation, omitting exposure to a hypotonic solution, is made from the same material.

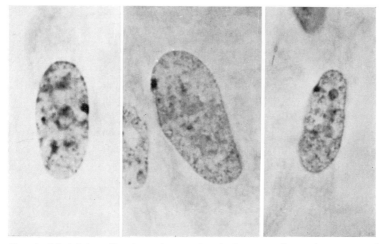

Fig. 4. Nuclei in cell culture from a female human embryo. (Preparation by Dr. D. H. Carr and Mr. J. E. Walker.)

C. PERIPHERAL BLOOD NEUTROPHILES

The neutrophile method of nuclear sex detection is based on the occurrence, in normal females, but not in normal males, of occasional neutrophile leucocytes that have a drumstick-shaped nuclear appendage. This accessory nuclear lobule is thought to contain sex chromatin which, perhaps because of its peripheral position, sometimes forms a small appendage in a type of cell that has, as one of its developmental characteristics, nuclear lobulation.

Those who are skilled in hematological techniques prefer the cover slip method of preparing a blood film (Davidson and Robertson Smith, 1954; Davidson, 1960). Others will perhaps prefer the microscope slide method that is used in many hospital laboratories. Care is needed in making the film, to ensure that parts of it are of moderate thickness. A film that is too thin makes tedious work when a large number of neutrophiles have to be examined, especially when there is a low neutrophile count, and a film that is too thick causes the neutrophiles to be distorted and shrunken. Films stained by the standard methods of Wright or Giemsa are quite satisfactory.

If large numbers of films are to be examined, staining with hematoxylin, as suggested by Carpentier *et al.* (1957), has the advantage of making their study less trying because of the pale staining of erythrocytes. Smears prepared from a buffy coat have the obvious advantage of neutrophile enrichment (Kosenow, 1956a; Pearce, 1960; Maclean, 1962).

Davidson and Robertson Smith (1954) recommend that neutrophiles be examined until six with a drumstick are found (female) and that the number examined be extended to 500 if drumsticks are not seen (male). The incidence of neutrophiles with drumsticks varies from one female to another. The range, in our experience, is of the order of 0.6–8.8%, with a mean of 3.1%. The cause of this variation has not been made clear, except that the frequency of neutrophiles with drumsticks is likely to be higher, the larger the Arneth Index of nuclear lobulation.

The distinctive drumstick appendage is about 1.2 × 1.6 μ in size. It is attached to a lobe of the nucleus by a filament or thread of variable thickness and length (Fig. 5). It is important not to confuse the true drum-

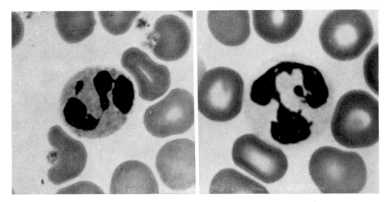

FIG. 5. Neutrophiles with a drumstick nuclear appendage.

stick with small club-shaped appendages, which are seen more often in blood films from normal males than from normal females. Sessile nodules occur in female neutrophiles and probably have the same significance as the drumstick. Kosenow (1956b) introduced a formula that takes into account the frequency of drumsticks, sessile nodules, and small clubs. This formula will prove useful in certain research projects, but is seldom needed when the neutrophile test is applied in clinical diagnosis.

The buccal smear and neutrophile methods should both be used if there is the slightest reason to suspect a sex chomosome mosaicism, which is likely to produce a discrepancy in the results of the two tests. For example, in an XO/XX/XXX mosaicism (Carr *et al.*, 1962) and an XY/XXXY mosaicism (Barr *et al.*, 1962), there were nuclei with duplicated sex chromatin in the buccal smears, but insufficient cells with two or more X chromosomes were in the blood to produce neutrophiles with drumsticks. When the patient's cells uniformly contain more than two X chromosomes (e.g., XXX, XXXX, XXXY, and XXXXY complexes), a prolonged search will usually reveal neutrophiles with two drumsticks (Maclean, 1962).

V. ORIGIN OF THE SEX CHROMATIN

The significance of the sex chromatin test depends on the relation between sex chromatin patterns and sex chromosome complexes which, in turn, is based on the origin of the sex chromatin.

The sexual dimorphism of interphase nuclei was, from the time of its first demonstration (Barr and Bertram, 1949), thought to be derived from the differing sex chromosome complexes of the two sexes. But 10 years elapsed before the problem of the origin of the sex chromatin was solved by Ohno and his collaborators (e.g., Ohno *et al.*, 1959; Ohno and Hauschka, 1960; Ohno and Makino, 1961). The study of early prophase nuclei showed that in somatic cells of males all chromosomes are isopycnotic, whereas in females a single chromosome of medium length is relatively dense or heteropycnotic. It was suggested that the heteropycnotic element was one of the two X's of female cells and that heteropycnosis persisted throughout interphase to form the sex chromatin. This was a revolutionary idea because there was no previous indication of differential behavior between homologous chromosomes.

The foregoing interpretation of prophase chromosomes and its extension to the chromatin pattern of interphase nuclei has been amply confirmed. For example, when abnormal sex chromosome complexes are included, the number of X chromosomes varies from one to five. The rule that the maximum number of sex chromatin masses at interphase is one less than the number of X chromosomes has proved to be reliable (Barr and Carr, 1962; Grumbach and Morishima, 1962). This relationship is best explained by one X being threadlike or euchromatic in all interphase nuclei, while X chromosomes in excess of one are potentially heteropycnotic.

The best confirmation of the single-X origin of sex chromatin comes from experiments involving exposure to tritiated thymidine of cells growing, and dividing, *in vitro* (German, 1962; Gilbert *et al.*, 1962; Morishima *et al.*, 1962). These studies show that the heteropycnotic or sex chromatin X (or X's) replicates later and faster than the other chromosomes of the complement.

The differential behavior of the two X chromosomes of female cells undoubtedly has biological implications that are as yet imperfectly understood. Differentiation of the two X's seems to occur when the embryo is in the blastocyst stage (Park, 1957), probably neither X^M nor X^P is favored for the heteropycnotic or sex chromatin role, and the isopycnotic or heteropycnotic state, once acquired, is probably "fixed," i.e., it is maintained in the chromosomes' descendants through successive cell generations (Grumbach and Morishima, 1962). If the foregoing concepts are correct, the female is an X chromosome mosaic, in the sense that X^M is heteropycnotic in some cells and X^P in the remainder. Judging from cytogenetic studies on plants and insects, heteropycnosis implies genetic inactivity. This is the basis of the Lyon hypothesis (Lyon, 1961, 1962; McKusick, 1962), which states that the female is a genetic mosaic, to the extent that X^M is genetically active in some cells and X^P in others. It is conceivable that such a mechanism may have an evolutionary value through limiting the genetic difference between the sexes, while at the same time taking advantage of XX/XY sex determination.

VI. SEX CHROMATIN PATTERNS AND SEX CHROMOSOME COMPLEXES

Because of the single-X origin of the sex chomatin and the potential heteropycnosis of X chromosomes in excess of one, the sex chromatin tests give valuable clues as to the number of X chromosomes in an individual's cells. The manner in which this works in practice will now be briefly outlined. References to the many sex chromosome abnormalities and the associated phenotypes, together with additional information on mosaicisms, X chromosome deletions, isochromosomes, etc., may be found in review articles (among others, those by Barr, 1959, 1963; Ford, 1961; Harnden and Jacobs, 1961; Haywood *et al.*, 1961; Miles, 1961; Polani, 1961; Robinson, 1961; Sohval, 1961, 1963; Ferguson-Smith, 1962; Moore, 1962; Eggen, 1963).

The correlations between sex chromatin patterns and sex chromosome complexes, as they are now known, are shown in Fig. 6. Nuclei are: (a) *chromatin-negative* when the complex is XY, as in normal males, male pseudohermaphrodites, females with testicular feminization, and XY "pure" gonadal dysgenesis. They are also chromatin-negative in females with Turner's syndrome and an XO sex chromosome "complex." Nuclei are: (b) *chromatin-positive,* with a single mass of sex chromatin, when two X chromosomes are present, whether XX as in the normal female

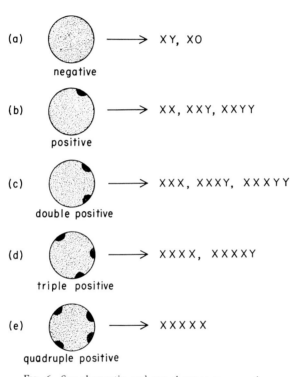

FIG. 6. Sex chromatin and sex chromosome complexes.

and in patients with the adrenogenital syndrome, or XXY and XXYY, both of the latter complexes being found in the chromatin-positive Kline-felter syndrome. The presence of a proportion of (c) *double chromatin-positive* nuclei indicates that there are three X chromosomes. These nuclei are found in the triple-X female and the variants of Klinefelter's syndrome that have XXXY or XXXYY sex chromosome complexes. Average figures (buccal smears and skin biopsy specimens combined) for seven triple-X females studied by our group were: no sex chromatin, 11%; one mass of sex chromatin, 42%; and two masses of sex chromatin, 47%, of nuclei. Some (d) *triple chromatin-positive* nuclei, together with others with fewer masses of sex chromatin, are found in the rare **XXXX** female and in the **XXXXY** variant of Klinefelter's syndrome. Average figures, combining the results from buccal smear and skin biopsy tests, for two **XXXX** and two **XXXXY** individuals studied by our group were: no sex chromatin, 7%; one mass of sex chromatin, 23%; two masses of sex chromatin, 47%; and three masses of sex chromatin, 23%. Finally, one female patient is on record (Grumbach *et al.,* 1963) who had an **XXXXX** sex chromosome complex; 10% of cultured cells derived from skin biopsy specimens were (e) *quadruple chromatin-positive.*

The correlations depicted in Fig. 6 show how the simple sex chromatin test can be a useful aid in differential diagnosis and a valuable adjunct to chromosome analysis.

Acknowledgments

Our studies on the sex chromatin and related subjects are supported by the Medical Research Council of Canada. Mr. J. E. Walker is responsible for many technical aspects of this work.

References

Barr, M. L. (1959). Sex chromatin and phenotype in man. *Science* **130**, 679-685.

Barr, M. L. (1963). Chromosomal abnormalities, with particular reference to sex. *Proc. 1st Inter-Am. Conf. Congenital Defects, Los Angeles, 1962* pp. 70-88. Lippincott, Philadelphia, Pennsylvania.

Barr, M. L., and Bertram, E. G. (1949). A morphological distinction between neurones of the male and female, and the behaviour of the nucleolar satellite during accelerated nucleoprotein synthesis. *Nature* **163**, 676-677.

Barr, M. L., and Carr, D. H. (1962). Correlations between sex chromatin and sex chromosomes. *Acta Cytol.* **6**, 34-35.

Barr, M. L., Bertram, L. F., and Lindsay, H. A. (1950). The morphology of the nerve cell nucleus, according to sex. *Anat. Record* **107**, 283-298.

Barr, M. L., Carr, D. H., Morishima, A., and Grumbach, M. M. (1962). An XY/XXXY sex chromosome mosaicism in a mentally defective male patient. *J. Mental Deficiency Res.* **6**, 65-74.

Beutler, E., Yeh, M., and Fairbanks, V. F. (1962). The normal human female as a mosaic of X-chromosome activity: Studies using the gene for G-6-PD-deficiency as a marker. *Proc. Natl. Acad. Sci. U. S.* **48**, 9-16.

Bohle, A., Stoll, P., and Vosgerau, H. (1957). Morphologische und Statistische Untersuchungen über die Intrauterine Absterbeordnung in der estern Hälfte der Schwangerschaft. *Klin. Wochschr.* **35**, 358-363.

Bradbury, J. T., Bunge, R. G., and Boccabella, R. A. (1956). Chromatin test in Klinefelter's syndrome. *J. Clin. Endocrinol. Metab.* **16**, 689, 1956.

Carpentier, P. J., Stolte, L. A. M., and Dobbelaar, M. J. (1957). The sex-linked difference in rabbit neutrophils. *Nature* **180**, 554-555.

Carr, D. H., and Walker, J. E. (1961). Carbol fuchsin as a stain for human chromosomes. *Stain Technol.* **36**, 233-236.

Carr, D. H., Morishima, A., Barr, M. L., Grumbach, M. M., Lüers, T., and Boschann, H. W. (1962). An XO/XX/XXX mosaicism in relation to gonadal dysgenesis in females. *J. Clin. Endocrinol. Metab.* **22**, 671-677.

Davidson, W. M. (1960). Sex determination: diagnostic methods. *Brit. Med. J.* **2**, 1901-1906.

Davidson, W. M., and Robertson Smith, D. (1954). A morphological sex difference in the polymorphonuclear neutrophil leucocytes. *Brit. Med. J.* **2**, 6-7.

Davidson, W. M., Fowler, J. F., and Smith, D. R. (1958). Sexing the neutrophil leucocytes in natural and artificial chimaeras. *Brit. J. Haematol.* **4**, 231-238.

DeMars, R. (1962). Sex chromatin mass in living, cultivated human cells. *Science* **138**, 980-981.

Eggen, R. R. (1963). Cytogenetics. Review of recent advances in a new field of clinical pathology. *Am. J. Clin. Pathol.* **39**, 3-37.

Eskelund, V. (1956). Determination of genetic sex by examination of epithelial cells in urine. *Acta Endocrinol.* **23**, 246-250.

Ferguson-Smith, M. A. (1962). Chromosome abnormalities as a cause of human infertility. *Fertility Sterility* **13**, 34-46.

Ford, C. E. (1961). The cytogenetic analysis of some disorders of sex development. *Am. J. Obstet. Gynecol.* **82**, 1154-1161.

Ford, C. E., Jones, K. W., Polani, P. E., de Almeida, J. C., and Briggs, J. H. (1959a). A sex-chromosome anomaly in a case of gonadal dysgenesis (Turner's syndrome). *Lancet* **I**, 711-713.

Ford, C. E., Polani, P. E., Briggs, J. H., and Bishop, P. M. F. (1959b). A presumptive human XXY/XX mosaic. *Nature* **183**, 1030-1032.

Gatenby, J. B., and Beams, H. W. (1950). "The Microtomist's Vade-Mecum (Bolles Lee)," p. 146. Churchill, London.

Geitler, L. (1937). Die Analyse des Kernbaus und der Kernteilung der Wasserläufer Gerris lateralis und Gerris lacustrus (Hemiptera Heteroptera) und die Soma-differenzierung. *Z. Zellforsch. Microskop. Anat.* **26**, 641-672.

German, J. L., III. (1962). DNA synthesis in human chromosomes. *Trans. N. Y. Acad. Sci.* **24**, 395-407.

Gilbert, C. W., Muldal, S., Lajtha, L. G., and Rowley, J. (1962). Time-sequence of human chromosome duplication. *Nature* **195**, 869-873.

Graham, M. A., and Barr, M. L. (1959). Sex chromatin in the opossum, *Didelphys Virginiana*. *Arch. Anat. Microscop. Morphol. Exptl.* **48**, 111-121.

Grumbach, M. M., and Morishima, A. (1962). Sex chromatin and sex chromosomes: On the origin of sex chromatin from a single X chromosome. *Acta Cytol.* **6**, 46-60.

Grumbach, M. M., Van Wyk, J. J., and Wilkins, L. (1955). Chromosomal sex in gonadal dysgenesis (ovarian agenesis). Relationship to male pseudohermaphrodism and theories of human sex differentiation. *J. Clin. Endocrinol. Metab.* **15**, 1161-1193.

Grumbach, M. M., Morishima, A., and Taylor, J. H. (1963). Human sex chromosome abnormalities in relation to DNA replication and heterochromatinization. *Proc. Natl. Acad. Sci. U. S.* **49**, 581-589.

Guard, H. R. (1959). A new technic for differential staining of the sex chromatin, and the determination of its incidence in exfoliated vaginal epithelial cells. *Am. J. Clin. Pathol.* **32**, 145-151.

Gurr, E. (1953). "A Practical Manual of Medical and Biological Staining Techniques," p. 78. Wiley (Interscience), New York.

Harnden, D. G., and Jacobs, P. A. (1961). Cytogenetics of abnormal sexual development in man. *Brit. Med. Bul.* **17**, 206-212.

Haywood, M. D., Cameron, A. H., and Wolff, O. H. (1961). Chromosomes in paediatrics. *Postgrad. Med. J.* **37**, 268-275.

Hunter, W. F., and Lennox, B. (1954). The sex of teratomata. *Lancet* **II**, 633-634.

Jacobs, P. A., and Strong, J. A. (1959). A case of human intersexuality having a possible XXY sex-determining mechanism. *Nature* **183**, 302-303.

Klinger, H. P., and Ludwig, K. S. (1957). A universal stain for the sex chromatin body. *Stain Technol.* **32**, 235-244.

Kosenow, W. (1956a). Untersuchungen zur hämatologischen Geshlechtsbestimmung: Kernanhangsdifferenzierung im Leukocytenkonzentrat. *Aerztl. Wochschr.* **11**, 320-325.

Kosenow, W. (1956b). Geschlechtsbestimmung auf Grund Morphologischer Leukocytenmerkmale. *Klin. Wochschr.* **34**, 51-53.

Lennox, B. (1956). A ribonuclease-gallocyanin stain for sexing skin biopsies. *Stain Technol.* **31**, 167-172.

Lyon, M. F. (1961). Gene action in the X chromosome of the mouse (*Mus musculus L.*). *Nature* **190**, 372-373.

Lyon, M. F. (1962). Sex-chromatin and gene action in the mammalian X-chromosome. *Am. J. Human. Genet.* **14**, 135-148.

Maclean, N. (1962). The drumsticks of polymorphonuclear leucocytes in sex chromosome abnormalities. *Lancet* **I**, 1154-1158.

McKusick, V. A. (1962). On the X chromosome of man. *Quart. Rev. Biol.* **37**, 69-175.

Marberger, E., Boccabella, R. A., and Nelson, W. O. (1955). Oral smear as a method of chromosomal sex detection. *Proc. Soc. Exptl. Biol. Med.* **89**, 488-489.

Miles, C. P. (1959). Sex chromatin in cultured normal and cancerous human tissues. *Cancer* **12**, 299-305.

Miles, C. P. (1961). Human chromosome anomalies: Recent advances in human cytogenetics. *Stanford Med. Bull.* **19**, 1-18.

Moore, K. L. (1962). The genetics of sex determination and sex differentiation in man. Historical review and discussion of new ideas. *Manitoba Med. Rev.* **42**, 497-514.

Moore, K. L., and Barr, M. L. (1953). Morphology of the nerve cell nucleus in mammals, with special reference to the sex chromatin. *J. Comp. Neurol.* **98**, 213-231.

Moore, K. L., and Barr, M. L. (1954). Nuclear morphology, according to sex, in human tissues. *Acta Anat.* **21**, 197-208.

Moore, K. L., and Barr, M. L. (1955). Smears from the oral mucosa in the detection of chromosomal sex. *Lancet* **II**, 57-58.

Moore, K. L., and Hyrniuk, W. (1960). Sex diagnosis of early human abortions by the chromatin method. *Anat. Record* **136**, 247.

Moore, K. L., Graham, M. A., and Barr, M. L. (1953). The detection of chromosomal sex in hermaphrodites from a skin biopsy. *Surg. Gynecol. Obstet.* **96**, 641-648.

Morishima, A., Grumbach, M. M., and Taylor, J. H. (1962). Asynchronous duplication of human chromosomes and the origin of sex chromatin. *Proc. Natl. Acad. Sci. U. S.* **48**, 756-763.

Myers, L. M. (1959). Sex chromatin in teratomas. *J. Pathol. Bacteriol.* **78**, 43-55.

Ohno, S. (1961). Properties of X chromosomes. *Lancet* **II**, 723-724.

Ohno, S., and Hauschka, T. S. (1960). Allocycly of the X-chromosome in tumors and normal tissues. *Cancer Res.* **20**, 541-545.

Ohno, S., and Makino, S. (1961). The single-X nature of sex chromatin in man. *Lancet* **I**, 78-79.

Ohno, S., Kaplan, W. D., and Kinosita, R. (1959). Formation of the sex chromatin by a single X-chromosome in liver cells of *Rattus norvegicus. Exptl. Cell Res.* **18**, 415-418.

Park, W. W. (1957). The occurrence of sex chromatin in early human and macaque embryos. *J. Anat.* **91**, 369-373.

Pearce, L. C. (1960). Sex chromatin in neutrophilic leucocytes. *Can. J. Med. Technol.* **22**, 97-102.

Peer, L. A. (1958). Sex chromatin study to determine the survival of cartilage homographs. *Transplant. Bull.* **5**, 404-406.

Plunkett, E. R., and Barr, M. L. (1956). Testicular dysgenesis affecting the seminiferous tubules principally, with chromatin-positive nuclei. *Lancet* **II**, 853-857.

Polani, P. E. (1961). Turner's syndrome and allied conditions. Clinical features and chromosome abnormalities. *Brit. Med. Bull.* **17**, 200-205.

Polani, P. E., Hunter, W. F., and Lennox, B. (1954). Chromosomal sex in Turner's syndrome with coarctication of the aorta. *Lancet* **II**, 120-121.

Robinson, A. (1961). The human chromosomes. *Am. J. Diseases Children* **101**, 379-398.

Sanderson, A. R. (1960). Rapid nuclear sexing. *Lancet* **I**, 1252.

Schultze, K. W. (1958). Zur Bedeutung der abortweier und über ihre Zellkernmorphologische Geschlechtsbestimmung. *Deut. Med. Wochschr.* **83**, 1818-1823.

Serr, D. M., Tricomi, V., and Solish, G. (1959). Nuclear sexing in embryonic tissues with observations on the sex ratio of human abortions. *Mod. Trends Gynaecol. Obstet.* **2**, 260-264.

Smith, D. W., Marden, P. M., McDonald, M. J., and Speckhard, M. (1962). Lower incidence of sex chromatin in buccal smears of newborn babies. *Pediatrics* **30**, 707-711.

Sohval, A. R. (1961). Recent progress in human chromosome analysis and its relation to the sex chromatin. *Am. J. Med.* **31**, 397-441.

Sohval, A. R. (1963). Chromosomes and sex chromatin in normal and anomalous sex development. *Physiol. Rev.* **43**, 306-356.

Sohval, A. R., and Casselman, W. G. B. (1961). Alteration in size of nuclear sex-chromatin masses (Barr body) induced by antibiotics. *Lancet* **II**, 1386-1388.

Tavares, A. S. (1955). On the sex of cancer and teratoma cells. *Lancet* **I**, 948-949.

Taylor, A. I. (1963). Sex chromatin in the newborn. *Lancet* **I**, 912-914.

Theiss, E. A., Ashley, D. J. B., and Mostofi, F. K. (1960). Nuclear sex of testicular tumors and some related ovarian and extragonadal neoplasms. *Cancer* **13**, 323-327.

Wagner, D. (1958). Zur Frage der chromosomalen Geschlechtsbestimmung bei Frühabborten und Tubargraviditäten. *Geburtsh. Frauenheilk.* **18**, 1460-1471.

Woodruff, M. F. A., and Lennox, B. (1959). Reciprocal skin grafts in a pair of twins showing blood chimaerism. *Lancet* **II**, 476-478.

Human Peripheral Blood
Leucocyte Cultures

WILLIAM J. MELLMAN

Department of Pediatrics, University of Pennsylvania, Philadelphia, Pennsylvania

I.	General	22
II.	The Mononuclear Leucocyte as the Mitotic Cell in Culture	23
III.	Collection of Peripheral Blood Leucocytes and Preparation of Cell Inoculum	26
	A. Collection and Storage of Cells	26
	B. Separation of Leucocytes from Whole Blood	27
	C. The Basis for Separation of Leucocytes from Other Formed Elements of the Blood	29
	D. Size of Cell Inoculum	30
IV.	Initiation of Mitosis in Blood Cultures: The Role of Phytohemagglutinin and Other Potentially Mitogenic Agents	33
V.	Influence of Culture Conditions on Cell Proliferation	36
	A. Culture Medium	36
	B. Serum Protein	37
	C. pH and CO_2 Control	37
	D. Incubation Temperature	38
	E. Antibiotics	38
VI.	Preparation of Metaphase Spreads for Cytogenetic Studies	38
	A. Colchicine Arrest of Mitoses at Metaphase	38
	B. Hypotonic Treatment	39
	C. Fixation	39
	D. Preparation of Slides and Staining	40
VII.	Life Span of PHA Initiated Cultures: Evidence for Secondary Mitoses in Culture	40
VIII.	Further Application of the Leucocyte Culture System	41
IX.	Methods for Culturing Human Peripheral Blood Leucocytes	42
	A. Macromethod	42
	B. Semimicro Procedure	45
	C. Procedures of Other Laboratories	46
	References	46

An abundant literature recording observations of the cytogenetic aspects of cultivated peripheral blood leucocytes in metaphase has now accumulated. This has rendered prophetic a suggestion made by Professor Haldane in 1932 in which he predicted that if peripheral blood leucocytes could be cultured, the human chromosome complex could be studied intensively (Chrustschoff, 1935). Such a practical tool for cytogenetic investigation is now available. It is now almost a certainty that, under the influence of phytohemagglutinin (PHA), as well as of more specific antigens, the small lymphocyte in peripheral blood morphologically alters into a blast-like cell that divides in culture. This paper attempts to bring together the methodological developments that have permitted the wide application of human leucocyte cultures for chromosome studies as well as to indicate the further applications of this system of primary human cell culture. Facets of methodology are discussed where there is specific knowledge as well as those where there is now only empiricism. Footnotes are included which offer practical experience concerning various elements of the culture method.

I. GENERAL

Utilizing the "gradient culture" of human leucocytes described by Osgood and Krippaehne (1955), Nowell (1960a) observed that mononuclear cells from the peripheral blood of normal individuals were mitotically active after a lag period of about 48–72 hours in culture. This confirmed the reports dating back to 1915 that *in vitro* mitosis of peripheral blood leucocytes does indeed occur (Bloom, 1938). However, to attain the high degree of mitotic activity observed, it soon became clear that a phytohemagglutinin extracted from the red kidney bean, *Phaseolus vulgaris,* was an essential element in the culture system employed (Nowell, 1960b).

Coincident with this "rediscovery" by Nowell, the now classic analyses of the human karyotype were being made by use of metaphases obtained from fibroblast cell cultures, bone marrow, and testicular tissue (Tjio and Levan, 1956; Ford and Hamerton, 1956a; Ford *et al.,* 1958). The peripheral blood culture method seemed a logical source of metaphase cells, and the first analysis of the human karyotype with this method was performed by Hungerford *et al.* (1959) on cultured leucocytes from a true hermaphrodite. The difficulties inherent in preparing uniformly high-quality metaphase spreads by the squash technique with cells from these cultures was quickly appreciated. Moorhead *et al.* (1960) found that the air-drying method of Rothfels and Siminovitch (1958), combined with the peripheral blood culture, provided a procedure that circumvented the need for the highly experienced "green thumb" of the tissue culturist and the "educated thumb" for squashing of the cytogeneticist. The skill of the microscopist has yet to be rendered redundant by any simple technical procedure.

The elements of the culture system are discussed in sequence. Some of the variations which have been suggestd by others are mentioned.

II. THE MONONUCLEAR LEUCOCYTE AS THE MITOTIC CELL IN CULTURE

There is considerable indirect evidence that mononuclear leucocytes, more specifically small lymphocytes, are the cells which divide in human blood cultures (Marshall and Roberts, 1963; Cooper et al., 1963). Although pure suspensions of lymphocytes that are still capable of division in culture have not been obtained, 90–98% lymphocyte preparations have

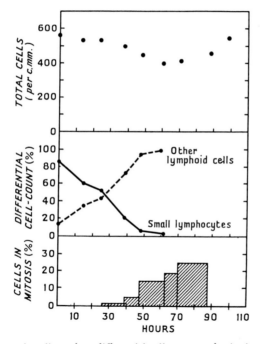

Fig. 1. Changes in cell number, differential cell count, and mitotic activity in relation to time in culture. Cell incubate is composed of peripheral blood leucocytes from which most of the polymorphonuclear leucocytes were removed after iron phagocytosis. (From Carstairs, 1962.)

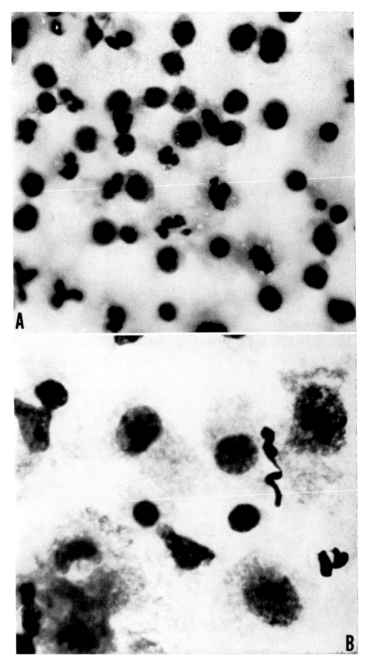

FIG. 2. Changes in cell morphology of cultured leucocytes. Four identical cultures initiated by semimicro method (see Section IX, B). Cultures harvested after 24 hours (A), 48 hours (B), 72 hours (C), and 96 hours (D) in culture. Cultures treated with colchicine for 2 hours before harvesting. Hypotonic pretreatment was *not* used before fixation.

Slides stained with Giemsa and photographed at the same magnification (2000 ×).

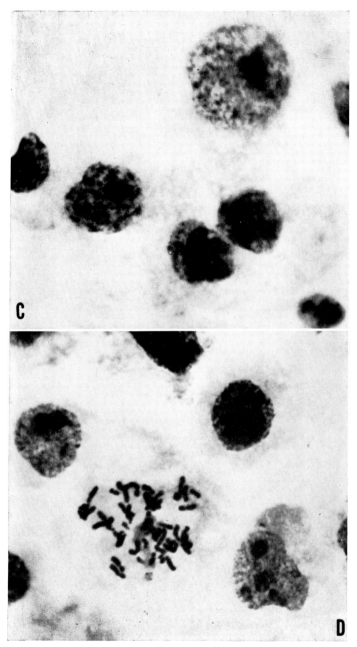

(A) 24-hour culture: small lymphocytes predominate; polymorphs and some larger mononuclear cells are seen. (B) 48-hour culture: mononuclear cells increasing in size and relative number. Polymorphs degenerating. Some small lymphocytes persist. (C) 72-hour culture: large mononuclear cells with prominent nucleoli and vacuolated cytoplasm. Mitoses present in other fields. (D) 96-hour culture: metaphase with chromosome scattered within large cell (spindle disrupted by colchicine). Multinucleolated cell in right lower field.

been prepared which are mitotically active. Serial observations by several workers of the changes in white blood cell (WBC) concentration, differential count, and the morphology of the surviving cells from the time of initiation of the culture through the period of mitotic activity have provided the most convincing circumstantial evidence that the small lymphocyte converts *in vitro* into the dividing cell (Tanaka *et al.,* 1963).

MacKinney *et al.* (1962) followed the course of a culture with a mixture of leucocytes. The cell number decreased by 45% over the first 36 hours. During this time the percentage of polymorphonuclear leucocytes (PMN) dropped from 59% to almost zero. Mature lymphocytes initially became the predominant cell type and then decreased as "young lymphocytes" and "large mononuclear cells" increased in the culture. Using a WBC suspension initially containing 95% mononuclear cells, of which 83% were "small lymphocytes," Carstairs (1962) demonstrated only a 10% decrease in total cell concentration over the first 36 hours, during which time the morphology of the lymphocytes shifted from predominantly small lymphocytes to other types of "lymphoid cells." By 48 hours very few small lymphocytes were present (see Fig. 1). Studies of the mitotic activity of these cultures and the timing of deoxyribonucleic acid (DNA) synthesis indicate synchronization with the time of alteration of lymphocyte morphology, from the mature "small lymphocyte" to the undifferentiated large mononuclear cell with vacuolated cytoplasm (see Fig. 2).

Further evidence that the lymphocyte is the potentially mitogenic cell in these cultures is afforded by studies of blood from infants with lymphocytic aplasia. Hauschteck and Hitzig (1963) failed to obtain mitosis in blood cells from an infant with "lympho-plasmocytic dysgenesis," and in the author's laboratory several unsuccessful attempts were made to obtain mitotic activity in cells from an infant with agammaglobulinemia and alymphocytosis (Lischner and Kaback, 1962).

III. COLLECTION OF PERIPHERAL BLOOD LEUCOCYTES AND PREPARATION OF CELL INOCULUM

A. COLLECTION AND STORAGE OF CELLS

Heparin has been found to be uniformly satisfactory for anticoagulation of blood collected for the preparation of leucocyte cultures.[1] Heparinized

---

[1] Excess heparin has on occasion produced clumping of the white cells which is noted when the cells are placed in a counting chamber (Walford, 1960). This ex-

whole blood can be stored at refrigerator temperatures for 12–24 hours before the white cells are separated, but after this period it is often impossible to separate viable white cells from the red cell mass, apparently because of the instability of heparin in the presence of blood. In another anticoagulant, acid–citrate–dextrose, cells still capable of mitosis have been recovered from banked whole blood for at least 2 weeks (Petrakis and Politis, 1962).

WBC separated from the red blood cells (RBC) maintained their mitotic potential for at least 96 hours at 5°C (Mellman *et al.,* 1962). At room temperature they lose their viability within 24 hours, although it has been reported that both separated white cells and whole blood survive at this temperature if culture medium is added (Edwards, 1962; Arakaki and Sparkes, 1963). These latter observations suggest that viability is preserved at metabolically active temperatures if nutrients are supplied. The ability to store WBC suspensions for several days at 5°C offers several advantages. The cells may be collected at a distance and shipped to the laboratory. The laboratory need not plant the cultures on the day the cells arrive. An aliquot of cells from a given subject may be stored until it is certain that the original culture of these cells has produced adequate metaphase preparations. Culture failures may be due to toxicity or contamination of the medium, or disturbances of incubator temperature regulation. When culture conditions are at fault, a second attempt at culturing the same cells should be successful and can be made without obtaining a second blood specimen.

B. Separation of Leucocytes from Whole Blood

Leucocytes may be separated from the red cells by centrifugation or by gravity sedimentation. Centrifugation may be done slowly, in which case the leucocytes are recovered in the supernatant plasma. The blood may also be spun rapidly: then the WBC must be recovered from the buffy coat.

Centrifugation of freshly drawn blood at slow speeds (about $25 \times g$) for 10–15 minutes at room temperature will produce a supernatant

---

cess heparin can be removed without affecting the viability of the cells by washing the WBC suspensions in serum or balanced salt solution. Preservatives, such as phenol, present in certain commercial preparations of heparin have been found to be toxic to leucocyte cultures. Several brands of heparin even with a preservative have been found to work satisfactorily. Commercial diluting fluids also may contain preservatives (e.g., benzyl alcohol) toxic to cell cultures.

containing WBC grossly free from RBC. If the blood is preincubated (30 minutes, 5°C) with PHA (Difco form M, 0.2 ml/10 ml), the agglutinated RBC can be more completely and more speedily sedimented (5–10 minutes at 25 $\times$ g, 5°C) (Moorhead *et al.*, 1960). Centrifuged specimens of PHA-treated blood provide supernatants which are free from platelets as well as from RBC, and the PMN compose a smaller percentage of the WBC than in the original blood. But as Skoog and Beck (1956) have shown, this method results in lower yields of WBC, so that a larger volume of whole blood is required to obtain an adequate WBC inoculum than with other methods.

Centrifugation at high speeds with resuspension of the buffy coat has also been found to be a suitable method of preparing cells for culture (Bender and Prescott, 1962).

Gravity sedimentation effectively removes the bulk of the RBC, leaving a WBC-rich supernatant plasma.[2] The property of rouleau formation permits the RBC to sediment more rapidly than the WBC. The influences on sedimentation rate are well known, yet poorly understood, and must be considered when predicting the time required for sedimentation. Temperature is the most common variable; the sedimentation rate is decelerated when the temperature is less than 20°C. Some workers have preferred to sediment blood at 37°C. At 20°–25°C, most heparinized blood will settle by gravity in 40–80 minutes, grossly clearing 25–30% of its original volume of RBC.[3]

---

[2] A typical experiment with 10 ml whole blood sedimented at room temperature using method A (see Section IX) produces at the end of 1 hour a supernatant containing 2.5–3.0 ml plasma with 12–24 $\times$ 10[6] WBC/ml, representing a 25–50% recovery of WBC from the original volumes of blood. Experiments have shown that the PMN sediment more rapidly than the lymphocytes. In one experiment, when the supernatant was separated into three equal fractions the following cell distribution was found:

	Total WBC/ml	PMN (%)	Lymphocytes
Upper layer	7.4 $\times$ 10[6]	32	68
Middle layer	19.4 $\times$ 10[6]	80	20
Lower layer	16.6 $\times$ 10[6]	91	9
Average	14.5 $\times$ 10[6]		

[3] The speed of sedimentation is also influenced by the surface tension of the container. If the blood is sedimented in a glass syringe or tube, it should be scrupulously clean or siliconized. Nonwettable containers such as disposable plastic syringes have been found most consistently satisfactory. Thorough anticoagulation

The WBC recovered in the supernatant plasma by gravity sedimentation are severalfold greater than when blood is slowly centrifuged. Depending on the WBC content of the blood obtained by venipuncture, gravity sedimentation recovers $12-24 \times 10^6$ WBC/ml of supernatant, whereas PHA treatment and centrifugation recover only $1-2 \times 10^6$ WBC/ml. Because of the relatively high yield by sedimentation, it is now possible to obtain inoculum for a single culture from as little as 1 ml of blood. A simple procedure that has proved practical and reproducible is described in Section IX, B.

Fibrinogen and dextran sedimentation have been found to be more efficient methods for separating WBC from the red cell mass (Skoog and Beck, 1956). The addition of these substances to the plasma does not interfere with growth in culture but makes the preparation of high-quality well-stained metaphase slides more difficult. This complication can be avoided by washing the cells at the time of harvesting the culture (Edwards, 1962). There appears to be little advantage to these sedimenting adjuvants with human blood, but they are finding important application where leucocytes are being cultivated from small animals (Nichols and Levan, 1962).

C. The Basis for Separation of Leucocytes from Other Formed Elements of the Blood

Within certain limits, RBC do not seem to interfere with the multiplication of WBC in culture. Excess RBC may be detrimental to the culture because they metabolize essential nutrients, especially glucose, since replenishment of the medium seems to obviate their adverse affect (Arakaki and Sparkes, 1963). In the author's laboratory, moderate numbers of intact

---

with adequate heparin is likewise important, as small clots impede sedimentation and trap WBC. Rinsing the syringe prior to venipuncture and leaving a small amount of heparin (0.1–0.2 ml containing 1000 units/ml) in the syringe assures complete anticoagulation.

When RBC morphology interferes with sedimentation (e.g., sickle cell anemia, acanthocytosis), gravity sedimentation is unsatisfactory and centrifugation is needed. The slow sedimentation rate of the blood of newborn infants is probably a function of the increased hematocrit as well as its serum protein composition. WBC can best be separated from newborn blood by diluting it with an equal volume of adult human serum or fetal calf serum.

All glassware used for cell collection or culture should be thoroughly rinsed of alkaline detergents. Epidemics of culture failures can often be traced to a breakdown in standards of glassware preparation.

RBC contaminating the WBC suspensions do not interfere with mitosis; a grossly hemolyzed supernatant plasma destroys the mitotic activity of the cultures. Recently, procedures for the production of metaphases in peripheral blood cultures utilizing whole blood inocula have been reported (Tips *et al.*, 1963). The number of metaphases that can be grown from whole blood cultures may be a function of the volume of blood that the culture medium will nourish. Despite this theoretical limitation of whole blood cultures, viz., fewer dividing mononuclear leucocytes, it may represent the most efficient way to utilize the WBC in a given volume of blood.

Although PMN are numerically less significant, the same considerations placed on the presence of RBC in culture may probably be applied to the PMN in the inoculum. A number of methods have been used to remove PMN from leucocyte suspensions. Except in circumstances with disproportionately high percentges of PMN, there seems to be no apparent need to remove them from the WBC suspensions. A simple procedure is to store the WBC suspensions at 5°C for 48 hours, during which time the PMN degenerate while the mononuclear cells remain viable. Alternatively, since PMN tend to adhere to glass, they can be removed by incubating the culture flask on its side with the cells exposed to a large glass surface for 30–60 minutes, and then standing the flask on end. This allows the cells which do not adhere to glass and the culture medium to settle to the bottom of the flask for the remaining period of incubation (Moorhead, 1964). Differential centrifugation and the use of iron or starch-coated iron granules to promote the magnetic removal of PMN following their phagocytosis of the iron have been used when it is desirable to obtain a suspension with a high percentage of mononuclear cells (Hastings *et al.*, 1961).

There appears to be no need to remove platelets before culturing insofar as they may affect the mitotic activity of the leucocytes. Platelets, like PMN leucocytes, and red cell stroma, become part of the fixed cell suspension. The cell preparations harvested and fixed from cultures made by inoculation with the supernatant plasma of PHA-treated and centrifuged blood contain the least cell debris and produce the best slide preparations. The high quality of these slides appears to be related to the relative absence of PMN, RBC, and platelets in these cultures. The chief disadvantage of this method of preparing cell incubates is the large volume of blood required to obtain an adequate cell culture population.

D. Size of Cell Inoculum

A discussion of the size of the cell inoculum must consider the other variables of culture conditions utilized by various workers. If specific cell interaction is critical, the concentration of WBC on the bottom surface of the culture vessel would be important, since the cells soon settle there. It seems unlikely that this is an important factor, as the cells fail to attach. Efficient multiplication of WBC has been shown to occur in whole blood where the mitotically active cells are significantly diluted with RBC; this is further evidence against the importance of the intimate association of the specific mitotic cell type.

Osgood and Krippaehne (1955) in their original studies of human blood cultures indicated that there is a "gradient factor" for different cell types which is an index of the ability of specific cell types to divide *in vitro*. They stated that mitotic activity is related both to the concentration of cells per unit area of growing surface and to the medium depth in the culture vessel; the presence of other actively dividing cells decreases this factor. Eagle and Piez (1962) have demonstrated that certain mammalian cell cultures require a number of nutrients which are dependent on the cell density, i.e., certain constituents need to be added to the medium only when the cell concentrations are low. The specific nutritional needs of WBC cultures have not been adequately evaluated. It has been shown that fewer WBC are needed to produce mitotic activity when they are introduced into the culture in the form of whole blood. Perhaps cells other than those which become mitotically active provide metabolic support for these cultures. The mechanism for this phenomenon may be analogous to the "conditioned medium" used for other mammalian cell systems. However, there may be the risk that an excess of the conditioning cell population exhausts the medium of essential nutrients before adequate mitotic activity is achieved.

When a large number of metabolizing cells is present in the culture, enough acid is produced to maintain a slightly acid pH. Moderate acidity is well tolerated, whereas alkalinity of the medium leads to cell degeneration. Cells other than those destined to divide, such as RBC and PMN, can function in endogenous acid production. The requirement for CO_2 by certain cell cultures also appears to be population-dependent; likewise, it has been shown that WBC cultures grown in an atmosphere of CO_2 are mitotically active at a lower cell density than where the cells depend on endogenously produced acid (McIntyre and Ebaugh, 1962). It is generally believed that exogenous CO_2 functions as a readily diffusible source of acid.

A further consideration in evaluating the optimum initial cell population is the desire to attain a maximum log phase in the culture. Nowell and others have shown that under certain conditions a minimum inoculum size is needed to produce a peak of mitotic activity limited to about a 48-hour period. Cells harvested for cytogenetic studies at this initial mitotic peak are likely to contain arrested metaphases in their first or possibly second division *in vitro*. These conditions offer the theoretic advantage that the metaphases analyzed will most closely approximate the chromosome situation *in vivo*. As will be described subsequently, evidence is available that a single cell may divide several times during the life of the culture. When smaller initial cell populations are used, it may be necessary to harvest the cells after a longer period in culture to obtain adequate metaphases for analysis. If harvesting is significantly delayed, it is possible that a high proportion of the mitoses may be other than the first or second division *in vitro*.

Experimental evidence has been obtained which shows that, with a sufficiently small initial WBC population, few mitoses are seen at 3 days, although highly active dividing populations are found after 9 days in culture without renewing the medium. When larger cell inocula are used, peak mitotic activity occurs at 3 days, and by 6 days few dividing cells can be found (Spina and Mellman, 1963).

Finally, when a WBC number is recommended as an inoculum, it must be appreciated that this does not allow for variations in the proportion of white cell types in individual specimens of blood, e.g., the increase in PMN with infections, the decrease in circulating lymphocytes with stress and corticosteroid therapy, and the normal higher percentage of lymphocytes in the blood of young children. For this reason, some have advocated preparing essentially pure suspensions of mononuclear cells so that more precise initial cell populations are used (Cooper and Hirschhorn, 1962). The improved frequency of successful cultures when PMN are removed from the initial cell suspension does not seem significant enough to warrant the extra procedure required.

Because of the vagaries of the centrifugation method of separation, Nowell and Hungerford (1963) have continued to recommend the estimation of inoculum size by determining the total white cell concentration in the supernatant plasma. With gravity sedimentation, there is generally less variation in cell concentration in the supernatant, so that persistence in determining the white cell concentration may be more traditional than necessary. With current procedures there appears to be a wide range of optimal white cell concentrations for adequate mitotic rates, yet there is still convincing evidence that there are minimum and maximum permissible limits.

IV. INITIATION OF MITOSIS IN BLOOD CULTURES: THE ROLE OF PHYTOHEMAGGLUTININ AND OTHER POTENTIALLY MITOGENIC AGENTS

Mononuclear leucocytes from the peripheral blood of nonleukemic humans divide in culture after a 2–3 day latent period when PHA is present in the medium, while immature leukemic cells divide in culture without this lag and without the addition of PHA. These differences are based on observations of blood cultures serially sampled for the presence of mitoses.

MacKinney et al. (1962), using tritiated thymidine labeling, have shown that only 0.1–0.5% of cells in normal peripheral blood are synthesizing DNA at the beginning of their time in culture and that there is no increase in the number of cells labeled until 24–48 hours later. This is consistent with the earlier findings of Bond et al. (1958). The maximum number of cells synthesizing DNA (about 45%) is reached at 72 hours (see Fig. 3). McIntyre and Ebaugh (1962), using P^{32} as their label, also found a significant increase in P^{32}-containing DNA at 24–48 hours; furthermore, they established that DNA synthesis as well as cell division failed to occur without the addition of PHA to the culture system.

The exact mechanism of action of PHA in peripheral blood cultures is still an enigma. PHA is a mucoprotein prepared by salt extraction of *Phaseolus vulgaris* (red kidney bean) or *Phaseolus communis* (navy bean) (Rigas and Osgood, 1955). It was originally used because of its potent hemagglutinating property and only fortuitously was noted to be mitogenic (Nowell, 1960b). Since Nowell's finding, attempts have been made to purify further this amorphous preparation in an attempt to identify the principle responsible for mitogenesis. Although there is increasing evidence that there are two principles in this material, one which is red cell-agglutinating and the other mitogenic, a completely purified mitogenic fraction has not yet been isolated (T. Punnett and H. H. Punnett, 1963). From attempts to separate the hemagglutinating function from that of mitotic stimulation has come the conclusion that hemagglutination is not correlated with mitogenesis, since the most potent RBC hemagglutinating preparations have failed to stimulate mitosis.

Several proposals have been made for the role of PHA in human peripheral blood cultures.

One suggestion is that PHA aggregates the leucocytes, and when WBC are in close association an interaction occurs which transforms them into dividing cells (Hirschhorn et al., 1963). An objection to this thesis is that

WBC multiply in cultures of whole blood even when the cells are agitated in spinner culture (Nowell, 1960b). Tests for the presence or absence of the hemagglutinating activity of PHA have generally used the RBC as the indicator cells. Unfractionated PHA preferentially agglutinates RBC in whole blood, although it will agglutinate WBC when added in sufficient

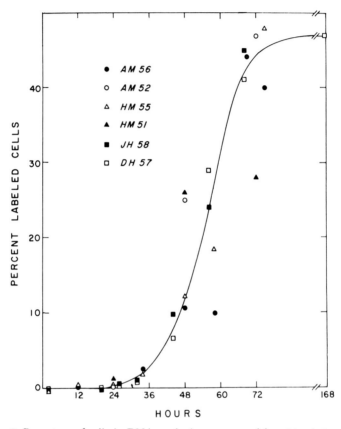

FIG. 3. Percentage of cells in DNA synthesis, as measured by tritiated thymidine uptake, during culture. Tritiated thymidine was added 2 hours prior to examination of cultures. (From MacKinney *et al.,* 1963.)

quantity to WBC suspensions. The factor in PHA that agglutinates RBC is different from that which aggregates WBC and is nonmitogenic. Therefore, the fraction of PHA which is leucoagglutinating and mitogenic may be identical (Barkhan and Ballas, 1963; Hirschhorn *et al.,* 1963).

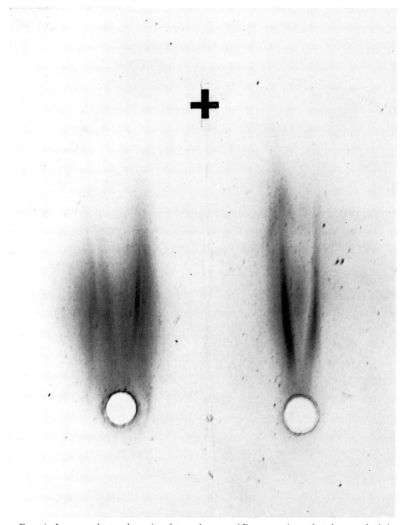

Fig. 4. Immunoelectrophoresis of two human AB sera using phytohemagglutinin (Difco P form, standard dilution) in center trough. Oil red O stain.

PHA has been shown to precipitate specific fractions of the serum proteins. By use of immunoelectrophoretic methods, at least three precipitin bands can be identified between PHA and human serum components. These bands can be seen to run electrophoretically in the β-globulin region and stain as lipoproteins (see Fig. 4) (Rawnsley and Mellman, 1963).

This precipitation pattern disappears when PHA is treated with RBC until no further RBC agglutination occurs. When PHA is absorbed by RBC in this manner it does not lose its mitogenic potency.

That PHA precipitates a serum protein which is a mitotic inhibitor has not been completely tested (Beckman, 1962). Since the WBC are effectively coated with serum protein, PHA reacting with this serum protein might alter the cell membrane permeability to substances in the media that promote cell division.

A further possibility is that PHA acts as an antigen which transforms the small lymphocyte into an antibody-producing cell as well as a dividing cell. Although these two processes seem to be concomitant, they need not be the same phenomenon (Pearmain et al., 1963).

Pearmain et al. (1963) observed that tuberculin can substitute for PHA in human lymphocyte cultures when donors of these cells were sensitive to tuberculin by the Mantoux test. A number of other antigens are being studied at the present time to determine their specificity as antigenic stimulants of mitosis in vitro.[4] It is tempting to assume, yet still uncertain, that PHA acts as a ubiquitous antigen, but it is hopeful that the riddle of PHA activity may be resolved by the study of antigens in human blood cultures.

V. INFLUENCE OF CULTURE CONDITIONS ON CELL PROLIFERATION

A. Culture Medium

The nature of the "defined media" that is part of the blood culture system is probably of little importance, since a significant part of the culture is serum or plasma which still defies definition as it is applied to the nutrition of the culture. Although TC 199 was the basal medium originally used by Osgood and Brooke and has continued to prove satisfactory, NCTC 109, Parker's, Waymouth's, and Eagle's ME media have all been found adequate. These media all have varying mixtures of amino acids, vitamins, and buffered salts. None of these media have been preferentially advan-

---

[4] It has occasionally been suggested that PHA is unnecessary in human blood cultures. Perhaps in these instances other antigenic substances were present in the culture medium that stimulated the mitoses of sensitized cells. The recent report that WBC of penicillin-allergic individuals may be stimulated to divide in culture by the usual addition of penicillin is one example of this phenomenon (Hirschhorn et al., 1963).

tageous, nor can they support the growth of blood cultures without supplementation with serum proteins.

B. SERUM PROTEIN

The addition of 10–40% serum to the culture medium is needed to support the metabolism of the cultures. It appears that when more serum is used the pH is more efficiently controlled, especially when the cultures are equilibrated with room air.

Both human and calf serum have been used with success in dividing cultures. Both autologous or homologous human serum can be used. When using homologous serum, AB donors have tended to be used, although the need for serum free from major blood group antibodies has not been systematically investigated. It has been the author's practice to add about half the volume of serum to be used as WBC-containing plasma and an equal volume as homologous AB serum. The extra serum may be obtained by rapidly centrifuging the blood which remains after separation of the WBC suspension. When calf serum has been used, commercially available fetal calf serum has been more consistently effective in supporting cell growth than ordinary calf serum.

Human AB serum and fetal calf serum can be stored at —20°C indefinitely without losing their effectiveness in supporting cell growth. Heparinized plasma when used fresh or refrigerated is an adequate substitute for serum, but it has been noted that after heparinized plasma has been frozen its growth-promoting activity is destroyed (Mellman et al., 1962). The exact mechanism of this instability of frozen heparinized plasma is not known. There are known effects of heparin on lipoprotein. This suggests that altered lipoprotein may be the element in serum critical to the life of the culture.

It has been found that there are certain AB donors who consistently and repeatedly provide serum which produces significantly higher mitotic rates with multiple different samples of human leucocytes. Biochemical comparison of the sera of these donors with other less mitotically active sera may eventually provide the key to the role of serum in these cultures.

C. pH AND CO_2 CONTROL

Alkalinity of the culture medium will adversely influence the health of these cultures. Air-tight bottles prevent the leakage of endogenously produced CO_2 from the atmosphere of the vessel, while open vessels incubated in the presence of 5% CO_2 in air also are satisfactory. Initial correction of the medium pH to 7.2 with 0.1 N HCl, with daily adjustments to maintain a pH of 7.2–7.4 with HCl or $NaHCO_3$ is practiced by Nowell. Others lightly gas the culture vessel with 5% CO_2 in air at the start of the culture. In the author's laboratory neither of these procedures is part of the routine practice.

D. Incubation Temperature

The rate of metabolism and the time of mitotic logarithmic activity are sensitive to environmental temperature. When incubated at 36–37°C, peak mitotic activity occurs at approximately 60–72 hours. Nowell and Hungerford (1963) have found that strictly controlled temperatures at 38°C will advance the mitotic peak to 48 hours. Temperatures above 39°–40°C usually have resulted in death of the culture.

E. Antibiotics

Penicillin and streptomycin have been added to human leucocyte cultures and effectively prevent most bacterial contamination. There is some evidence that mammalian cell cultures may be sensitive to toxic levels of streptomycin (Metzgar and Moskowitz, 1963) as well as to other antibiotics, in particular chloramphenicol (Ambrose and Coons, 1963). Assuming that reasonably sterile precautions are taken, the addition of antibiotics may be needless.

Commercial PHA is now provided bacteria-free, although mold contamination has been an occasional problem. The overgrowth of mold is usually not a problem with cultures of 48–72 hours duration. When cultures are being maintained for longer periods, it is best to filter the PHA. A Swinney-type filter attached to the syringe containing reconstituted PHA has been the most convenient method of removing mold spores at the time of planting the cultures.

VI. PREPARATION OF METAPHASE SPREADS FOR CYTOGENETIC STUDIES

A. Colchicine Arrest of Mitoses at Metaphase

Both Tjio and Levan (1956) and Ford and Hamerton (1956b) adapted the technique from plant cytogenetics (P. Gavaudan *et al.*, 1937) of using colchicine to prevent spindle formation and thereby to promote dispersion of metaphase chromosomes. Either colchicine or its analog deacetymethyl-colchicine (Colcemid, CIBA) is now routinely added to blood cultures. The longer the culture is exposed to colchicine the greater the potential number of arrested metaphases. However, this advantage of prolonged colchicine treatment is offset by the risk of marked condensation and contraction of the chromosomes. This aspect of the metaphase process proceeds independently of the colchicine effect on the spindle, resulting in poorer definition of the fixed chromosomes.

B. Hypotonic Treatment

Hsu's (1952) fortuitous observation and promotion of the use of hypotonic solutions before fixation of cultured cells have been a great boon to human cytogenetics. This treatment in synergy with the effect of colchicine swells the cell and promotes dispersion of metaphase chromosomes. The usual procedure is to dilute the balanced salt solution used to wash the harvested cells with distilled water, then to incubate the cells in this environment for a period before fixation.

With human fibroblast cultures, Lejeune (1960) has recommended the use of a solution containing one part human serum to five parts of distilled water. This treatment, he found, preserves the fine morphology of the chromosomes. Hungerford and Nowell (1963) have used this solution with cultured leucocytes and have had similar gratifying results.

C. Fixation

The quality of chromosome morphology and stainability is influenced by fixation procedures. The less the water present in the fixative and surrounding the cells at the time of initial fixation, the better the fixation. For this reason the cells should be spun into a small button and all the supernatant liquid removed. The fixative is then added and allowed to filter through the pellet of cells and left undisturbed for about 30 minutes. Although this procedure has been found effective, some prefer to agitate the cells when first adding the fixative. A freshly made solution of three volumes of absolute methanol to one volume of glacial acetic acid works well. If the alcohol has been exposed to air, it will have absorbed water and not dehydrate the cells as well. The optimal time that the cells sit in the first fixative varies with the size of the button of cells harvested. Using the procedures outlined in Section IX, 30 minutes is usually correct. When there are fewer cells the initial fixation time should be shortened proportionately. Fresh fixative should then be added to the cells. If the original fixative is removed before resuspending the cells, a small volume of fresh solution should be added so that the cells can be thoroughly dispersed. When the original fixative is used, only 0.5 ml should have been layered on the cells. At this stage multiple changes of fixative may be needed before the metaphase chromosomes are clear of coating substances that interfere with their flattening on glass and their affinity for stain.

The nature of the fixation procedure was illustrated by Saksela and Moorhead (1962), who showed that chromosome morphology was altered by the use of equal volumes instead of the usual 3:1 dilution of alcohol and acetic acid. The volatility of alcohol is an important factor in the flattening and dispersion of chromosomes with the air-drying or ignition techniques of preparing slide preparations.

D. Preparation of Slides and Staining

The ease of mastering the air-dried technique of preparing chromosome spreads is a distinct advantage over the traditional squashing procedure. There is already some evidence that the details of chromosome morphology and the distributions of chromosome number described by various workers cannot be compared unless the same procedure for fixing and spreading the cells on slides is used.

A number of stains have been employed. These include Feulgen, aceto-orcein, Giemsa, Unna's blue, and methylene blue. The Feulgen stain specifically identifies DNA and may provide finer detail of chromosome structure than the others. The remaining ones have been adopted because they stain the chromosomes more intensely. The use of phase contract optics has intensified the paler chromosome stains.

VII. LIFE SPAN OF PHA INITIATED CULTURES: EVIDENCE FOR SECONDARY MITOSES IN CULTURE

As has already been discussed, for cytogenetic studies that best reflect the *in vivo* state of chromosome morphology, the first division *in vitro* should ideally be harvested. When optimal primary cell populations are cultured for this purpose, there are usually few further mitoses after a 24–48 hour wave of mitotic activity. The stationary phase that occurs is presumably due to exhaustion of nutrients or accumulation of toxic metabolites.

When fewer cells are planted, cell division begins on schedule, but mitoses continue to appear for more prolonged periods of time. Using tritiated thymidine pulse labeling, Bender and Prescott (1962) have suggested that cells may undergo as many as four divisions in culture. Availability of nutrients does not seem to be the only limiting factor, for despite dilution of cell population and replenishment of medium, there has been no consistent success in getting actively dividing human nonleukemic cell cultures to survive for more than 14–21 days (Moorhead, 1964).

To date there have been no reports of prolonged cultures of human leucocytes except for those in which heteroploid transformation occurs. Heteroploid strains have been derived from both nonleukemic (Berman and Stulberg, 1958) and leukemic (Osgood and Brooke, 1955) bloods. Petrakis *et al.* (1961) have placed normal human leucocytes in subcutaneous millipore diffusion chambers and observed that the surviving mononuclear cells are able to transform into fibroblast-like cells. It may be necessary to use mononuclear leucocytes after they have become fibroblastic in order to maintain them for prolonged periods in culture.

VIII. FURTHER APPLICATION OF THE LEUCOCYTE CULTURE SYSTEM

The usefulness of the peripheral blood cultures for human cytogenetic studies is established. Despite the short life span of these cultures, the ability to establish readily available primary human cells in active metabolism and replication naturally suggests that this culture system be adopted for other experiments. An immunological study involving the response of cultured leucocytes to specific antigens with the production of possibly specific γ-globulin has been reported (Elves *et al.*, 1963). The effect of physical and chemical agents, including hormones, chemical mutagens, and X-rays, on these cultures is under active examination. The responses of cultured cells to these agents are being investigated by observing the chromosomes for evidence of morphological alterations, and by determining their effects on the rate of mitotic activity (mitotic index) (Nowell, 1961; Jackson and Lindahl-Kiessling, 1963; Bender and Gooch, 1963). There is reason to believe that intermediary metabolism may be examined in this system, since this may be a better source of cultured cells for study of inborn errors of metabolism than has been the experience thus far with human fibroblast cultures.

IX. METHODS FOR CULTURING HUMAN PERIPHERAL BLOOD LEUCOCYTES

(As performed at the Chromosome Laboratory of the Children's Hospital, Philadelphia, Pennsylvania.)

A. MACROMETHOD (Fig. 5)

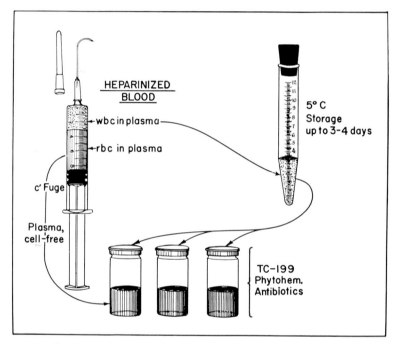

FIG. 5. Peripheral blood leucocyte culture macromethod according to procedure outlined in text. (Diagram from Klevit, 1962.)

1. Place 0.1 ml aqueous heparin (1000 units/ml) into a 10 ml plastic disposable syringe. Aseptically draw 5–10 ml of venous blood and mix the heparin thoroughly by inverting the syringe.

2. Aspirate the blood from the needle and a small space below the hub of the syringe. Wipe the needle with alcohol, cover with a needle cover, and stand the syringe on the end of the plunger with the needle pointed up. Let stand at room temperature (over 68°F) for about 1 hour. Observe periodically until about 30–40% of the blood volume has visibly cleared of red cells.

3. Bend the needle at right angles and extrude the plasma into a sterile calibrated centrifuge tube. (The leucocyte-containing plasma may then be stored at 5°C for 3–4 days if indicated before planting the cultures.)

4. If autologous plasma is to be used, the remaining volume of blood can be centrifuged rapidly in another sterile tube and the supernatant plasma removed for use in the cultures.

5. Count the white cells in the leucocyte-containing plasma. Determine the volume of cell suspension containing $8–12 \times 10^6$ WBC.

6. Into a sterile culture vessel (20 ml vial, 24×50 mm), add the volume of cell suspension containing 10^7 leucocytes (usually 0.5–1·0 ml). Then add:

   a. 1 ml of additional autologous plasma, AB human serum, *or* fetal calf serum
   b. 6 ml of basal medium TC 199
   c. 0.03–0.05 ml of Bactophytohemagglutinin (P form, Difco—1 vial constituted in 5 ml of distilled water)
   d. 0.02 ml of a solution containing penicillin (100,000 units/ml) and streptomycin (100 mg/ml) (these amounts are not critical)

7. Incubate at 37°C with an air-tight cap.

8. On the third day of culture (60–70 hours), add 0.05 ml of either colchicine to give a final culture concentration of 0.4 µg/ml, or Colcemid to a final concentration of 0.05 µg/ml.

9. After 2–4 hours, suspend the cells in the medium, transfer to a calibrated conical centrifuge tube, and spin for 5 minutes at 500–800 rpm (International centrifuge SB). Remove medium and wash in 5 ml of Hank's balanced salt solution and re-spin. Remove the supernatant salt solution to the 0.5 ml mark on the tube. Suspend the cells thoroughly in this volume with a Pasteur pipet. Add 2 ml of distilled water, periodically mixing the cells. Allow to stand for 8–10 minutes at room temperature.

10. Resuspend the cells and centrifuge as before. Remove *all* hypotonic supernatant fluid without disrupting the button.

Prepare fixative by adding 1 volume of glacial acetic acid (reagent grade) to 3 volumes of absolute methyl alcohol just before adding to cell button. (Both reagents should be used from a small stock bottle and renewed periodically, as they absorb moisture with repeated exposure to air.)

11. Add fixative dropwise gently to top of cell button (about 0.5 ml). Allow to stand undisturbed for 20–30 minutes. Remove fixative. Add a small volume of fresh fixative and suspend cells thoroughly. (Take care

that fluid is not aspirated more than a short distance into the stem of the pipet, as cells tend to stick to the pipet wall, and mitoses may be lost in this way.) Recentrifuge and change fixative. Repeat this procedure until suspension is cloudy and less flocculent. (Clumps may be reduced in size by repeated aspiration through a finely drawn pipet.)

12. Dip a thoroughly clean slide (commercially precleaned slides are recommended) into distilled water. Observe for cleanliness of slide by adherence of the water film.

13. Place a drop of the cell suspension on the center of the wet slide, then:

a. *Blowing Technique.* Immediately tilt slide on long edge, touching absorbent paper, and blow directly on the slide to promote evaporation. Complete drying of the slide by laying it on a warm surface.

b. *Flaming Technique.* Immediately pass through a small flame, igniting the alcohol fixative. Hold horizontally until the flame extinguishes itself and the drop of fixative is dry.

14. Examine the dried slide under a phase contrast microscope (an ordinary light microscope with the illumination reduced and condenser lowered will do). Observe for the following:

a. *Cells Are Scarce.* Concentrate the cell suspension from step 11 by centrifuging and removing part of the fixative and repeat steps 12–14.

b. *Chromosomes Insufficiently Spread or Shredded.* Resuspend the cells from step 11 in fresh fixative one or more times and repeat steps 12–14. A larger drop will also promote spreading. Flaming is usually more effective than blowing if the degree of spreading is inadequate.

c. *Chromosomes Are Overspread or Scattered.* Use a smaller drop from step 11 and repeat 12–14. Do not evaporate fixative as quickly, i.e., blow gently or not at all; do not warm slide.

15. Having made sufficient slides with adequate well-spread mitoses, store the remaining cell suspension at 5°C. The suspension can be stored indefinitely. To make more slides after storage, change fixative several times and repeat procedure from step 12.

16. Stain (Giemsa)

a. Mix 10 ml of Giemsa stain with 90 ml of distilled water and 3–5 ml of 0.15 N NH$_4$OH (to pH 7.2 approx.). Use Giemsa stain only once and then discard.

b. Stain slides 5–6 minutes.

c. Dehydrate slides through two dishes of acetone, one of ½ acetone, ½ xylol; and finally xylol. (Excessive agitation in acetone may destain slides.)

d. Mount in permount.

B. SEMIMICRO PROCEDURE

1. To a 2 ml plastic disposable syringe, add 0.1 ml of aqueous heparin (1000 units/ml) and 1 ml of human AB serum (or fetal calf serum, although AB is preferable). Fill the syringe to the 2 ml mark with venous blood (Fig. 6A,B).

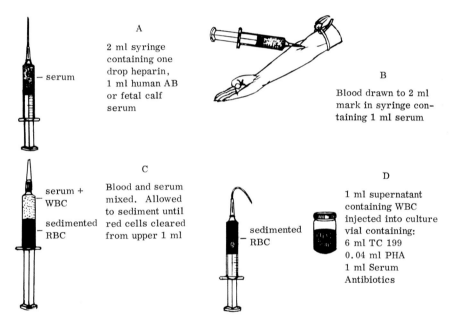

A

2 ml syringe containing one drop heparin, 1 ml human AB or fetal calf serum

— serum

B

Blood drawn to 2 ml mark in syringe containing 1 ml serum

C

serum + WBC

sedimented RBC

Blood and serum mixed. Allowed to sediment until red cells cleared from upper 1 ml

sedimented RBC

D

1 ml supernatant containing WBC injected into culture vial containing:
6 ml TC 199
0.04 ml PHA
1 ml Serum
Antibiotics

FIG. 6. Semimicro method for culturing peripheral blood leucocytes from 1 ml of blood.

2. Mix the syringe contents. Empty the needle by aspiration. Stand at room temperature as above (Section A, step 2) until the supernatant cleared of red cells is about 1 ml (30–60 minutes) (Fig. 6C).

3. Bend the needle and inject into the culture vessel directly without

doing a WBC count.[5] The vessel should contain the ingredients described under Section A (step 6 a–d) which can be prepared in advance and stored at —20°C, and brought to room temperature before adding the cell suspension (Fig. 6D).

4. Proceed as in Section A (steps 7–16).

C. PROCEDURES OF OTHER LABORATORIES

1. *Laboratory of Dr. P. C. Nowell.* Blood (10–20 ml) is obtained in a syringe containing 0.2 ml heparin. PHA (M form) (0.2 ml/10 ml of blood) is added to the blood which is mixed and refrigerated for 30–45 minutes. Blood is centrifuged at $25 \times g$ for 10 minutes at 5°C, the supernatant removed, and leucocytes are counted. Leucocytes (10^7) are planted with 3 ml autologous plasma, 5 ml medium, and antibiotics. The pH is adjusted to 7.2 with 0.1 N HCl and, if needed, daily adjustments are made with either HCl or $NaHCO_3$ to maintain a pH of 7.2–7.4. The culture is incubated at 37°C for 3 days and the remaining procedure is as above with the exception of hypotonic treatment (1:5 dilution of serum is used; see Section VI, B).

2. *Other Micromethods.* For descriptions, see Edwards (1962), Frøland (1962), Tips *et al.* (1963), and Arakaki and Sparkes (1963). The latter two methods use whole blood as the cell inoculum.

Acknowledgments

This study was aided by U.S. Public Health Service grants AM-02231 and HD-00588 and a Research Career Development Award, National Institutes of Health.

References

Ambrose, C. T., and Coons, A. H. (1963). Studies on antibody production. VIII. Inhibitory effect of chloramphenicol on synthesis of antibody in tissue culture. *J. Exptl. Med.* **117**, 1075-1088.

Arakaki, D. T., and Sparkes, R. S. (1963). Microtechnique for culturing leukocytes from whole blood. *Cytogenetics* **2**, 57-60.

Barkhan, P., and Ballas, A. (1963). Phytohaemagglutinin: Separation of haemagglutinating and mitogenic principles. *Nature* **200**, 141-142.

Beckman, L. (1962). Effect of phytohaemagglutinin on human serum and cell proteins. *Nature* **195**, 582-583.

Bender, M. A., and Gooch, P. C. (1963). Chromatid-type aberrations induced by X-rays in human leukocyte cultures. *Cytogenetics* **2**, 107-116.

---

[5] Counting of the cell-containing supernatant has been found superfluous, and in a series of 10 samples obtained by this method the average WBC count is 5.8×10^6 ml (range 4.0–7.8) with an average differential of 56% lymphocytes (range 40–68%) and 44% PMN (range 32–60%) (Loftus and Spina, 1963).

Bender, M. A., and Prescott, D. M. (1962). DNA synthesis and mitosis in cultures of human peripheral leukocytes. *Exptl. Cell Res.* **27**, 221-229.

Berman, L., and Stulberg, C. S. (1958). The Detroit strains of human epithelial-like cells from nonleukemic peripheral blood. *Blood* **13**, 1149-1167.

Bloom, W. (1938). Tissue cultures of blood and blood-forming tisues. *In* "Handbook of Hematology" (H. Downey, ed.), Vol. II, p. 1499. Harper (Hoeber), New York.

Bond, V. P., Cronkite, E. P., Fliedner, T. M., and Schork, P. (1958). Deoxyribonucleic acid synthesizing cells in peripheral blood of normal human beings. *Science* **128**, 202-203.

Carstairs, K. (1962). The small lymphocyte, its possible pluripotential quality, *Lancet* **I**, 829.

Chrustschoff, G. K. (1935). Cytological investigations on cultures of normal human blood. *J. Genet.* **31**, 243-261.

Cooper, H. L., and Hirschhorn, K. (1962). Improvements in white cell culture including differential leukocyte separation. *Blood* **20**, 102.

Cooper, E. H., Barkhan, P., and Hale, A. J. (1963). Observations on the proliferation of human leucocytes cultured with phytohaemagglutinin. *Brit. J. Haematol.* **9**, 101-111.

Eagle, H., and Piez, K. (1962). The population-dependent requirement by cultured mammalian cells for metabolites which they can synthesize. *J. Exptl. Med.* **116**, 29-43.

Edwards, J. H. (1962). Chromosome analysis from capillary blood. *Cytogenetics* **1**, 90-96.

Elves, M. W., Roath, S., Taylor, G., and Israëls, M. C. G. (1963). The *in vitro* production of antibody lymphocytes. *Lancet* **I**, 1292-1293.

Ford, C. E., and Hamerton, J. L. (1956a). The chromosomes of man. *Nature* **178**, 1020-1023.

Ford, C. E., and Hamerton, J. L. (1956b). A colchicine hypotonic citrate squash sequence for mammalian chromosomes. *Stain Technol.* **31**, 247.

Ford, C. E., Jacobs, P. A., and Lajha, L. G. (1958). Human somatic chromosomes. *Nature* **181**, 1565-1568.

Frøland, A. (1962). A micromethod for chromosome analysis of peripheral blood cultures. *Lancet* **II**, 1281-1282 (letter).

Gavaudan, P., Gavaudan, N., and Pomriaskinsky-Kobozieff, N. (1937). Sur l'influence de la colchicine sur la caryocinèse dans les méristèmes radiculaires de l'Allium cepa. *Compt. Rend. Soc. Biol.* **125**, 705-707.

Hastings, J., Freedman, S., Rendon, O., Cooper, H. L., and Hirschhorn, K. (1961). Culture of human white cells using differential leucocyte separation. *Nature* **192**, 1214-1215.

Hauschteck, E., and Hitzig, W. H. (1963). Failure of mitosis in cultures of blood from a girl with lymphoplasmocytic dysgenesia. Personal communication.

Hirschhorn, K., Bach, F., Kolodny, R., Firschein, I. L., and Hashem, N. (1963). Immune response and mitosis of human peripheral blood lymphocytes *in vitro*. *Science* **142**, 1185-1187.

Hsu, T. C. (1952). Mammalian chromosomes *in vitro*. I. The karyotype of man. *J. Heredity* **43**, 167-172.

Hungerford, D. A., and Nowell, P. C. (1963). Personal communication.

Hungerford, D. A., Donnelly, A. J., Nowell, P. C., and Beck, S. (1959). The chromosome constitution of a human phenotypic intersex. *Am. J. Human Genet.* **11**, 215-236.

Jackson, J. F., and Lindahl-Kiessling, K. (1963). Polyploidy and endoreduplication in human leukocyte cultures treated with β-mercaptopyruvate. *Science* **141**, 424-425.

Klevit, H. D. (1962). The sex chromosomes in abnormalities of sexual differentiation. *Am. J. Med. Sci.* **243**, 790-807.

Lejeune, J. (1960). Le mongolisme trisomie dégressive, p. 17. Thésis, Faculté des Sciences. Université de Paris.

Lischner, H., and Kaback, M. M. (1962). Unpublished observations.

Loftus, J., and Spina, J. (1963). Unpublished data.

McIntyre, O. R., and Ebaugh, F. G. (1962). The effect of phytohemagglutinin on leukocyte cultures as measured by P^{32} incorporation in the DNA, RNA, and acid soluble fractions. *Blood* **19**, 443-453.

MacKinney, A. A., Stohlman, F., and Brecher, G. (1962). The kinetics of cell proliferation in cultures of human peripheral blood. *Blood* **19**, 349-358.

Marshall, W. H., and Roberts, K. B. (1963). The growth and mitosis of human small lymphocytes after incubation with a phytohaemagglutinin. *Quart. J. Exptl. Physiol.* **48**, 146-155.

Mellman, W. J., Klevit, H. D., and Moorhead, P. S. (1962). Studies on phytohemagglutinin-stimulated leukocyte cultures. *Blood* **20**, 103 (abstr.).

Metzgar, D. P., and Moskowitz, M. (1963). Studies on the effect of streptomycin on mammalian cells in culture. *Exptl. Cell Res.* **30**, 379-387.

Moorhead, P. S. (1964). The blood technique and human chromosomes. *Symp. Mammalian Tissue Culture Cytol. São Paulo 1962.* Pergamon Press, New York. In press.

Moorhead, P. S., Nowell, P. C., Mellman, W. J., Battips, D. M., and Hungerford, D. A. (1960). Chromosome preparations of leukocytes cultured from human peripheral blood. *Exptl. Cell Res.* **20**, 613-616.

Nichols, W. W., and Levan, A. (1962). Chromosome preparations by the blood tissue culture technique in various laboratory animals. *Blood* **20**, 106 (abstr.).

Nowell, P. C. (1960a). Differentiation of human luekemic leukocytes in tissue culture. *Exptl. Cell Res.* **19**, 267-277.

Nowell, P. C. (1960b). Phytohemagglutinin: An initiator of mitosis in cultures of normal human leukocytes. *Cancer Res.* **20**, 462-466.

Nowell, P. C. (1961). Inhibition of human leukocyte mitosis by prednisolone *in vitro. Cancer Res.* **21**, 1518-1521.

Nowell, P. C., and Hungerford, D. A. (1963). Personal communication.

Osgood, E. E., and Brooke, J. H. (1955). Continuous tissue culture of leukocytes from human leukemic bloods by application of "gradient principles." *Blood* **10**, 1010-1022.

Osgood, E. E., and Krippaehne, M. L. (1955). The gradient tissue culture method. *Exptl. Cell Res.* **9**, 116-127.

Pearmain, G., Lycette, R. R., and Fitzgerald, P. H. (1963). Tuberculin-induced mitosis in peripheral blood leucocytes. *Lancet* **I**, 637-638.

Petrakis, N. L., and Politis, G. (1962). Prolonged survival of viable, mitotically competent mononuclear leukocytes in stored whole blood. *New Engl. J. Med.* **267**, 286-289.

Petrakis, N. L., Davis, M., and Lucia, S. P. (1961). The *in vivo* differentiation of human leukocytes into histiocytes, fibroblasts and fat cells in subcutaneous diffusion chambers. *Blood* **17**, 109-118.

Punnett, T., and Punnett, H. H. (1963). Induction of leucocyte growth in cultures of human peripheral blood. *Nature* **198**, 1173-1175.

Rawnsley, H., and Mellman, W. J. (1963). Unpublished observations.

Rigas, D. A., and Osgood, E. E. (1955). Purification and properties of the phytohemagglutinin of *Phaseolus vulgaris. J. Biol. Chem.* **212**, 607-609.

Rothfels, K. H., and Siminovitch, L. (1958). An air drying technique for flattening chromosomes in mammalian cells grown *in vitro. Stain Technol.* **33**, 73-77.

Saksela, E., and Moorhead, P. S. (1962). Enhancement of secondary constrictions and the heterochromatic X in human cells. *Cytogenetics* **1**, 225-244.

Skoog, W. A., and Beck, W. S. (1956). Studies on the fibrinogen, dextran and phytohemagglutinin methods of isolating leukocytes. *Blood* **11**, 436.

Spina, J., and Mellman, W. J. (1963). Unpublished observations.

Tanaka, Y., Epstein, L. B., Brecher, G., and Stohlman, F. (1963). Transformation of lymphocytes in cultures of human peripheral blood. *Blood* **22**, 614-629.

Tips, R. L., Smith, G., Meyer, D. L., and Ushijima, R. N. (1963). Karyotype analysis of leukocytes as a practical laboratory procedure. *Texas Rept. Biol. Med.* **21**, 581-586.

Tjio, J. H., and Levan, A. (1956). The chromosome number of man, *Hereditas* **42**, 1-6.

Walford, R. I. (1960). "Leukocyte Antigens and Antibodies," p. 3. Grune & Stratton. New York.

Direct Chromosome Preparations of Bone Marrow Cells[*]

J. H. TJIO

National Institute of Arthritis and Metabolic Diseases, Bethesda, Maryland

AND

J. WHANG

National Cancer Institute, Bethesda, Maryland

I. Introduction 51
II. Procedures 52
III. Discussion 53
     References 56

I. INTRODUCTION

Studies of mammalian chromosomes have advanced rapidly since the introduction of preliminary treatment of cells with colchicine and hypotonic solutions, especially when used for the study of established cell lines and cultured cells from connective tissue, bone marrow, and peripheral blood. Direct processing of bone marrow cells has also aided progress since this enables one to identify the cell line from which the analyzed cells are derived (Whang *et al.*, 1963). The technique has proven to be very useful in the study of leukemia because leukemic cells do not grow under the *in vitro* conditions of marrow tissue culture (Sandberg *et al.*, 1962b). Satisfactory chromosome preparations have been obtained by several investigators with the use of short-term cultures (Ford *et al.*, 1958) or immediately after direct aspiration (Bottura and Ferrari, 1960; Meighan and Stich, 1961; Sandberg *et al.*, 1962a) of bone marrow cells.

Due to the great cellularity and inherent high mitotic activity of the marrow, the amount of required material is small, the use of mitotic inducers is superfluous, and sterile techniques are unnecessary in processing the sample. In fact, the two direct methods to be described here are short, simple, and reliable. The first, similar to that used for chromosomes in meristematic tissue of plants (La Cour, 1941), permits preparations

[1] The techniques described here are based on those given by the authors in *Stain Technology* **37**, 17-20 (1962).

to be made without prior *in vitro* culture or *in vivo* colchicine administration, but requires squashing. This method is especially suited for use
where laboratory facilities are limited. The second method dispenses with
squashing but requires use of a centrifuge. In this second method, the
cells are fixed and then attached to slides by the air-drying method of
Rothfels and Siminovitch (1958) for cells in suspension. This minimizes
mechanical distortion and ruptures, and ensures uniform flattening of
the cells in division. These preparations are especially suitable for analysis
from photomicrographs.

II. PROCEDURES

Solutions for the preliminary treatment

Colchicine solution: 0.85% NaCl solution containing $6.6 \times 10^{-3} M$
phosphate, pH 7, to which is added either colchicine or diacetylmethyl
colchicine (Colcemide, Ciba) 0.3 μg/ml.

Hypotonic solution: Sodium citrate, 1% in distilled water.

Staining solutions

Orcein stain: Orcein (G. T. Gurr's natural or synthetic orcein), 2 gm;
hot glacial acetic acid, 45 ml; and distilled water, 55 ml (see La Cour,
1941).

Orcein-HCl: Orcein stain, 9 vol.; 1 *N* HCl, 1 vol.

Squash preparations

1. Aspirate about 0.5 ml sternal, iliac crest, or tibial marrow and
drop immediately into 2–3 ml of colchicine solution. Transfer the marrow
pieces to a second change of colchicine solution, taking care to free them
of blood clots as much as possible. Leave for 1–2 hours at 20–30°C.

2. Transfer to 2–3 ml of hypotonic solution and leave for 20 minutes
at 20–30°C.

3. Transfer the material to a watch glass containing a few drops of
orcein-HCl and heat it over a small flame to effect rapid fixing, staining,
and softening. The solution must not boil.

4. Transfer a piece of marrow to a slide, add a drop of orcein stain,
and place a 22-mm square cover slip in position. Tap the cover slip gently
and repeatedly with the point of a blunt pencil or needle. Remove excess
fluid from the edges of the cover slip with filter paper and express the
remainder by pressure applied to the cover slip through blotting paper.
Avoid sidewise movements of the cover slip.

5. Seal with a waterproof cement. We use Krönig cement (Fisher Scientific Co., Rt. 23, Philadelphia, Pennsylvania).

If stored in a cold place these slides keep for about 3 months. They can be made permanent by the usual dry-ice freezing method (Schultz *et al.,* 1949) and mounted with Permount.

Air-dried preparations

1. As for squashes, except that the second change of colchicine solution may be omitted if the marrow pieces are very small.

2. Centrifuge at room temperature at 400 rpm for 4–5 minutes. Remove supernatant and add 2–3 ml of hypotonic solution. Shake to loosen cells and leave for 0.5 hour.

3. Centrifuge and remove the supernatant. Add 5 ml of Carnoy's fixative (alcohol-acetic, 3:1), resuspend by shaking, and leave for 2–5 minutes. Repeat this procedure a second time.

4. Centrifuge and remove all the supernatant; add approx. 0.2–0.5 ml (depending on the volume of the cell button) of fresh fixative and agitate to resuspend the cells.

5. With a Wintrobe or similar pipette put 1–2 mm droplets of the cell suspension on chemically clean slides. Blow on each droplet gently as soon as the cells are attached to the glass surface to assist in spreading and drying. Leave to dry thoroughly.

6. Immerse slides 10–20 minutes in a Coplin jar containing orcein stain.

7. Dehydrate in grades of alcohol. Clear in 2 changes of absolute alcohol-xylene (1:1) to avoid excessive extraction of stain, 2 changes of xylene, and mount in a synthetic resin (Permount used). Staining can also be performed with the Feulgen reaction, Wright's or Giemsa stain, or crystal violet.

III. DISCUSSION

Chromosome preparations from marrow cells made without prior *in vitro* culture exclude the possibility of nonrepresentational development in the artificial condition of *in vitro* culture. Results from leukemia marrow grown *in vitro* may not be representative due to selective growth of certain cell types. Thus interpretation problems of findings after culture growth are avoided by the direct marrow preparations. It may be assumed with some certainty that the findings from these preparations represent the situation in the cells of the marrow at the moment of sampling.

We have obtained satisfactory results with several hundred marrow aspirates from patients with leukemia and developmental defects examined with the techniques described above. The number of reliable metaphase plates per aspirate have varied between 10 and more than 100. The

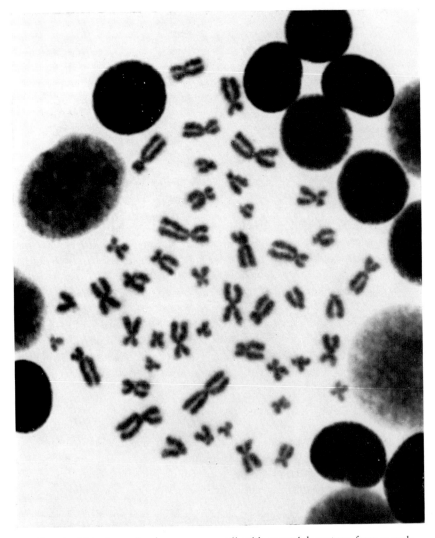

FIG. 1. Metaphase of a bone marrow cell with normal karyotype from a male patient with chronic lymphocytic leukemia. Squash method.

authors prefer the air-dried technique because of its simplicity for slide preparation and because the number of ruptured cells is rare. The quality of the preparations obtained with both methods is illustrated in Figs. 1 and 2. The techniques described are rapid and simple since slides can be ready for screening within 3 hours after aspiration or biopsy.

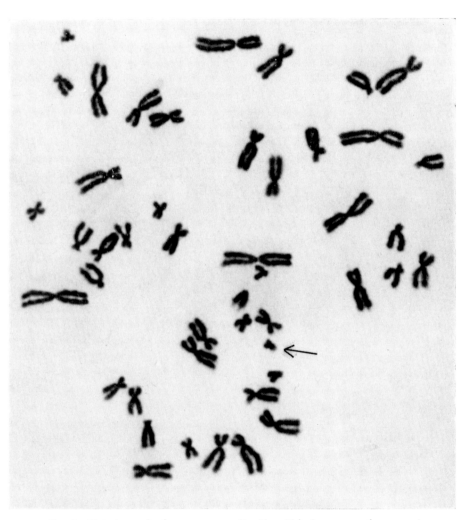

FIG. 2. Metaphase of a bone marrow cell with a Ph[1] chromosome from a male patient with chronic granulocytic leukemia. Air-drying method.

References

Bottura, C., and Ferrari, I. (1960). A simplified method for the study of chromosomes in man. *Nature* **186**, 904-905.

Ford, C. E., Jacobs, P. A., and Lajtha, L. G. (1958). Human somatic chromosomes. *Nature* **181**, 1565-1568.

La Cour, L. F. (1941). Acetic-orcein: a new stain-fixative for chromosomes. *Stain Technol.* **16**, 169-174.

Meighan, S. S., and Stich, H. F. (1961). Simplified technique for examination of chromosomes in the bone marrow of man. *Can. Med. Assoc. J.* **84**, 1004-1006.

Rothfels, K. H., and Siminovitch, L. (1958). An air-drying technique for flattening chromosomes in mammalian cells grown *in vitro. Stain Technol.* **33**, 73-77.

Sandberg, A. A., Ishihara, T., Crosswhite, L. H., and Hauschka, T. S. (1962a). Comparison of chromosome constitution in chronic myelocytic leukemia and other myeloproliferative disorders. *Blood* **20**, 393-423.

Sandberg, A. A., Ishihara, T., Crosswhite, L. H., and Hauschka, T. S. (1962b). Chromosomal dichotomy in blood and marrow of acute leukemia. *Cancer Res.* **22**, 748-756.

Schultz, J., MacDuffee, R. C., and Anderson, T. F. (1949). Smear preparations for the electron microscopy of animal chromosomes. *Science* **110**, 5-7.

Whang, J., Frei, E. III, Tjio, J. H., Carbone, P. P., and Brecher, G. (1963). The distribution of the Philadelphia chromosome in patients with chronic myelogenous leukemia. *Blood* **20**, 664-673.

The Skin Culture Technique

D. G. HARNDEN AND SHEILA BRUNTON

*Medical Research Council, Clinical Effects of Radiation Research Unit,
Western General Hospital, Edinburgh, Scotland*

I.	Introduction	57
II.	Media and Materials	58
III.	Step by Step Procedure	63
IV.	General Discussion of Method	66
	Appendix	72
	References	73

I. INTRODUCTION

There are now three main methods for examining human chromosomes. The simplest and most widely used is the short-term peripheral blood culture technique of Moorhead *et al.* (1960). For the study of diseases of the reticuloendothelial system the direct bone marrow technique of Tjio and Whang (1962) is an excellent one. The third method is the use of relatively long-term cultures of fibroblasts. Although the blood culture method is now the technique used routinely for the determination of the karyotype, fibroblast cultures still have a useful complementary role in this field and they are also well suited for work in the rapidly expanding field of somatic cell genetics.

The main uses to which fibroblast cultures can be put are:

(1) Corroboration of a new or unexpected karyotype discovered by the examination of blood cells.

(2) Diagnosis of mosaicism, where it is essential to examine more than one tissue.

(3) Checking the normality of the karyotype where an abnormality is found in peripheral blood or bone marrow cells of a patient with a disease of the reticuloendothelial system.

(4) Determination of the karyotype of very small babies from whom

it is not practicable to take a large sample of peripheral blood. (However, microtechniques for peripheral blood are already taking over this function.)

(5) Determination of the karyotype of embryos or cadavers.

(6) Experimental work where cytogenetic studies are combined with biochemical, virological, or other studies. In this latter field some elegant studies have already been done, notably the transformation of human cells in culture with simian vacuolating virus (SV4O) by Koprowski *et al.* (1962) and the study of the X chromosome inactivation hypothesis by Davidson *et al.* (1963).

The purpose of this paper is to present the details of the techniques used, rather than to discuss the results obtained. There will be three main sections dealing with the media and materials, a stepwise outline of the method currently used in our laboratory, and a discussion of the various modifications that are available.

II. MEDIA AND MATERIALS

Cockerel Plasma (CP)

This is used because it can be stored at $+4°C$ for several weeks without anticoagulant if all the glassware with which the blood or plasma comes into contact is coated with paraffin wax or silicone. Another advantage is that it forms a firm, clear clot which is not digested too rapidly by cellular enzymes.

(1) Coat all glassware with wax or silicone.

(2) Using an oiled syringe, draw 20 ml of blood from the wing vein of a young bird (under 1 year old).

(3) Transfer the blood to centrifuge tubes which have been precooled in iced water.

(4) Spin at 1500 rpm for 30 minutes at $+4°C$.

(5) Remove the plasma and place in fresh, chilled tubes.

(6) Stopper tightly and store at $+4°C$.

Chicken Embryo Extract (CEE)

If large quantities of embryo extract are required, it is preferable to prepare an ultrafiltrate. This makes full sterile precautions unnecessary during the preparation, but care should be taken to avoid gross contamination (Bryant *et al.*, 1953). If only small quantities are required, the preparation of an ultrafiltrate is too laborious and a simpler method may be used, taking full sterile precautions (Paul, 1959). Commercial CEE is available, but we find our own product to be better and cheaper.

For large quantities:

(1) Arrange for a supply of hens eggs incubated for 10 days.

(2) Carefully remove the embryos from the eggs and place them in a measuring cylinder.

(3) When all the embryos have been collected, homogenize in a tissue grinder or by forcing through a syringe.

(4) Add 1.25 volumes of BSS (see below).

(5) Mix and distribute into universal containers (or large centrifuge tubes).

(6) Spin at 2500 rpm for 30 minutes at $+4°C$.

(7) Pour the supernatant into a beaker and add 2 mg hyaluronidase per 100 ml extract. (Dissolve the hyaluronidase in 2 ml distilled water.)

(8) Incubate for 1 hour at $37°C$.

(9) Ultracentrifuge at 25,000 rpm for 60 minutes in the No. 30 rotor of a Spinco model L ultracentrifuge.

(10) Filter through a No. 03 porosity Selas candle filter[1] under positive pressure of 8–10 lb per square inch (psi).

(11) Distribute in sterile bottles and store at $-10°C$.

For small quantities (sterile procedure):

(1) Remove the embryos from the eggs.

(2) Homogenize by chopping with curved scissors or by forcing through a syringe.

(3) Mix the embryo pulp with 1.25 volumes of BSS.

(4) Spin at 3000 rpm for 15 minutes.

(5) Remove the supernatant and store at $-10°C$.

Serum

(1) A pint of human AB venous blood is allowed to coagulate at $+4°C$. (The serum is removed more easily if the bottle stands at an angle during the period of coagulation.)

(2) The serum is removed under negative pressure using a long, wide-bore needle.

(3) Spin at 1500 rpm for 30 minutes at $+4°C$.

(4) Filter through No. 03 porosity Selas candle filter.

(5) Distribute in small volumes and store at $-10°C$.

---

[1] See Appendix.

Eagle's Medium

This is obtained as a $10\times$ strength solution from Burroughs Wellcome.[1]

(1) To 100 ml of $10\times$ strength medium add 800 ml of sterile glass-distilled water or water from "Elgastat"[1] deionizer (GDW).

(2) Add 0.5 ml kanamycin (see below).

(3) Bring the pH to 7.2 by adding approximately 3.5 ml 10% $NaHCO_3$ solution.

(4) Make up to 1000 ml with GDW.

(5) Store in screw-capped bottles at $+4°C$.

Hank's Basic Salt Solution (BSS)

$CaCl_2$	0.14 gm
Glucose	1.00 gm
NaCl	8.00 gm
KCl	0.40 gm
$MgSo_4 \cdot 7H_2O$	0.20 gm
KH_2PO_4	0.06 gm
$Na_2HPO_4 \cdot 2H_2O$	0.06 gm
Phenol red (0.2%)	10.00 ml

Dissolve the $CaCl_2$ in 200 ml GDW. Dissolve all the other components in 790 ml GDW and add the phenol red. Mix the two solutions. Distribute in 200 ml volumes in screw-capped prescription bottles. Autoclave at 15 psi for 20 minutes. Store at $+4°C$. Approximately 5 ml sterile 1.4% sodium bicarbonate is added to each 200 ml bottle immediately before use to adjust the pH to 7.2.

BSS may be made up at $10\times$ concentration. If this is done, do not autoclave but add 3–4 ml chloroform to each liter and store at $+4°C$. For use, dilute $10\times$ with GDW and heat to $57°C$ to remove the chloroform. Autoclave and adjust the pH as before.

$Ca^{++} + Mg^{++}$-Free Hank's Solution (Solution A)

This is made up as for Hank's solution, but the calcium and magnesium salts are omitted.

Glucose	1.00 gm
NaCl	8.00 gm
KCl	0.40 gm
KH_2PO_4	0.06 gm
$Na_2HPO_4 \cdot 2H_2O$	0.06 gm
Phenol red (0.2%)	10.0 ml

---

[1] See Appendix.

Make up to 1 liter with GDW. Distribute in 200 ml volumes in screw-capped bottles and autoclave at 15 psi for 20 minutes. Store at +4°C. Adjust the pH to 7.2 by adding to each 200 ml approximately 5 ml of sterile 1.4% sodium bicarbonate solution immediately before use.

Trypsin (0.25%)

Dissolve 2.5 gm trypsin (Nutritional Biochemical's Bacto-trypsin 1-300)[1] in a few milliliters of solution A. Add sufficient normal NaOH to adjust the pH to 8.0. Make the volume up to 100 ml with solution A. Filter through a Seitz filter using Carlson filter sheets, grade E.K.[1] Store at —10°C in small aliquots. Dilute 10× with solution A immediately before use. Trypsin should be warmed to 37°C before use on the cultures.

Sodium Bicarbonate (1.4%)

NaHCO$_3$	3.5 gm
Phenol red (0.2%)	2.5 ml
GDW	247.5 ml

Distribute in 5 ml volumes in screw-capped bottles and autoclave with the caps tightly closed for 20 minutes at 15 psi. Store at +4°C. One 5 ml bottle is added to each 200 ml bottle of BSS or solution A before use.

Phenol Red

Mix 0.4 gm phenol red with approximately 22 ml N/20 NaOH. Bring to a final volume of 200 ml with GDW and sufficient N/20 HCl to bring the pH to 7.0. Autoclave in a screw-capped bottle at 15 psi for 20 minutes. Store at +4°C.

This is a 100× stock. Add 0.1 ml to each 10 ml of solution requiring an indicator.

Kanamycin[1]

Add 5 ml sterile GDW to a vial containing 1 gm kanamycin. Add 0.5 ml of this solution to each liter of Eagle's medium to give a final concentration of 100 µg/ml of kanamycin. Store stock solution at —10°C.

Mycostatin[1]

Add 5 ml sterile GDW to a vial containing 500,000 units of mycostatin. Withdraw 0.1 ml and dilute to 10 ml in BSS giving a final concentration

---

[1] See Appendix.

of 1000 units/ml. Add 20 units for each milliliter of growth medium. Store stock solution at —10°C.

Neomycin[1]

Add 5 ml sterile GDW to a vial containing 0.5 gm neomycin sulfate (350,000 units). Dissolve and remove 1 ml. Add this to 13 ml sterile GDW. Distribute in 1 ml amounts and store at —10°C. Use 1 ml for every 100 ml of growth medium to give a final concentration of 50 units/ml.

Penicillin[1]

Use 20 ml sterile GDW to dissolve the contents of 2 vials of penicillin, each containing 100,000 units. This gives a concentration of 10,000 units/ml. Distribute in 1 ml amounts and store at —10°C. To each 100 ml of growth medium, add 1 ml of this solution to give a final concentration of 100 units/ml.

Streptomycin[1]

Add 4.25 ml sterile GDW to a vial containing 1 gm streptomycin. Withdraw 1 ml and add to 19 ml sterile GDW. Distribute in 1 ml amounts and store at —10°C. Add 1 ml of this solution to each 100 ml of growth medium to give a final concentration of 100 units/ml.

Colchicine[1]

Make up a stock solution of 10 ml of 0.5% colchicine in sterile GDW. From this make up a working solution of 0.005% colchicine in BSS. Store at +4°C. Add 0.5 ml the working solution to each 10 ml culture, to give a final concentration of 0.00025%.

Fixative (3:1)

> 3 parts absolute ethyl alcohol,
> 1 part glacial acetic acid.

Make up immediately before use.

Hypotonic Solution

Make up a stock solution of 3.8% sodium citrate (50 ml). For use dilute with GDW to 0.95% and warm to 37°C.

---

[1] See Appendix.

Orcein

Gurr's[1] synthetic orcein	2 gm
Glacial acetic acid	60 ml
GDW	40 ml

Heat the acetic acid but do not boil. Add the orcein and stir. Cool and add the GDW. Filter through Whatman No. 1 filter paper. Store at $+4°C$ and refilter frequently.

Growth Medium

The same growth medium is now used for all cultures.

Eagle's medium with antibiotics	70%
Human AB serum	20%
CEE	10%

The three components of the growth medium are distributed in small amounts such that when they are mixed they will give 20, 50, or 100 ml of complete growth medium. Any unused complete growth medium is discarded.

These values are not critical and considerable variability will be tolerated by the cells.

III. STEP BY STEP PROCEDURE

A. OBTAINING SKIN BIOPSY

(1) Clean skin with surgical spirit.

(2) Inject local anaesthetic.

(3) Make a small X or V shaped incision with a scalpel blade.

(4) Hold point of V with forceps and cut off small piece of tissue 2–3 mm in diameter.

(5) Place tissue in small screw-capped bottle with about 4 ml Eagle's medium.

(6) Cover incision with a Band-Aid.

B. PRIMARY CULTURES

(1) Tip contents of bottle into glass dish.

(2) Cut tissue into small pieces using forceps and scissors (about 0.5 mm diameter).

(3) Place a number of drops of CEE into one petri dish and an equivalent number of drops of CP into another.

---

[1] See Appendix.

(4) Using a Pasteur pipette, lift one piece of tissue into a third petri dish and withdraw the surplus medium.

(5) Mix one drop of CEE and one drop of CP and draw into the pipette along with the piece of tissue.

(6) Place tissue in a culture flask and spread the CEE/CP mixture in a thin layer round about it.

(7) Repeat with other pieces of tissue to set up a minimum of 2 culture flasks. (A 4 cm diameter culture flask should have approximately 5 pieces of tissue, while a 9 cm diameter flask should have 10–15 pieces.)

(8) Leave for a few minutes to ensure that the plasma has clotted firmly.

(9) Add 5 ml of growth medium (or sufficient to cover the clots).

(10) Flush out the flask with 5% CO_2 in air and close with a silicone rubber stopper.

(11) Incubate at 37°C.

(*Note:* Carrel flasks are ideal for this type of culture; babies' feeding bottles are also suitable and much cheaper, although the progress of the cultures cannot be observed quite so well in these, as compared with Carrel flasks.)

C. MAINTENANCE (FOR BOTH PRIMARY CULTURES AND SUBCULTURES)

(1) Cultures are checked every 2 days for state of growth, sterility, and pH.

(2) At the same time the liquid medium is changed by discarding the spent medium and replacing it with fresh growth medium.

(3) Adjust the pH with 5% CO_2 or with sodium bicarbonate solution (1.4%) if this is necessary.

(4) Add additional antibiotics if necessary.

D. FIRST SUBCULTURE

(1) Remove growth medium.

(2) Add 10 ml of 0.25% prewarmed trypsin solution.

(3) Incubate for approximately 15 minutes at 37°C.

(4) Check that the cells have been released from the plasma.

(5) Transfer entire contents of flask to centrifuge tube and spin at 500 rpm for 5–10 minutes.

(6) Discard trypsin.

(7) Resuspend pellet of cells in 1 ml fresh growth medium.

(8) Transfer entire contents of tube to fresh culture flask containing 9 ml fresh growth medium.

(9) Flush out flask with 5% CO_2 in air and stopper tightly.

(10) Incubate at 37°C.

E. OTHER SUBCULTURES

Proceed as for the first subculture but with two modifications:

(a) Use trypsin for only 5 minutes.

(b) After suspending cells in 1 ml growth medium, use only 0.1 ml for each subculture (i.e., 10-fold dilution of cells).

F. PROCESSING CELLS FOR MAKING CHROMOSOME PREPARATIONS

(1) Select a moderately heavy culture showing numerous dividing cells. (Usually a culture is used approximately 20 hours after a subculture or change of medium.)

(2) Add 0.5 ml 0.005% colchicine solution (prewarmed).

(3) Reincubate for approximately 2–4 hours.

(4) Prepare cell suspension with trypsin as described under subculture.

(5) Spin in a siliconized centrifuge tube at 500 rpm for 10 minutes.

(6) Discard supernatant and resuspend cells in prewarmed BSS.

(7) Spin at 500 rpm for 10 minutes.

(8) Discard supernatant and resuspend cells in prewarmed 0.95% sodium citrate solution.

(9) Place in 37°C water bath and leave 20 minutes.

(10) Spin at 500 rpm for 10 minutes.

(11) Discard supernatant.

(12) Flick the bottom of the tube till the cells become resuspended in the small quantity of fluid remaining.

(13) Add freshly mixed 3:1 (ethyl) fixative drop by drop, agitating between each drop.

(14) Once a good suspension is obtained, add an excess of fixative.

(15) Leave at least 30 minutes (normally cells are left overnight at this stage at —10°C).

G. PREPARATION OF SLIDES

(1) Place carefully cleaned microscope slides in iced water.

(2) Spin the suspension of cells in fixative at 500 rpm for 10 minutes.

(3) Discard supernatant and resuspend in fixative.

(4) Spin 10 minutes at 500 rpm.

(5) Discard supernatant and resuspend in a few drops of 75% acetic acid.

(6) Shake excess water from a cold, wet slide.

(7) Place 3 or 4 drops of the cell suspension on the slide and immediately heat it over a spirit flame till it is quite hot.

(8) When dry, cool and place in 2% acetic orcein for 2–3 hours at 37°C.

(9) Rinse quickly in 45% acetic acid.

(10) Dehydrate in Cellosolve.[1]

(11) Place in Euparal Essence for 2 minutes.[1]

(12) Mount in Euparal.[1]

IV. GENERAL DISCUSSION OF METHOD

The method described above is the one currently in use in our laboratory. This does not, however, necessarily mean that this is the best method. There are now in use in several laboratories a large number of variations of the skin culture technique, and since good results are being obtained it is obvious that there are many different ways of establishing a culture and making satisfactory chromosome preparations.

There are, however, a number of essential points, most of which apply to all tissue culture work (see Paul, 1959; Parker, 1961).

(a) All glassware must be scrupulously clean and carefully rinsed free of detergents or cleaning fluids.

(b) Sterile precautions must be taken throughout. This has not been stressed in the procedure section since it is assumed that the cultures will be handled sterilely at all times. The use of antibiotics allows a little more freedom than was at one time possible with tissue cultures, but even so we do have trouble with infection in our laboratory from time to time. The antibiotic used is changed periodically and others are kept in reserve. It is rare to lose a culture because of contamination but, especially in the case of yeast infections, it may not be possible to free the cultures entirely of the contaminating organism. Care must be taken in interpreting results from cultures which have been treated with high doses of antibiotics, since there appears to be a tendency for some of them to cause chromosome breakage. This is especially true of mycostatin, while Cohen

---

[1] See Appendix.

et al. (1963) have found serious chromosome damage in cultures treated with streptonigrin.

(c) Careful control of the pH is essential at around pH 7.2. Although the cells will tolerate acidity down to about 6.5, this slows the growth considerably; short periods at alkaline pH (>7.8) are likely to prove lethal. Most workers use a bicarbonate buffer system which necessitates the use of a 5% CO_2 in air atmosphere. This can be achieved either by gassing the incubator or by keeping the cultures in tightly stoppered flasks which have been flushed out with 5% CO_2 in air.

Let us now consider the various stages of the technique.

A. THE BIOPSY

The techniques which were developed for growing tissue from skin biopsies can be used with very little modification for growing any kind of solid tissue. Since most of these can only be obtained during surgery, we will consider mainly skin tissue. (However, if fascia is available there is no doubt that a culture can be more quickly established from this tissue.) The biopsy should be about 2–4 mm in diameter and should take the full thickness of skin since the cells which eventually form the cultures are fibroblasts from the connective tissue and not epithelial cells. One can work with less tissue, but it takes much longer to establish a culture from a small biopsy and the chances of failure are higher. A local anesthetic is not always necessary but may be used without fear that it will hamper the growth of the culture. There are of course a variety of different ways of taking the biopsy. A "painless" method is described by Edwards (1960), while Davidson *et al.* (1963) advocate the use of a punch.

The tissue should be placed immediately in a sterile screw-capped bottle containing tissue culture medium. The best results are achieved when the tissue is set up in culture immediately. Some delay, however, is permissible so that biopsies taken at an inconvenient hour can safely be left at room temperature till the following day. Biopsies can be sent by post and indeed have been received in Edinburgh and grown successfully from Australia, Germany, India, Nigeria, South Africa, and the United States. Biopsies have been grown after a delay of 5 days but delays of more than 2 days should be avoided if possible.

Successful cultures can also be established from specimens taken up to 5 days post mortem provided that the body has been refrigerated. In such cases contamination by bacteria or fungi is the main problem and biopsies should be taken as soon as possible after death and certainly before the pathologists have taken over. Fascia is more likely to be sterile than skin, and if it can be obtained is to be preferred to skin.

B. PRIMARY CULTURES

The establishment of the primary cultures is the stage at which the various methods differ most from each other. Puck *et al.* (1958) digested the tissue with trypsin and plated out the resulting cell suspension. This method, however, requires great care and very delicate handling of the cells and, unless these precautions are taken, the success rate is not high (with adult as opposed to fetal cells). For many purposes it is an advantage to use a technique which does not require too rigorous adherence to exact procedures. Most other methods rely on cutting the tissue into smaller pieces and placing these in culture medium without trypsinization. The tissue must be held in position so that growth can occur. This can be achieved by using a plasma clot (Harnden, 1960; Lejeune *et al.*, 1959), by holding the tissue down with a sheet of perforated cellophane (Hsu and Kellogg, 1960), or by placing the tissue on a metal grid (Koprowski *et al.*, 1962). Recently DeMars (1963, personal communication) has obtained good results by pinning pieces of tissue down under a microscope cover slip. Davidson *et al.* (1963) do not describe their technique in detail, but appear to have established cultures successfully by methods previously used for fetal tissue. The tissue was minced and placed in culture vessels without plasma or any other means of immobilizing the tissue fragments.

Whichever method is used a liquid medium is then added which consists basically of a complex synthetic medium such as medium 199 (Morgan *et al.*, 1950) or Eagle's medium (Eagle, 1955) supplemented by serum and in most cases a growth stimulant such as chick or beef embryo extract. Here, as in all other stages, each group of workers has its own preference. We have found the commercially available media (199 from Glaxo[1] and Eagle's medium from Burroughs Wellcome[1]) to be convenient, relatively inexpensive, and to give satisfactory results. Human AB serum, pooled human serum, calf serum, and fetal calf serum have all been used with apparently good results. Fetal calf serum is claimed to have potent growth-promoting properties (Puck *et al.*, 1958). Occasionally it is found that a particular batch of serum from one individual is toxic to the cells. For this reason many workers prefer to use pooled serum. This problem

---

[1] See Appendix.

arises only infrequently and we find it more convenient to use serum from a single donor. We do however take the precaution of having a second batch of serum available at all times. There is some discussion as to whether or not chick embryo extract is necessary. It has been our experience that its use gives very much better results both in terms of the speed with which the culture is established and the number of dividing cells found in the final preparations.

Usually some outgrowth of cells is observed between 1 and 4 days after setting up the culture. However, some cultures may fail to show any growth for much longer periods, and if a particular piece of tissue is valuable it should not be discarded because no growth is observed for several weeks. Commonly only some of the explanted pieces of tissue grow, but successful cultures can be established even if only one piece grows. During this initial period of growth the maintenance of the correct pH is of special importance. The medium should be replenished every 2 or 3 days. When adequate growth has occurred, the first subcultures are made. What is "adequate growth" can really only be judged from experience. There should be a good halo of cells around the explanted tissue; and the fewer the pieces of tissue growing the larger the halo should be allowed to grow before subculture. The average time to the first subculture using the technique described here is 10–14 days.

C. Subcultures

The methods of subculture do not differ much, except for that of Lejeune et al. (1959), who set up the primary cultures in plasma clots on cover glasses in culture tubes. In this method subculture is effected by cutting the original piece of tissue free from the outgrowth and replanting it in a fresh clot in a new culture tube. The cells of the original culture are allowed to grow back into the "window" created by the removal of the explant, and chromosome preparations are made from this culture. All the other methods employ trypsin to digest the cells free from the clot or off the glass of the vessel. After washing, the cells are seeded out into a new culture vessel and allowed to adhere to the glass as a monolayer. Thereafter these cultures can be handled by the techniques which have become routine for the handling of cell cultures. The medium is renewed every few days and subcultures are made whenever the confluent monolayer becomes too heavy. This should be done before the cells start to peel up from the glass in a sheet. Should this happen, however, the cells can still be trypsinized to give good subcultures. The time spent in each subculture can be controlled by adjusting the inoculum of cells. Using the 1 in 10 dilution suggested here, subcultures have to be made, on the average, once a week.

The length of time for which cells can be cultured is the subject of some debate. Puck and his colleagues maintain their cultures for periods of over a year without any apparent deterioration or the occurrence of any aneuploidy. However, Hayflick and Moorhead (1962), using fetal material, find that the cells have a finite life in culture. Also, Moorhead and Saksela (1963) find increasing aneuploidy in the last few subcultures before the cultures completely cease proliferation. We have not attempted to carry our cultures for many passages, but we do observe the slowing down reported by Hayflick and Moorhead.

D. CHROMOSOME PREPARATIONS

The basic principle here is to fix the cells when the largest possible number are dividing. Two devices are used to enhance the number of dividing cells. Firstly, methods of synchronization are used and secondly, drugs are added to the cultures which prevent the completion of mitosis but do not prevent the entry of cells into mitosis. Although methods of synchronization commonly used for microorganisms can be applied to mammalian cells (e.g., the cold shock method of Newton and Wildy, 1959), most of the techniques for skin culture use the partial synchrony or wave of divisions which follows a change of medium or a subculture. Most commonly the cells are exposed to colchicine (or one of its derivatives) for a short period about the time when it is judged that the maximum number of divisions is occurring. Here again the method of Lejeune et al. differs from the others in that it does not involve the use of colchicine. The cultures are allowed to become acid, the medium is then replenished and the pH restored to 7.4 by the addition of sodium bicarbonate solution and a few drops of embryo extract. It is found that if the cells are fixed about 16 hours later, an adequate number of mitoses can be found without the use of colchicine. One can frequently get many mitoses without the use of colchicine using the technique described in this paper; however, it is felt that a greater consistency can be achieved if it is used, and that no serious disadvantage results from its use.

The use of a hypotonic treatment is common to all of the methods. Dilute sodium citrate, dilute Hank's solution, diluted serum, and even distilled water have all been used with apparently good results.

Two main methods have been used for making chromosome preparations from skin cultures. In the first the cells are grown on cover slips and the complete processing of the cells is then carried out with the cells attached to the coverslips (e.g., Harnden, 1960). In the second, the cells are brought into suspension using trypsin; they are then processed in much the same way as peripheral blood cells (Hsu and Kellogg, 1960; Frøland, 1961). Although the former method can give good results, it has been found that, after experience with both methods, the second method gives consistently better results and this is now the method used in our laboratory. After hypotonic treatment the cells are fixed and there is general agreement that 3:1 (ethyl alcohol:glacial acetic acid) fixative gives the best results. We prefer to fix the cells in suspension, adding the fixative extremely slowly. Hsu and Kellogg, however, get their best results by fixing the pellet of cells without breaking it up. The fixed cells in suspension do not, however, respond to treatment in exactly the same way as peripheral blood cells. We have found that the cells are more resistant to spreading by air drying than are blood cells. We therefore transfer the cells to 75% acetic acid immediately before drying them. This gives greatly improved spreading. If, however, it is found that this method gives too many broken cells the standard air drying from 3:1 fixative should be used. The squashing techniques for flattening the cells have now been almost entirely replaced by modifications of the air drying technique.

All our preparations are stained with orcein and made permanent by mounting in Euparal. The use of orcein has two minor disadvantages: firstly it precipitates rapidly in solution and has to be refiltered frequently, and secondly it is not absolutely specific for chromatin. If it is carefully applied, these features are no great disadvantage. Its great merits are the simplicity of its use and its permanence when compared with, for example, Feulgen. Other stains have been used and some of these can give good results, e.g., Unna blue as recommended by Lejeune.

The length of time taken from the biopsy to the making of the final chromosome preparations varies considerably. The best that has been achieved using the method described here is 10 days, with an average between 14 and 21 days. Lejeune et al. (1959) and Puck et al. (1958) both give their average time taken to be 7 days. Lejeune et al. employed fascia which, as already pointed out, is established in culture more quickly than skin, while Puck et al. eliminated the slow-growing explant stage which delays the plasma clot cultures, by employing a direct trypsinization technique.

Material	Source

Selas candle filters,
  1" × 6" porosity No. 03
  Catalog No. FPS 86
	Selas Corporation of America,
	  Philadelphia 34,
	  Pennsylvania, U.S.A.

Eagle's Tissue Culture Medium,
  10× strength
	Burroughs Wellcome & Co.,
	  Wellcome Foundation Ltd.,
	  The Wellcome Building,
	  Euston Road,
	  London, N.W.1, England

"Elgastat" deionizer B102	Elga Products Ltd.,
	  Lane End,
	  Bucks., England

Trypsin Hyaluronidase }	Nutritional Biochemical Corporation, Cleveland, Ohio, U.S.A.

Kanamycin	Bayer Products,
	  Division of Winthrop Group Ltd.,
	  Surbiton-upon-Thames, England

Mycostatin	E. R. Squibb and Son.,
	  Woodend Avenue,
	  Speke, Liverpool, 19, England

Neomycin	Upjohn of England Ltd.,
	  Fleming Way,
	  Crawley, Sussex, England

Penicillin
Streptomycin }
Medium 199
	Glaxo Laboratories
	  Greenford,
	  Middlesex, England

Colchicine	British Drug Houses Ltd., Poole, England

Silicone stoppers
"Escorubber bungs"
  sizes 5, 9B, and 20
	Esco (Rubber) Ltd.,
	  2 Stothard Place,
	  Bishop's Gate,
	  London, E.C.2, England

Euparal
Euparal Essence }
	Flatters & Garnett Ltd.,
	  309 Oxford Road,
	  Manchester, 13, England

Cellosolve
  (ethylene glycol monoethyl ether)
	Hopkin & Williams Ltd.,
	  Chadwell Heath,
	  Essex, England

E.K. 6 cm asbestos filter pads	John C. Carlson, Ltd.,
	  Great Eastern Street,
	  London, E.C.2

Synthetic orcein	G. T. Gurr, Ltd.,
	  136/138 New King's Road,
	  London, S.W.6, England

References

Bryant, J. S., Earle, W. R., and Peppers, E. V. (1953). The effect of ultracentrifugation and hyaluronidase on the filterability of chick embryo extract for tissue culture. *J. Natl. Cancer Inst.* **14**, 189.

Cohen, M. M., Shaw, M. W., and Craig, A. P. (1963). The effects of streptonigrin on cultured human leucocytes. *Proc. Natl. Acad. Sci. U. S.* **50**, 16.

Davidson, R. G., Nitowsky, H. M., and Childs, B. (1963). Demonstration of two populations of cells in the human female heterozygous for glucose-6-phosphate dehydrogenase variants. *Proc. Natl. Acad. Sci. U. S.* **50**, 481.

DeMars, R. I. (1963). Personal communication.

Eagle, H. (1955). Nutrition needs of mammalian cells in tissue culture. *Science* **122**, 501.

Edwards, J. (1960). Painless skin biopsy. *Lancet* **i**, 496.

Frøland, A. (1961). A simplified method for making chromosome preparations from skin biopsies. *Acta Pathol. Microbiol. Scand.* **53**, 319.

Harnden, D. G. (1960). A human skin culture technique used for cytological examinations. *Brit. J. Exptl. Pathol.* **41**, 31.

Hayflick, L., and Moorhead, P. S. (1962). The serial cultivation of human diploid cell strains. *Exptl. Cell Res.* **25**, 585.

Hsu, T. C., and Kellogg, D. S. (1960). Primary cultivation and continuous propagation *in vitro* of tissues from small biopsy specimens. *J. Natl. Cancer Inst.,* **25**, 221.

Koprowski, H., Ponten, J. A., Jensen, F., Ravdin, R. G., Moorhead, P., and Saksela, E. (1962). Transformation of cultures of human tissue infected with simian SV40 virus. *J. Cell. Comp. Physiol.* **59**, 281.

Lejeune, J., Turpin, R., and Gautier, M. (1959). Le Mongolisme, premier exemple d'aberration autosomique humaine. *Ann. Génét.* **1**, 41-49.

Moorhead, P. S., Nowell, P. C., Mellman, W. J., Battips, D. M., and Hungerford, D. A. (1960). Chromosome preparations of leucocytes cultured from human peripheral blood. *Exptl. Cell Res.* **20**, 613.

Moorhead, P. S., and Saksela, E. (1963). Aneuploidy in the degenerative phase of serial cultivation of human cell strains. *Proc. Natl. Acad. Sci. U.S.* **50**, 390.

Morgan, J. F., Morton, H. J., and Parker, R. C. (1950). Nutrition of animal cells in tissue culture. I. Initial studies on a synthetic medium. *Proc. Soc. Exptl. Biol. Med.* **73**, 1.

Newton, A. A., and Wildy, P. (1959). Parasynchronous division of HeLa cells. *Exptl. Cell Res.* **16**, 624.

Parker, R. C. (1961). "Methods of Tissue Culture," 3rd ed. Harper (Hoeber), New York.

Paul, J. (1959). "Cell and Tissue Culture." E. and S. Livingstone, Edinburgh and London.

Puck, T. T., Cieciura, S. J., and Robinson, A. (1958). Genetics of somatic mammalian cells. III. Long term cultivation of euploid cells from human and animal subjects. *J. Exptl. Med.* **108**, 945.

Tjio, J. H., and Whang, J. (1962). Chromosome preparations of bone marrow cells without prior *in vitro* culture or *in vivo* colchicine administration. *Stain Technol.* **37**, 17.

Direct Handling of Germ Cells

SUSUMU OHNO

Department of Biology, City of Hope Medical Center, Duarte, California

I.	Introduction	75
II.	Fixing, Squashing, and Staining Gonadal Material	76
III.	Various Methods of Pretreatment	77
	A. For Mitotic Prophase and Telophase Figures of Germ Cells	77
	B. For Mitotic Metaphase and Anaphase Figures of Germ Cells	79
	C. For First Meiotic Prophase Figures of Germ Cells	79
	D. For First and Second Meiotic Metaphase Figures of the Male	81
	E. For First and Second Meiotic Metaphase Figures of the Female	83
IV.	Interpreting the Findings	85
	A. The Hazard of Estimating Cytologically the Frequency of Meiotic Nondisjunction	85
	B. Analysis of Translocations from Chromosomal Configurations at Meiosis	86
V.	Summary	90
	References	90

I. INTRODUCTION

Short-term culturing of skin and of peripheral blood provide a relatively simple and painless means of analyzing the human chromosome constitution. Since the anomalies so detected most likely arose in the germ cells of the parents, future advances in this field can only follow a considerable increase in our knowledge of germ cell behavior at various stages of development.

Fortunately, a technique for obtaining satisfactory cytological preparations directly from mammalian gonads was first developed in 1952 by Makino and Nishimura. Various modifications based on similar principles have been used successfully since then for studies of mammalian germ cells.

Herein are described several methods used in this laboratory to investigate human germ cells at different developmental stages.

Although the mitotic process in general is familiar to most investigators, the configurations presented by meiotic chromosomes are more difficult to interpret. Thus, the last two sections of this paper are devoted to what I feel is a sound approach to estimating the incidence of meiotic nondisjunction for a given chromosome, and to discerning the nature of a given translocation from the configurations seen in meiosis.

II. FIXING, SQUASHING, AND STAINING GONADAL MATERIAL

While the kind of pretreatment selected for gonadal tissue depends on the developmental stage of the germ cells to be studied, the procedure for fixing, squashing, and staining is the same for all stages and will be described first.

Several minutes prior to use, fresh fixative is prepared by mixing equal volumes of glacial acetic acid and distilled water. At least 50 times the volume of tissue to be fixed is necessary for adequate fixation.

Small cubes ($2 \times 2 \times 2$ mm) of pretreated gonadal tissue are immersed in fresh fixative for 15 minutes at least, 45 minutes at most. One cube of fixed tissue is placed on a glass slide along with about 0.1 ml of fixative. To release most of the free cells, the cube is gently tapped with a blunt metal instrument, such as the end of a diamond glass pencil. The stringy connective tissue remaining in the free cell suspension is removed with watchmaker's forceps. If clumps of tissue are left, no amount of pressure will effectively flatten individual cells. After removal of the connective tissue, less than 0.1 ml of free cell suspension remains on the slide, which is gently covered with a No. 1 cover slip (24×40 mm), great care being taken to avoid formation of air bubbles.

For protection during the squashing process, and to provide a surface on which the fingers can find a grip, the covered slide is placed in the center of four layers of No. 1 filter paper folded in the middle. So enveloped, the slide is placed on a completely flat surface and both thumbs aligned on top of the paper-covered slide. The full weight of the body is brought evenly upon the two thumbs, the pressure directed straight downward for at least 1 minute, preferably 2. At this crucial stage, a preparation can be completely ruined by the slightest movement of the thumbs, or by directing the pressure obliquely. After squashing, when the slide is removed from the filter paper, the presence of Newton rings between the cover slip and the slide indicate a successful squash.

For 1 minute the slide is immersed in a mixture of dry ice and methanol in a large beaker; this permits the cover slip to be pried off the frozen fixative with a razor blade and discarded. (Several years of experience have taught us that neither coating the cover slip with silicon nor the slide with albumin is necessary to keep well-squashed cells on the slide. We simply rub a clean slide vigorously with a coarse paper towel several minutes before its use.)

After the slide dries in the air, it is immersed in methanol for 15 minutes to extract the fatty substances usually found in gonadal tissue. Again the slide is dried, washed in tap water, and hydrolyzed in 1 N HCl at 60°C for 15 minutes to remove most of the ribonucleic acid (RNA) from the chromosomes and flattened cytoplasm.

The slide is now ready for staining. In our laboratory, we obtain equally good results by staining 3 hours with Feulgen reagent, 5 minutes with Giemsa solution, or 1 minute with 0.25% basic fuchsin solution. After drying in air, the slide is mounted with a No. 1 cover slip and synthetic balsam.

III. VARIOUS METHODS OF PRETREATMENT

A. For Mitotic Prophase and Telophase Figures of Germ Cells

To obtain good mitotic prophase and telophase figures of germ cells, cut the gonadal tissue into pieces no larger than $2 \times 2 \times 2$ mm and suspend them in isotonic solution, such as Medium 858, or Hank's basal salt solution (Difco), at 3°C. After 10 minutes, transfer the pieces to fresh cold solution; repeat this two more times. The pieces are now ready to be fixed, squashed, and stained. Hypotonic pretreatment should be avoided at all costs.

In males, mitotic figures of definitive spermatogonia can be obtained at all ages of postnatal life. Mitotic figures of primordial germ cells come only from prenatal gonads. Although no distinctive characteristics set apart prophase nuclei of germ from somatic cells, the heteropycnosis of the Y chromosome appears to be more conspicuous in the germ cells. A prophase nucleus of a primordial germ cell often contains one enormous nucleolus organized by 11 or 12 autosomes, mostly members of the D(13–15) and G(21–22) groups (Fig. 1).

In females, only the fetal ovary contains mitotic figures of germ cells,

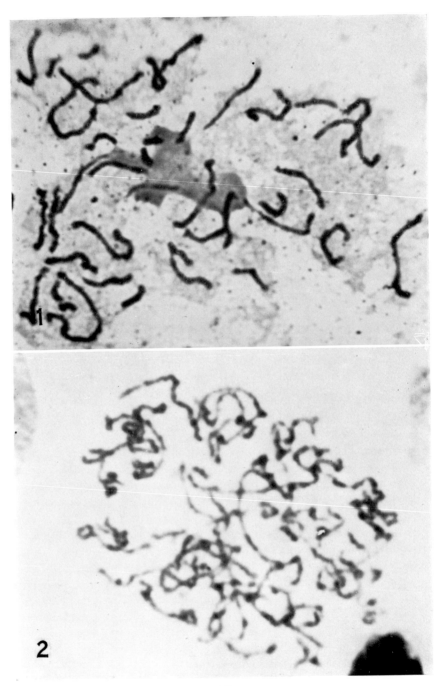

since in the postnatal ovary germ elements are represented by dictyate oocytes which have already completed first meiotic prophase (Ohno *et al.,* 1962). Although primordial germ cells first seen in yolk sac and later in the gonadal ridges of early embryos are sex chromatin-positive, showing a condensed X at prophase, oogonial prophase nuclei from fetal ovaries 3–6 months old are easily distinguished from somatic cells, since both X chromosomes are in an extended state (Fig. 2); thus, interphase nuclei of definitive oogonia are sex chromatin-negative.

B. FOR MITOTIC METAPHASE AND ANAPHASE FIGURES OF GERM CELLS

Gonadal tissue, minced into two millimeter cubes $2 \times 2 \times 2$ mm, is immersed into neutral (pH 7) double-distilled water at room temperature. After 10 minutes, the tissue is transferred to fresh distilled water; this is repeated two more times. By then the material, swollen to 3 times its original volume, is ready for fixing, squashing, and staining. The usual quality of metaphase figures obtained by this method is illustrated in Fig. 5.

Primordial germ cells differentiate into spermatogonia in the neonatal testis, into oogonia in 2-month embryonic ovaries. This period of transition is brief but turbulent; after it, many germ cells degenerate. Lagging chromosomes and nondisjunction are often demonstrated in anaphase figures from this period.

C. FOR FIRST MEIOTIC PROPHASE FIGURES OF GERM CELLS

Figures in leptotene, zygotene, pachytene, and diplotene can be found in the male testis between the ages of 13 and 81. Such material, usually secured by testicular biopsy, should receive the pretreatment described in Section A.

In primary spermatocytes, both the X and Y manifest positive heteropycnosis from the onset of meiosis (Sachs, 1954). Thus, at pachytene the sex vesicle containing the heavily condensed XY bivalent sharply contrasts with the 22 autosomal bivalents demonstrating fine chromomeric patterns (Fig. 3).

In the female, first meiotic prophase figures are found only in the fetal ovary, although a newborn ovary occasionally yields several pachytene and

FIG. 1. Mitotic prophase of a primordial germ cell from the gonad of a 1½-month-old male embryo. A huge nucleolus may be noted. About 12 chromosomes are participating in nucleolus organization (Giemsa stain).

FIG. 2. Mitotic prophase nucleus of an oogonium from the ovary of a 3-month-old female fetus. Both X chromosomes are in an extended state (Feulgen stain).

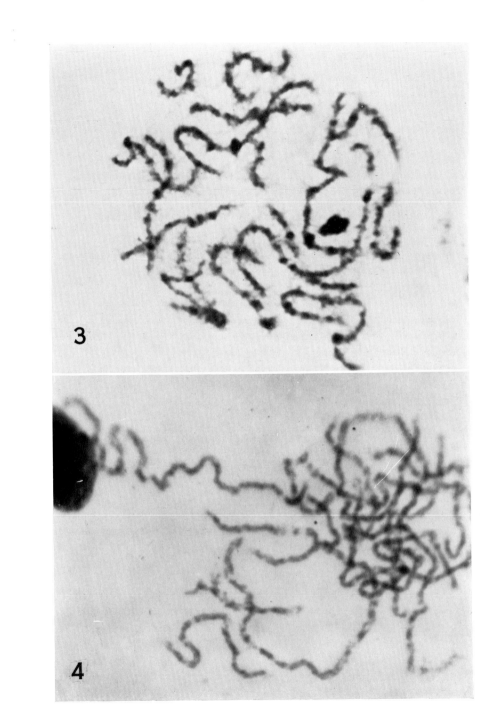

diplotene figures. A few leptotene and zygotene figures can be recovered from an embryo of only $2\frac{1}{2}$ months, but meiotic prophase figures at all stages are most numerous in fetal ovaries between the fourth and eighth months. Individual oocytes which have progressed to pachytene and diplotene are invariably surrounded by a single layer of follicular cells, the removal of which is an essential part of pretreatment. The fetal ovary is immersed in isotonic solution. Under the dissecting microscope, the cortical area is removed and cut into pieces no larger than 2 mm square. This material is placed in a 10% trypsin solution and incubated for 30 minutes at 37°C. After the material has received three 10-minute rinsings in isotonic solution, it is ready for fixing, squashing, and staining. (The trypsin which works best in our hands is Trypsin 1:250, Difco certified. A 10% solution made with distilled water is oversaturated.)

Unlike the male XY-bivalent, the XX-bivalent in fetal oocytes does not condense; thus, the female pachytene nucleus contains 23 bivalents, each demonstrating an intricate chromomeric pattern (Fig. 4). Another conspicuous difference between male and female pachytene nuclei is the pronounced tendency in female nuclei for autosomal bivalents to form non-homologous associations at their centromeric regions.

D. For First and Second Meiotic Metaphase Figures of the Male

Hypotonic pretreatment will greatly improve the quality of diakinesis, first meiotic metaphase, interkinesis, and second meiotic metaphase figures obtained from the testis of a sexually mature male. However, precautions must be taken to prevent the loss of cells in the late stages of meiosis. As spermatocytes advance in the meiotic process, they progressively move away from the basement membrane toward the center of the lumen of the seminiferous tubules where they become free cells. These cells are easily lost if the tubule is cut into very short pieces; during pretreatment they will simply float away.

A block of fresh testicular tissue is immersed in isotonic solution. Under the dissecting microscope, individual seminiferous tubules at least 2 cm long are removed (I use a pair of watchmaker's forceps in each hand).

Fig. 3. Pachytene nucleus of a spermatocyte obtained by testicular biopsy of a 63-year-old man. The sex vesicle embedding the positively heteropycnotic XY-bivalent is seen right center (Feulgen stain).

Fig. 4. Pachytene nucleus of an oocyte from the ovary of a $5\frac{1}{2}$-month-old female fetus. Unlike the XY-bivalent of the male, the XX-bivalent is isopycnotic to the autosomal bivalents and demonstrates a fine chromomeric pattern (Feulgen stain).

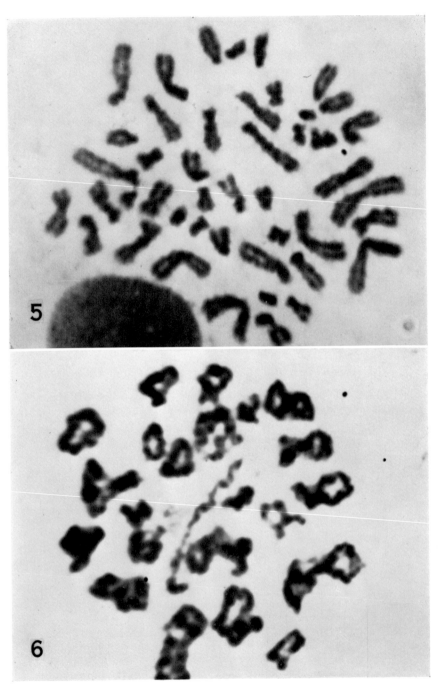

One long piece of tubule is placed in the middle of a glass slide, covered with 2 ml of double-distilled water, and allowed to set for 30 minutes. If the room is unusually warm and too much evaporation is feared, the slide should be covered by a small glass cylinder.

At the end of the hypotonic pretreatment, the tubule is swollen to 3 times its original size. Distilled water remaining on the slide is absorbed out from the periphery by strips of filter paper. On the tubule is placed 0.5 ml of 50% acetic acid; after 15 minutes of fixation, the tubule is teased into minute fragments with the watchmaker's forceps. Squashing and staining follow.

The most conspicuous feature of diakinesis and first meiotic metaphase nuclei in the male is the end-to-end association of the X and Y (Fig. 6). Because of this terminal association, first meiosis is always reductional to the two sex elements. Thus, in a pair of sister interkinesis nuclei, one contains the X, the other the Y, both heavily condensed and in sharp contrast to the extremely extended isopycnotic autosomes (Fig. 7).

Each secondary spermatocyte in second meiotic metaphase contains 22 autosomes and either the X or the Y. The sex element is still heavily condensed, while the sister chromatids of autosomes, fuzzy in outline, are completely split apart except at the centromeric region (Fig. 8).

E. FOR FIRST AND SECOND MEIOTIC METAPHASE FIGURES OF THE FEMALE

An individual dictyate oocyte resumes meiosis from diakinesis only after the follicle has grown full size, increasing quite suddenly in volume 80- to 90-fold. Thus, a first meiotic metaphase figure of an oocyte can be obtained only from a mature follicle in the ovary of a woman in her reproductive span on the day of ovulation. An ovulated but unfertilized ovum that has moved into the Fallopian tube will yield only second meiotic metaphase figures.

We have not yet had the good fortune to obtain such fresh material. Should the occasion arise, however, we would use the following procedure, which is quite successful with smaller mammals.

Fig. 5. A spermatogonial mitotic metaphase figure (Giemsa stain).

Fig. 6. First meiotic metaphase figure of a spermatocyte. In addition to the 22 autosomal bivalents, each demonstrating a number of chiasmata, the X and Y seen in the center are in characteristic end-to-end association (Feulgen stain).

(All photomicrographs were taken by Leitz Panphoto; 100×10.)

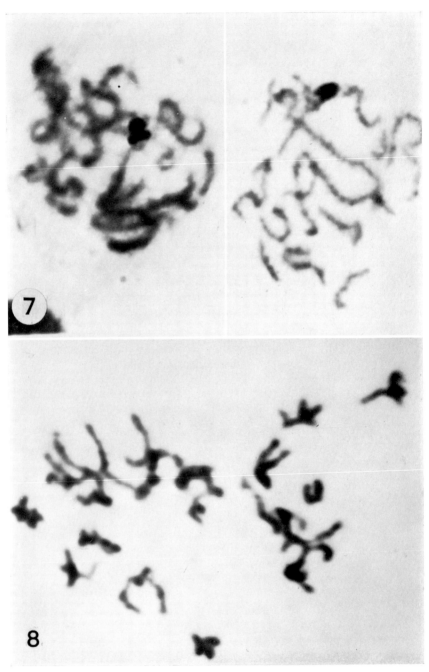

The mature follicle is punctured with the sharp points of the watchmaker's forceps, and the liquor folliculi poured out into a petri dish. Under the dissecting microscope, an ovum surrounded by the cells of corona radiata is easy to locate. The petri dish is incubated at 37°C until most of the corona radiata cells detach themselves from the ovum (about 50 minutes). Under the dissecting microscope, the ovum is sucked out with a small pipet and deposited with a small amount of fluid into a drop of 50% acetic acid on a glass slide. After 15 minutes of fixation, the slide is covered. Only a gentle squashing is needed to spread apart the bivalents of an oocyte in first meiotic metaphase.

IV. INTERPRETING THE FINDINGS

A. The Hazard of Estimating Cytologically the Frequency of Meiotic Nondisjunction

Meiotic nondisjunction can occur either at first meiotic anaphase on a given bivalent, or at second meiotic anaphase on a given chromosome. Subsequent to the alignment of bivalents on the equatorial plate of the first meiotic spindle, the X and Y tend to segregate from each other ahead of the autosomes and move toward opposite division poles, a phenomenon known as "positive allocycly." Figures squashed at this stage have been misinterpreted to be first meiotic metaphase figures with the X and Y existing as univalents which move independently of each other. We observed 300 pairs of male second meiotic metaphase figures and failed to find a single instance of nondisjunction of the X and Y at first meiosis (Ohno, 1963). The frequency of nondisjunction at first meiosis can only be ascertained by observing second meiotic chromosomes of secondary spermatocytes or oocytes and not by observation of first meiotic metaphase figures. Since even the best testicular preparations will yield only a few second meiotic anaphase figures of analyzable quality, it is obviously impractical to use cytological methods to estimate the frequency of nondisjunction at second meiosis.

Fig. 7. A pair of interkinesis nuclei. The nucleus at the left contains the condensed X, the nucleus at the right the condensed Y chromosome (Feulgen stain).

Fig. 8. Second meiotic prometaphase figure of a spermatocyte. Two sister chromatids of each autosome are completely separated, except at the centromere locus. The X seen at center bottom still stands out by virtue of positive heteropycnosis (Feulgen stain).

(Figures 5–8 are from a testicular biopsy specimen obtained from a 71-year-old man.)

B. ANALYSIS OF TRANSLOCATIONS FROM CHROMOSOMAL CONFIGURATIONS AT MEIOSIS

Translocation usually involves two segments of two nonhomologous chromosomes. Reciprocal translocation requires that each chromosome have one break; insertion requires that one chromosome have two breaks and the other but one (Fig. 9).

The nonhomologous chromosomes involved in the translocation tend to form a quadrivalent during first meiosis in a germ cell of an individual heterozygous for the translocation (Fig. 9). If because of its small size one chromosome is lost, a trivalent is formed (Fig. 10). This is often the case in the Robertsonian type of translocation, such as D(13–15)/G(21) in man.

The frequency with which the quadrivalent is detected in late stages of first meiosis (diakinesis and first meiotic metaphase) depends upon the size of the chromosomal segments involved in the translocation. If both are large, almost every figure will demonstrate 21 bivalents and 1 quadrivalent, while if one segment is small, only a fraction of the figures will contain a quadrivalent (Fig. 11).

If a translocation is suspected but cannot be proved by observation of mitotic metaphase figures from blood cultures, a request for a testicular biopsy specimen from the patient is certainly warranted, since the detection of a quadrivalent in even a small percentage of first meiotic figures would confirm the suspicion beyond doubt. Furthermore, observation of the quadrivalent's configuration would answer the following questions: (1) Is this a terminal translocation or an insertion? (2) Is the sex element involved? (3) Is there a major disparity in size between the two non-homologous chromosomes involved in translocation?

An individual whose complement contains 45 chromosomes, including an extra metacentric in Group C(6–12) formed at the expense of one small and one medium acrocentric, may with equal likelihood be a carrier for G-trisomy (21–22) or for D-trisomy (13–15). He is a carrier for G-trisomy if a breakpoint is on the short arm of the D-chromosome; then it is a G-chromosome which moves at random to either division pole at first meiotic anaphase (upper row, Fig. 10). However, if the breakpoint on the G-chromosome is on its short arm, the D-chromosome moves at random (bottom row, Fig. 10).

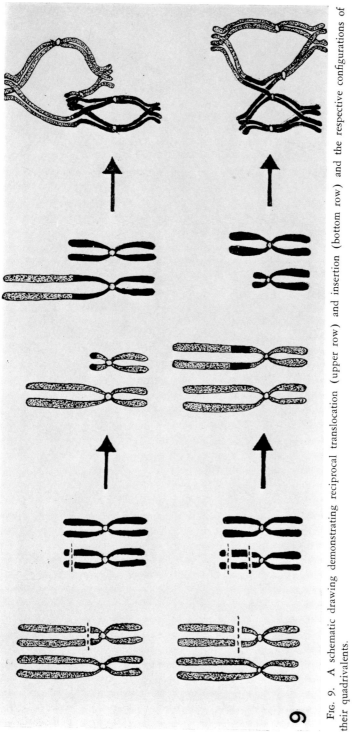

FIG. 9. A schematic drawing demonstrating reciprocal translocation (upper row) and insertion (bottom row) and the respective configurations of their quadrivalents.

87

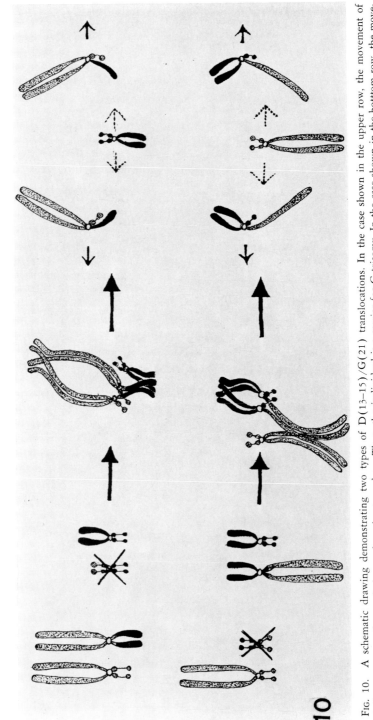

FIG. 10. A schematic drawing demonstrating two types of D(13–15)/G(21) translocations. In the case shown in the upper row, the movement of a G-chromosome at first meiotic anaphase is at random. Thus, the individual is a carrier for G-trisomy. In the case shown in the botttom row, the movement of a D-chromosome is at random, and the individual is a carrier for D-trisomy.

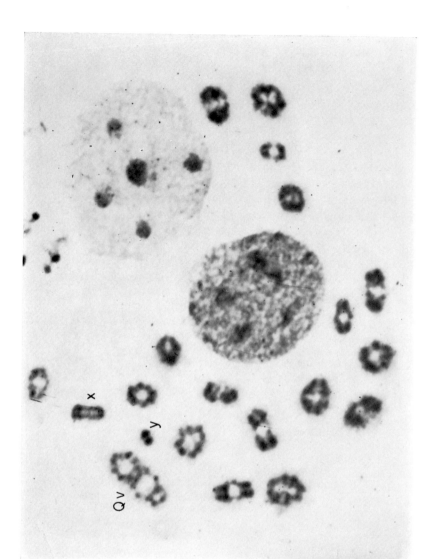

Fig. 11. First meiotic metaphase figure of the male mouse (*Mus musculus, 2n = 40*) heterozygous for T6 translocation (Carter *et al.*, 1955). Instead of having 19 autosomal bivalents and an XY-bivalent, there are 17 autosomal bivalents and one quadrivalent (Qv). The end-to-end association of the X and Y has been disrupted in this figure.

89

V. SUMMARY

There seems to be a widespread belief that human germ cells and meiotic figures are much more difficult to handle than those of other mammals, requiring an almost mystical mastery of technique. We have found that human materials are neither harder nor easier to handle than those of, say, laboratory mice. The central problem is the scarcity of fresh material. Since a lone investigator is unlikely to accumulate a significant number of interesting cases (i.e., translocations) in a limited span of time, it is hoped that many more workers will acquire the necessary skills to study germ cells, always keeping their eyes open for persons with unusual inherited defects. Only then might an investigator have the good fortune to detect by analysis of meiotic figures certain subtle translocations which defy detection by analysis of colchicinized mitotic metaphase figures.

Acknowledgments

This work was supported in part by grant CA-05138 from the National Cancer Institute, U. S. Public Health Service. The author acknowledges with gratitude the editorial assistance of Patricia A. Ray.

Contribution number 20-63, Department of Biology, City of Hope Medical Center, Duarte, California.

References

Carter, T. C., Lyon, M. F., and Phillips, R. J. S. (1955). Gene-tagged chromosome translocations in eleven stocks of mice. *J. Genet.* **53**, 154-166.

Makino, S., and Nishimura, I. (1952). Water pre-treatment squash technique. *Stain Technol.* **27**, 1-7.

Ohno, S. (1963). Relative instability of the mitotic process in zygotes of mice and man. *Ann. Meeting Am. Assoc. Pathol. Bacteriol. 60th Cincinnati 1963 Program and Abstracts.*

Ohno, S., Klinger, H. P., and Atkin, N. B. (1962). Human oögenesis. *Cytogenetics* **1**, 42-51.

Sachs, L. (1954). Sex linkage and the sex chromosomes in man. *Ann. Eugen.* **18**, 255-261.

Suggested Reading

Edwards, R. G. (1962). Meiosis in ovarian oöcytes of adult mammals. *Nature* **196**, 446-450.

Ford, C. E., and Hamerton, J. L. (1956). A colchicine, hypotonic citrate, squash sequence for mammalian chromosomes. *Stain Technol.* **31**, 247-251.

Ohno, S., Kaplan, W. D., and Kinosita, R. (1958). A photomicrographic representation of mitosis and meiosis in the male of *Rattus norvegicus*. *Cytologia (Tokyo)* **23**, 422-428.

Welshons, W. J., Gibson, B. H., and Scandlyn, B. J. (1962). Slide processing for the examination of male mammalian meiotic chromosomes. *Stain Technol.* **37**, 1-5.

Autoradiography of Human Chromosomes

WERNER SCHMID

with technical contributions by JOHN D. CARNES

*Section of Cytology, Department of Biology, The University of Texas,
M. D. Anderson Hospital and Tumor Institute, Houston, Texas*

I.	Introduction	91
II.	Methodology	94
III.	Synopsis and Sequence of Technical Procedures for Autoradiography of Human Chromosomes	97
IV.	Techniques	98
	A. Tissue Culture	98
	B. Continuous Labeling and Pulse-Labeling	99
	C. Harvest of Cultures and Preparation of Slides	100
	D. Autoradiographic Procedures	102
	E. Removal of Autoradiographic Film from Preparations	107
	Appendix	108
	A. Equipment Used for Autoradiography	108
	B. Materials	108
	C. Stepwise Procedures Used for Autoradiography	108
	References	109

I. INTRODUCTION

Studies on the kinetics of deoxyribonucleic acid (DNA) replication in chromosomes have been furthered significantly by the use of radioactive thymidine and autoradiography. Basic features of chromosome organization and duplication were revealed when Taylor *et al.* (1957) introduced tritiated thymidine in their study on *Vicia faba* chromosomes. Asynchronous DNA replication among chromosomes was first reported by Lima-de-Faria (1959), who applied the autoradiographic technique to an investigation of the timing of DNA replication; this study utilized a cell type that possesses a chromosome grossly out of phase, in respect to the cycle of division and condensation. This allocyclic element, found in spermatocytes of the grasshopper *Melanoplus differentialis,* is the X chromosome in the prophase of the first meiotic division. Lima-de-Faria was able to demonstrate that DNA replication in this condensed chromosome was continuing after replication in the autosomes had ceased. He extended his studies to the chromosomes of *Secale,* in which he demonstrated asynchrony of DNA synthesis within individual chromosomes. Further studies on the timing of DNA replication revealed asynchronous patterns, e.g., in root tip cells of *Crepis* (Taylor, 1958), in fibroblasts of a near-diploid tissue culture cell line of Chinese hamsters (Taylor, 1960), and in root tip cells of *Tradescantia paludosa* (Wimber, 1961). The study by Wimber describes essentially the same basic features that make the autoradiographic method useful for human chromosome identification and characterization, namely, the observation that specific portions of the chromosomes continue DNA replication near the end of the DNA synthetic period after other parts of the chromosomes have ceased to synthesize. Obtrusive instances of asynchronous replication of DNA were also found in polytene chromosomes of *Rhynchosciara* (Ficq and Pavan, 1957).

A number of investigators have applied the autoradiographic method to human chromosomes (e.g., Morishima *et al.,* 1962; German, 1962; Gilbert *et al.,* 1962; Moorhead and Defendi, 1963; Rowley *et al.,* 1963; Giannelli, 1963; Grumbach *et al.,* 1963). Much attention was focused on the asynchronous DNA replication pattern of the X chromosomes in females and in human sex anomalies having increased numbers of X chromosomes. Results of these studies showed that, in cells having two or more X chromosomes, only one X completes synthesis of DNA at a rate and time comparable with the general patterns of the autosomes; the additional X chromosomes show a much higher rate of DNA synthesis toward the end of the DNA synthetic period, and are the last chromosomes in the complement to complete DNA replication. The "$n-1$" rule governing the formation of sex chromatin bodies is therefore followed exactly by the late-replicating X chromosomes.

The same studies strongly suggested that some autosomes exhibit replication patterns that might be highly useful for chromosome characterization, and might permit identification of morphologically not distinguishable chromosomes. Some modifications in the technique of chromosome autoradiography indeed provided consistent and clear-cut results, demonstrating that the method is feasible for this purpose. Using the so-called "continuous-labeling technique," to be described later, instead of the customary pulse-labeling method, it was possible to demonstrate that, near the end of the DNA-synthetic period, different segments of specific chromosomes complete DNA replication in very regular sequences. Homologous chromosomes of autosome pairs show the same sequences, usually in synchrony, but sometimes slightly out of phase, in the sense that replication is sometimes more advanced in one homolog than in the other. Whereas pulse labeling tends to emphasize the degree of asynchrony among these patterns, the continuous labeling beginning in late S-period underlines the common patterns. Furthermore, it was found advisable to photograph the chromosomes systematically before superimposing the autoradiographic film. This precaution allows the investigator to expose the radioactive chromosomes to the autoradiographic film for a longer time. With this longer exposure, the resulting heavy grain patterns (which are easily related to the pictures of the previously photographed chromosomes) are much more significant than patterns consisting of only a few scattered silver grains. Chromosome figures which are covered only by a small number of silver grains often do not even permit differentiation between early and later replication patterns which are qualitatively completely different. By applying these improved methods in the human karyotype, it was soon possible to demonstrate that chromosome pairs 1, 2, 3, and 16, which are unequivocally identifiable by their morphology, show essentially identical, late DNA replication patterns among homologs (Schmid, 1963). These observations were soon confirmed in morphologically well-defined chromosome pairs of Chinese hamster (Hsu et al., 1964) and in macrochromosomes of the chicken (Schmid, 1962).

In some of the larger chromosomes exhibiting complex and well-defined patterns of completion of DNA synthesis, the patterns most likely can be used to decipher structural rearrangements which are not recognizable morphologically, such as translocations or large inversions. No such findings have yet been reported, and in this connection much basic research remains to be done. Especially necessary is the study of DNA replication patterns in translocation chromosomes which involve pieces from two chromosomes, the individual DNA replication patterns of which are well known. It is not yet possible to state whether these chromosome parts independently retain their original patterns or, in a rearranged order, one segment influences the DNA replication sequences in the attached "foreign" chromosome piece.

The patterns of specific, late-replicating chromosome regions have an interesting counterpart in observations made in human chromosomes by using two other new techniques. Sasaki and Makino (1963) and Saksela and Moorhead (1962) have described methods by which secondary constrictions in specific regions of certain chromosomes can easily be demonstrated. The method of Saksela and Moorhead (1962) uses a modified fixation procedure, and that of Sasaki and Makino (1963) involves incubation of cells during the last several hours of cultivation in a calcium-free medium. The results of both methods are strikingly similar. The secondary constrictions, which look puffy by the fixation method and more like achromatic gaps by the other method, are located, for the greater part, in the same specific regions. Interestingly, in almost all of these regions, localized, delayed DNA replication is observed by using the autoradiographic method. Constrictions which are found with a high incidence usually correspond to regions that replicate very late. Other constrictions of which only a low incidence is reported to occur correspond to regions which complete DNA synthesis earlier (Schmid, 1963).

II. METHODOLOGY

For the autoradiographic study of DNA synthesis in chromosomes, two main requirements are necessary. A compound must be utilized which is incorporated into DNA only, and not simultaneously into the ribonucleic acid (RNA), which is chemically very similar. Furthermore, due to the small size of the chromosomes, only an isotope that exposes very limited film areas overlaying the chromosomes is suitable.

DNA and RNA share three common bases: adenine, guanine, and cytosine. They differ in one base, which is thymine in DNA and uracil in RNA. To render only the chromosomes radioactive, radioactive thymine must be utilized. In mammalian systems, the deoxyriboside of thymine (thymidine) can be effectively incorporated into cellular DNA by the activity of thymidine kinase, although normally the cells synthesize thymidylic acid via deoxyuridylic acid.

The isotope that fulfills the requirements for the autoradiographic study of small cytological structures is tritium (H^3). Tritium emits β-radiation only; in water, the maximum range of the emitted electrons is 3 μ, and the average range, 1.5 μ. If a photographic emulsion is placed over a pointlike source containing tritium, only an area averaging 3 μ in diameter will be exposed to the β-rays. Tritium has a half-life of 12.3 years, with a disintegration rate of 0.016% each day.

To date, somatic human chromosomes can be identified and characterized only when in their condensed metaphase state; the same also holds true if the chromosomes are labeled with tritiated thymidine. Mitotic chromosomes as such cannot be labeled with tritiated thymidine, since no DNA is replicated during mitosis. In order to obtain labeled metaphase chromosomes, the cells must be offered the radioactive thymidine several hours before they divide, and harvested when these cells reach metaphase.

Cells which multiply double their DNA during a specific period of interphase—the DNA synthetic or the S-period. The time which a cell spends in interphase can vary greatly. Many cells that are still capable of proliferation remain in interphase for prolonged periods, e.g., lymphocytes, which can be stimulated to divide in culture by use of phytohemagglutinin. On the other hand, continuously growing cells move from one division to the other in less than 24 hours. This variation in the duration of interphase is not, or very little, reflected in the length of the DNA synthetic period. The S-period has a duration which, under given environmental conditions, is species- and cell line-specific. For human leucocytes in short-term tissue cultures made up from peripheral blood, Bender and Prescott (1962) reported for the S-period preceding the first *in vitro* division a minimum duration of 12 hours; a few cells observed by Bender and Prescott had an S-period as long as 30 hours. Moorhead and Defendi (1963) found an S-period of 7–7½ hours in cells of long-term fibroblast cultures derived from human embryos. For HeLa cells, the S-period is approximately 6 hours (Stubblefield, 1962).

More precisely timed for a given cell line is the interval between cessation of DNA synthesis and the onset of mitosis (Fig. 1). In human lymphocytes and fibroblasts this lag period, designated G_2 (G_1 being the

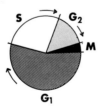

FIG. 1. Diagram representing the cell cycle for cells of a logarithmically growing population. At any given moment a small portion of the cell population is in mitosis (M), while the interphase cells are in the G_1-period, the DNA-synthetic (S) period and in the G_2-period. Individual cells move like the hand of a clock from M over G_1, S, G_2, to the next mitosis. (After Hsu, 1964.)

designation of the period between the preceding mitosis and S-period), has an average duration of 4–6 hours.

The conventional method of applying tritiated thymidine has been the so-called pulse-labeling. In this method, the radioactive compound is introduced to a cell population at a desired strength, and the cells are allowed to incorporate it into their DNA for a short duration. After this period, the cells are allowed to grow in a medium without radioactive thymidine in order to stop further labeling. Thus, the exact duration of the labeling period is known, and after desired time intervals the cells can be fixed. However, for the study of the DNA replication sequences at the end of the S-period, this method is not satisfactory, as was pointed out earlier; more satisfactory is the so-called continuous-labeling method.

The principle of this continuous-labeling technique is illustrated in Fig. 2. The symbols of three nonhomologous chromosomes of a cell proceed from the G_1-period, to the S-period, and into G_2. According to metaphase morphology and late replication pattern, these three chromosomes might be human chromosomes 1, 17, and 18. The lines across the chromosomes represent sites at which DNA replication is supposedly taking place at a given moment. DNA replication along the chromosomes is always focalized, but since during the greater part of the S-period too many sites replicate DNA simultaneously, it is extremely difficult to recognize the patterns by autoradiographic means. However, this situation changes late in the S-period. Some specific chromosome segments that are large enough to be recognizable in the condensed metaphase state complete DNA replication about 2 hours before the end of the S-period. Soon, other large segments follow in a specific sequence. During the critical last two hours, the later the uptake of tritiated thymidine begins, the fewer chromosome segments will become radioactive; finally, a pattern of a few, specific, late-replicating chromosome regions can be observed (e.g., Fig. 5).

Differences in the DNA replication patterns between morphologically similar, nonhomologous chromosomes in some cases occur early, and in other cases, late during the last 2 hours of the S-period. Also, if the chromosomes are large, a stepwise sequence of patterns can, in some cases, be followed. If all the labeling patterns occurring during this time period are to be studied in a given karyotype, the different stages can be obtained conveniently in a single preparation by using a 2-hour Colcemid treatment. If Colcemid is added to a culture 4 hours after the beginning of the tritiated thymidine treatment, first those cells which had almost reached the G_2-period when the tritiated thymidine became available will be arrested in metaphase. During the next 2 hours, progressively earlier stages will reach metaphase and be arrested. By modifying onset and duration of the Colcemid treatment, a higher proportion of early or of late DNA replication stages can be selected.

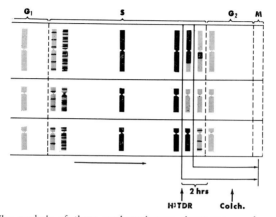

FIG. 2. The symbols of three nonhomologous chromosomes of a cell proceed from G_1 through S, into the G_2-period. The lines across the chromosomes represent sites at which DNA replication is supposedly taking place at a given time interval. DNA replication along the chromosomes is always focalized, but during the greater part of the S-period too many sites replicate DNA simultaneously, making it extremely difficult to recognize patterns by means of autoradiography. The situation changes late in the S-period. Some specific chromosome segments that are large enough to be recognizable in the condensed metaphase state complete DNA replication about 2 hours before the end of the S-period; other large segments follow in a specific sequence. During the critical last 2 hours, the later the uptake of tritiated thymidine (H³TDR) begins, the fewer chromosome segments will become radioactive. Differences in the DNA replication patterns between morphologically similar, nonhomologous chromosomes may occur early in some cases, but late in other cases. By modifying onset and duration of the colchicine treatment, a higher proportion of early or of late DNA replication stages can be selected.

III. SYNOPSIS AND SEQUENCE OF TECHNICAL PROCEDURES FOR AUTORADIOGRAPHY OF HUMAN CHROMOSOMES

1. *Tissue Culture.* Conventionally prepared, short-term blood cultures or logarithmically growing, long-term fibroblast cultures are conveniently used.
2. *Labeling with Tritiated Thymidine.* Continuous labeling beginning in the late part of the S-period, or pulse-labeling.

3. *Colchicine Treatment.* (If continuous labeling is applied, variation of onset and duration of colchicinization permits selection for metaphase cells with chromosomes in specific DNA replication stages.)

4. *Preparations.* Conventional procedures are applied for squash preparations or air-dried preparations.

5. *Photomicrography.* Mitotic figures to be studied later are photographed at high magnification before autoradiographic film is superimposed.

6. *Removal of Cover Slips* from squash preparations *by freezing* on dry ice.

7. *Stripping Slides with Autoradiographic Film,* or coating with liquid emulsion. Exposure.

8. *Developing Autoradiographic Film.*

9. *Restaining* of preparations. Mounting.

IV. TECHNIQUES

A. TISSUE CULTURE

Routinely, we have grown short-term cultures of peripheral leucocytes, bone marrow cells, and fibroblast cultures in McCoy's medium 5a (McCoy *et al.*, 1959), supplemented with 20% fetal calf serum. Also, for labeling experiments, we have successfully used Eagle's minimal medium supplemented with 20% calf serum. It is likely that different tissue culture media have a different influence on the duration of the specific periods (G_1, S, G_2) in the cell cycle. Furthermore, the amount of nonradioactive thymidine in the medium definitely influences the rate of uptake of the added tritiated thymidine. For any given medium, and the cells that are grown in it, it seems advisable to explore, in preliminary experiments, the rate of uptake of tritiated thymidine and the duration of the G_2-period.

We prepare our blood cultures by (1) letting the red cells of the heparinized blood sample (10 ml blood plus 200 units heparin) sediment for 2–3 hours at room temperature, (2) transferring 2–4 ml of the supernatant plasma to a 2-ounce prescription bottle, and (3) adding medium up to the 10 ml mark. Phytohemagglutinin (Difco) M and P (0.10 ml of each) are added and the cultures incubated at 37°C. In cultures made from blood of patients with abnormal white cell counts, the number of white cells is adjusted to 2–4 million cells per milliliter of medium. The incubation temperature is critical, especially during the time when the isotope is incorporated.

Only cultures with an abundance of mitotic cells are worthwhile for a detailed autoradiographic study. Much time can be saved if, instead of attempting to use a mediocre preparation, the culturing is repeated. In blood cultures, more mitoses often are observed on the fourth day than on the third day of culturing; thus, two cultures are usually made, with one labeled and harvested on the third and one on the fourth day. The slides from the better sample are then selected for further processing.

B. Continuous Labeling and Pulse-Labeling

For continuous labeling, a concentration of the tritiated thymidine of 1 µc/ml medium proves to be practical. When this concentration is used, the preparations later require an exposure to the autoradiographic film for average periods of 5–10 days. This exposure time is long enough that the time at which the slides must be developed does not become too critical, at least not for qualitative studies. On the other hand the incidence of chromatid breaks caused by the radiation effect of the incorporated tritiated thymidine at this concentration remains within tolerable limits. For short pulse-labeling experiments, a higher concentration of tritiated thymidine may sometimes be desirable in order to obtain reasonably short exposure times. This would, e.g., be considered if after a tritiated thymidine pulse of 15 minutes duration an exposure time of 2–3 weeks were found to be still insufficient.

For routine experiments, we used tritiated thymidine of a specific activity of 1.9 curies/mmole. In handling tritiated compounds, it must be remembered that contaminations caused by careless handling or accidents cannot be detected easily with scintillation counters, because tritium does not emit γ-radiation.

In experiments using *continuous labeling,* tritiated thymidine (1 µc/ml medium) is usually added about 6 hours (exact timing must be explored) prior to termination of the cultures. Chromosome segments which have completed DNA replication no longer incorporate any thymidine, nor is tritiated thymidine stored in the cells in an amount that would cause undue background radioactivity. The excess isotope is therefore left in the cultures until harvest, when it is removed automatically with the culture medium. Two hours before termination of the cultures, or at another selected time, Colcemid, at a final concentration of 0.03 µg/ml, is added.

Pulse-labeling experiments are, for technical reasons, much more easily carried out on monolayer cultures than on suspended cell cultures. If suspension cultures are used, the cells must be centrifuged in order to remove the medium containing the tritiated thymidine and the media used for washing. If no special precautions are taken, the temperature of the cultures will drop during these procedures and the cell metabolism will slow down, a factor that must be taken into account. A means of avoiding centrifugation of suspension cultures during pulse-labeling consists of stopping the incorporation of tritiated thymidine into the cells by diluting the radioactive compound and offering the cells a hundred- or thousandfold amount of nonradioactive thymidine. This method works satisfactorily, except that such high concentrations of thymidine may have the effect of inhibiting DNA replication to some extent, and therefore prolong the duration of the DNA synthetic period of the cells. Stubblefield (1962) estimates, on the basis of his experiments with HeLa cells, that a concentration of 10 µg of thymidine per milliliter of medium will cause an approximate 2-hour prolongation of the total S-period. Any delay in the duration of the S-period will enhance asynchrony between individual cells, i.e., the longer the race, the less likely the competitors will arrive at the finish line at the same time, or, in the case of cells, at metaphase.

When monolayer cultures are used, no centrifugations and no addition of cold thymidine are necessary; the cells will remain almost undisturbed, especially if a few precautions are taken. The medium containing the tritiated thymidine and the medium used for washing the cultures (very gently) are prewarmed in the incubator before use. The original culture medium is saved, and this "conditioned" medium is added to the cultures again after the pulse-labeling is over. For most pulse studies, a short colchicinization with a relatively high colchicine concentration (e.g., Colcemid: 0.06 µg/ml for 1 hour) is desirable.

C. HARVEST OF CULTURES AND PREPARATION OF SLIDES

1. Squash Preparations

The white cells suspended in the medium (or fibroblasts detached with 0.2% trypsin solution) are centrifuged for 4 minutes in 12-ml conical tubes in a clinical centrifuge at $400 \times g$. The supernatant is poured off, 10 ml of hypotonic solution (1% sodium citrate) added, and the cells suspended with a pipet. The tube is left in this state for 10 minutes, after which the cells are centrifuged again. The supernatant is decanted and 10 ml of 50% acetic acid are added very carefully by using a pipet in order not to disturb the cell pellet. After a minimum of 20 minutes, the fixative is decanted and the tube put upside down on a filter paper in order to remove the last few drops of acetic acid. About as many drops of aceto orcein stain (2%) are added as corresponds to the volume of the cell pellet (usually 2 to 3 drops). With a capillary pipet, cells and stain are mixed. The cells are then ready for squash preparations.

The slides to be used are alcohol-cleaned, but the cover glasses are simply wiped clean with a lint-free cloth. If this is done, more cells will adhere to the slide when, later in the procedure, the cover slips are removed. There are certain brands of cover glasses that have to be siliconized. If the cell suspension contains large particles or debris which prevent a complete flattening of the cells, a drop can first be placed on a slide where these particles will attach to the glass. Then the remaining fluid is permitted to flow to the surface of another slide where it will be squashed. A filter paper is placed over the cover slip; squashing is then begun very gently by using a thumb. When stain can no longer be pressed out from under the cover glass, a final strong pressure is applied. Every sideways movement of the cover glass will destroy the preparation. Air pockets under the cover glass should be avoided because, later in the freezing procedure, cells near the air pockets will be dislodged and lost.

Microscopic inspection of the slide at this stage will reveal whether the preparation has the necessary high quality to be of use in an autoradiographic study. If so, the slide is immediately sealed with Kroenig's wax along the edges of the cover slip to prevent desiccation.

When not in use, the temporary slides should be stored in a refrigerator. We found that slides kept at room temperature for a period of time show a high background in the eventual autoradiographs. It is possible that some DNA becomes decomposed, thus allowing the label to diffuse into the cytoplasm. At 4°C the temporary slides can be stored safely for at least 4 weeks. From each culture, several good slides are generally used for observation and photography; from each slide, the best mitotic figures, preferably those without overlapping chromosomes, are chosen. A total of about 30 photographed figures is necessary for most studies. The reason for scattering suitable cells over several slides is to avoid severe loss in case of accidents that can happen through a variety of manipulations for autoradiography. The coordinates of each cell in relation to the microscope stage are recorded to allow future relocation of the same.

As soon as a sufficient number of cells have been photographed, the preparations must be processed further, i.e., the acetic acid must be removed and the slides air-dried. For this purpose, a freezing procedure (Conger and Fairchild, 1953) is applied. The slides are placed, right side up, on the smooth surface of a block of dry ice, where they are left for approximately 5 minutes. During this time, the wax edges will crack. With a scalpel, the cover glass is flipped off with a single quick movement, and the slide is placed in a staining jar containing absolute alcohol. After 4 minutes, the remnants of wax are removed from the slides with a razor blade and the slides are placed into another jar with absolute alcohol for 2 additional minutes. Careless handling during this procedure will cause loss of cells. The slides are then placed into a slide box, permitted to dry, and protected from dust. In this stage, the slides can be stored for months without deteriorating.

2. Air-Dried Preparations

Anyone who is accustomed to the air-drying method, and is getting sufficiently high numbers of overlap-free chromosomes spreads by his technique, can apply the method also for autoradiography of chromosomes. Whether the chromosome figures are then observed and photographed by putting immersion oil directly on the preparations or whether the slides are mounted with cover glasses in any temporary way, in the end, the preparations have to be dry and free of any oil or mounting media over the cells.

D. AUTORADIOGRAPHIC PROCEDURES

For autoradiography of chromosomes, it is usually preferable to employ the stripping film technique. For beginners, this technique may appear somewhat complicated, but it gives highly satisfactory results of consistent quality. There is no doubt that excellent results are also achieved by using the liquid emulsion (NTB-2) technique, which is easier, but has the disadvantage of not always producing a film membrane of constant thickness. A detailed description of the coating technique is given by Kopriwa and Leblond (1962). These authors mention another factor of importance: they state that the liquid emulsion cannot be stored for more than 2 months, whereas the plates with the stripping film can be kept under refrigeration for long periods of time—up to a year—without the fog (background grains) becoming unduly high. Kopriwa and Leblond conclude that for this reason and because little special equipment is needed, the stripping film technique is more convenient when autoradiographic work is done intermittently and with a small number of slides. These are conditions which normally prevail in laboratories involved in chromosome autoradiography. There can, however, be no doubt that particularly for large-scale continued work, the coating technique is the method of choice.

In applying the stripping technique, Kodak stripping film AR.10 can be used. The following manipulations are carried out in a darkroom illuminated by red safelight (e.g., Kodak filter, Wratten, series 2). The film, which is mounted on glass plates, has to be cut into squares of approximately 40 × 40 mm. In order to keep the background grains to a minimum, the cutting is performed by using a frame on top of which a ruler can be moved without touching the film. The cutting is done with a scalpel, and a new blade is used for each film plate (Fig. 3). In order to render superfluous a strict control of humidity and temperature in the darkroom, the autoradiographic film is then treated as follows.

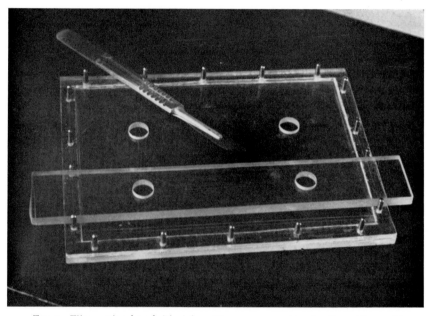

Fig. 3. Film cutting board. Plexiglass. Pins serve as guides for the cutting guide. (Film cutting board available through its designer, J. D. Carnes.)

The plate is placed in a tray containing 75% alcohol. After 3 minutes, it is transferred to a second tray containing absolute alcohol. At this stage, the cut film squares are still attached to the glass plate. With a pair of small forceps, a single square is lifted and removed from the plate. The film must loosen easily without distortion and without curling up. It is then dropped, with the emulsion side down, into a third tray containing distilled water at room temperature. The film will swirl momentarily and spread out completely on the surface of the water. With one hand, the experimenter dips a slide into the water, and with the other hand maneuvers the film square into position, with one end of the film touching the slide near its frosted end. When the slide is lifted out of the water, the film will cover the preparation and its overlapping ends will fold to the underside of the slide. The slide is then put on a glass plate and attached to it with a clip. For about 3 minutes, this plate is placed back into the tray with the distilled water; this is conveniently done in batches of half a dozen slides. After they are taken out of the water, the slides are removed from the glass plate, one by one, and the film square is straightened out by using a camel hair brush and fingers. The slides are placed into a rack for drying. For this purpose, we use a slide box (22 × 16 × 3 cm) with large openings sawed in the bottom and lid so that only a frame structure remains. This drying rack is inserted into a light-proof drying box which is provided with a small electric blower that moves air through the box at a slow speed (Fig. 4). The built-in light trap system also keeps dust from settling on the wet slides. The drying must be done at room temperature and usually takes about 3 hours. As soon as the slides are dry, they are transferred to a small slide box (Bakelite or metal) which can be closed hermetically and taped around the lid to prevent light leakage. In this box, space must be left for about 1 teaspoonful of a dehydrating agent, such as a silica gel desiccant, wrapped in some gauze. The box is kept in a refrigerator until the slides are ready to be developed. If the exposure time must be tested, some pilot slides are placed in separate boxes so that most of the slides can be left undisturbed if the exposure time needs to be extended.

Before the slides are developed, their reverse sides are painted with a mounting medium (e.g., Permount) in order to prevent any shifting of the film squares during the developing process and the subsequent staining. To dry the mounting medium, the same drying apparatus as described previously is used. About 2 hours are sufficient for this drying. For developing and staining, the slides are conveniently placed in a rack holding some 10 or 20 slides to facilitate moving simultaneously from one fluid to the other. Kodak developer D-19b is adjusted to 20°C. The developing time of 5 minutes recommended by the manufacturer for conventional use is too long for chromosome autoradiography. Two minutes are sufficient and give considerably smaller silver grains than the 5 minutes' developing time. The slides are dipped in water and fixed in acid fixer for twice the time required for the film to clear—about 2 minutes. They are then washed in a 20°C running water bath for 5–10 minutes. For drying the slides, rack and drying box are again conveniently used.

The dry slides are stained with a diluted and buffered solution of Giemsa blood stain. The desirable light-blue staining of the chromosomes,

FIG. 4. Light-proof drying box. A small electric blower moves air through a light trap system. Also: drying rack for slides which is being inserted into the drying box. (Drying box available through its designer, J. D. Carnes.)

which provides a good contrast to the black silver grains, is achieved by the following procedure. The stain must be made up in these proportions: distilled water, 100 ml; 0.1 M citric acid, 3 ml; 0.2 M Na_2HPO_4, 3 ml; methyl alcohol, 3 ml; and stock solution of Giemsa's blood stain (e.g.,

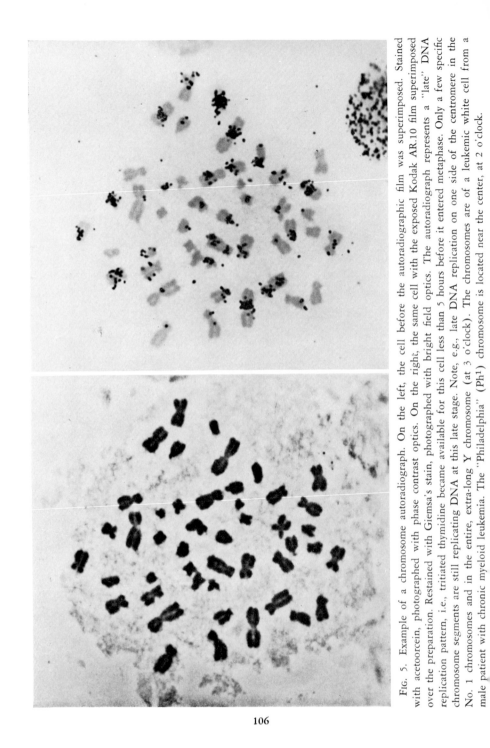

Fig. 5. Example of a chromosome autoradiograph. On the left, the cell before the autoradiographic film was superimposed. Stained with acetoorcein, photographed with phase contrast optics. On the right, the same cell with the exposed Kodak AR.10 film superimposed over the preparation. Restained with Giemsa's stain, photographed with bright field optics. The autoradiograph represents a "late" DNA replication pattern, i.e., tritiated thymidine became available for this cell less than 5 hours before it entered metaphase. Only a few specific chromosome segments are still replicating DNA at this late stage. Note, e.g., late DNA replication on one side of the centromere in the No. 1 chromosomes and in the entire, extra-long Y chromosome (at 3 o'clock). The chromosomes are of a leukemic white cell from a male patient with chronic myeloid leukemia. The "Philadelphia" (Ph[1]) chromosome is located near the center, at 2 o'clock.

106

Curtin), 5 ml. In this solution, which is used only once, the slides are stained at room temperature for 4–7 minutes. Then, they are dipped twice in distilled water and dried at room temperature. A new razor blade is used for each slide to remove the overlapping ends of the film on the back side of the slides. The absolutely dry slides are mounted, e.g., with Euparal, preferably by using cover glasses one size larger than those used originally. The chromosome figures (Fig. 5) are then studied by using bright field optics.

E. Removal of Autoradiographic Film from Preparations

Autoradiographic film can be removed from preparations without damaging the chromosomes. For some special purposes, e.g., for studying DNA replication of the allocyclic X in very late S-phase, it is more convenient to omit photographing the chromosomes before autoradiography and to get control pictures of the chromosomes later, by taking the autoradiographic film off. If, however, replication stages are to be studied in which all or most of the chromosomes are expected to be labeled, this method has no advantage. In heavily labeled chromosome figures it is not possible to determine whether underneath the silver grains the chromosome figures are complete and free from overlaps. Therefore, once again it is necessary to take an excess of photographs, this time of labeled chromosome figures.

One of the methods to remove autoradiographic film from preparations has been related to us by Dr. N. O. Bianchi, La Plata, Argentina, and is reproduced with his kind permission:

(1) Cover glasses mounted with Euparal or Permount are removed with a scalpel after the slides are soaked overnight in xylene. The rest of the mounting medium is removed by washes in xylene and absolute alcohol.

(2) Distilled water, 10 minutes.

(3) Potassium ferricyanide (7.5%), 3–4 minutes.

(4) Sodium thiosulfate (20%), 5 minutes.

(5) Two changes in distilled water, 1 minute each.

(6) Trypsin (Difco, 1:250) 0.1% in phosphate buffer (pH 7.2–7.8) at 37°C, 10 minutes.

(7) Wash in tap water, 10 minutes.

(8) Wash in distilled water, dry.

For some purposes, it is satisfactory to remove the silver grains only, by use of steps 1–5 and to leave the cleared film on the preparations.

If tryptic digestion, which at the same time removes film and part of the cytoplasm, should be avoided, the film can be peeled off after soaking the preparations in warm water (about 40°C). Removal of the film without previous treatment with potassium ferricyanide will leave some of the silver grains attached to the chromosomes.

APPENDIX

A.   EQUIPMENT USED FOR AUTORADIOGRAPHY

Darkroom, illuminated by red safelight (Kodak filter, Wratten, series 2)

Film cutting board (see Fig. 3)

Three trays (approx. 5×7 inches) for immersion of film plates

Glass plates (approx. 4×7 inches) ; clips to attach slides

Camel hair brush

Drying rack for slides (slide box with openings in bottom and lid)

Drying box with electric blower (see Fig. 4)

Staining dishes for developer, fixative, and stain

Staining racks

Slide boxes (Bakelite or metal)

B.   MATERIALS

Tritiated thymidine

Kodak AR.10 fine grain autoradiographic stripping film

Kodak developer D-19b

Acid fixer

Dehydrating agent (e.g., Drierite)

Gauze squares

Mounting medium (e.g., Permount) ; brush to apply it

Razor blades

C.   STEPWISE PROCEDURES USED FOR AUTORADIOGRAPHY

1. Stripping Slides with Film

1. Cut film (AR.10) and place in 75% alcohol bath for 3 minutes.
2. Transfer film plate into absolute alcohol bath.
3. Remove one film square and place in water bath upside down.
4. Place microslide in bath and maneuver film on top of preparation, then lift film out of bath.
5. Place slide on glass plate and attach with clip. Repeat until plate is full. Then place plate in water bath for 3 minutes.
6. Remove plate from water bath and take off clips.

7. With camel hair brush and fingers, straighten film square over slide and place in drying rack.

8. Place rack in drying box approximately 3 hours.

9. Transfer slides to storage boxes, leaving space for dehydrating agent. (Put pilot slides into separate boxes.)

10. Put about 1 teaspoon of dehydrating agent on opened gauze square and roll it into a ball. Place in slide box.

11. Place slide box in refrigerator until ready to develop.

2. Developing Slides and Staining

1. Paint back side of slides with mounting medium (e.g., Permount). Put in drying box for approximately 2 hours.

2. Place slides in staining rack and develop in staining dish in D-19b for 2 minutes at 20°C. Dip up and down a few times.

3. Dip in water.

4. Place in acid fixer for 2 minutes.

5. Place in 20°C running water bath for 5–10 minutes.

6. Dry in drying box for 1–2 hours.

7. Place slides in staining rack and stain for 4–7 minutes in Giemsa stain (see recipe in text).

8. Dip twice in distilled water.

9. Dry until absolutely dry.

10. Remove film and mounting medium from back side of slides using new razor blades.

11. Mount cover glass on dry film with mounting medium (e.g., Permount).

Acknowledgments

This investigation was supported by research grant G-16241 from the National Science Foundation.

The author wishes to thank Dr. T. C. Hsu who introduced him to the autoradiographic techniques for suggestions and criticism in the preparation of the manuscript. It is also a pleasure to thank Mrs. S. Connelly for her editorial assistance.

References

Bender, J. A., and Prescott, D. M. (1962). DNA synthesis and mitosis in cultures of human peripheral leukocytes. *Exptl. Cell Res.* **27**, 221-229.

Bianchi, N. O. (1963). Personal communication.

Conger, A. D., and Fairchild, L. M. (1953). A quick-freeze method for making smear slides permanent. *Stain Technol.* **28**, 281-283.

Ficq, A., and Pavan, C. (1957). Autoradiography of polytene chromosomes of *Rhynchosciara angelae* at different stages of larval development. *Nature* **180**, 983-984.

German, J. L. (1962). DNA synthesis in human chromosomes. *Trans. N. Y. Acad. Sci.* **24**, 395-407.

Giannelli, F. (1963). The pattern of X-chromosome deoxyribonucleic acid synthesis in two women with abnormal sex-chromosome complements. *Lancet* **I**, 863-865.

Gilbert, C. W., Muldal, S., Lajtha, L. G., and Rowley, J. (1962). Time-sequence of human chromosome duplication. *Nature* **195**, 869-873.

Grumbach, M. M., Morishima, A., and Taylor, J. H. (1963). Human sex chromosome abnormalities in relation to DNA replication and heterochromatinization. *Proc. Natl. Acad. Sci. U. S.* **49**, 581-589.

Hsu, T. C. (1964). Genetic cytology. In "The Biology of Cells and Tissues in Culture" (E. N. Wilmer, ed.). Academic Press, New York. In press.

Hsu, T. C., Schmid, W., and Stubblefield, E. (1964). DNA replication sequences in higher animals. In press.

Kopriwa, B. M., and Leblond, C. P. (1962). Improvements in the coating technique of radioautography. *J. Histochem. Cytochem.* **10**, 269-284.

Lima-de-Faria, A. (1959). Differential uptake of tritiated thymidine into hetero- and euchromatin in *Melanoplus* and *Secale*. *J. Biophys. Biochem. Cytol.* **6**, 457-466.

McCoy, T. A., Maxwell, M., and Kruse, P. F. (1959). Amino acid requirements of the Novikoff hepatoma *in vitro*. *Proc. Soc. Exptl. Biol. Med.* **100**, 115-118.

Moorhead, P. S., and Defendi, V. (1963). Asynchrony of DNA synthesis in chromosomes of human diploid cells. *J. Cell. Biol.* **16**, 202-209.

Morishima, A., Grumbach, M. M., and Taylor, J. H. (1962). Asynchronous duplication of human chromosomes and the origin of sex chromatin. *Proc. Natl. Acad. Sci. U. S.* **48**, 756-763.

Rowley, J., Muldal, S., Gilbert, C. W., Lajtha, L. G., Lindstein, J., Fraccaro, M., and Kaijser, K. (1963). Synthesis of deoxyribonucleic acid on X-chromosomes of an XXXXY male. *Nature* **197**, 251-252.

Saksela, E., and Moorhead, P. S. (1962). Enhancement of secondary constrictions and the heterochromatic X in human cells. *Cytogenetics* **2**, 225-244.

Sasaki, M. S., and Makino, S. (1963). The demonstration of secondary constrictions in human chromosomes by means of a new technique. *Am. J. Human Genet.* **15**, 24-33.

Schmid, W. (1962). DNA replication patterns of the heterochromosomes in *Gallus domesticus*. *Cytogenetics* **1**, 344-352.

Schmid, W. (1963). DNA replication patterns of human chromosomes. *Cytogenetics* **2**, 175-193.

Stubblefield, E. (1962). Personal communication.

Taylor, J. H. (1958). The mode of chromosome duplication in *Crepis capillaris*. *Exptl. Cell Res.* **15**, 350-357.

Taylor, J. H. (1960). Asynchronous duplication of chromosomes in culture cells of Chinese hamster. *J. Biophys. Biochem. Cytol.* **7**, 455-463.

Taylor, J. H., Woods, P. S., and Hughes, W. L. (1957). The organization and duplication of chromosomes as revealed by autoradiographic studies using tritium-labeled thymidine. *Proc. Natl. Acad. Sci. U. S.* **43**, 122-128.

Wimber, D. E. (1961). Asynchronous replication of deoxyribonucleic acid in root tip chromosomes of *Tradescantia paludosa*. *Exptl. Cell Res.* **23**, 402-407.

Bright Field, Phase Contrast, and Fluorescence Microscopy

WALTER J. RUNGE

Department of Medicine, University of Minnesota, Minneapolis, Minnesota

I.	Introduction	111
II.	Theory of Light Microscopes	112
	A. Size of Image	112
	B. Numerical Aperture and Lens Aberrations	113
	C. Resolving Power of the Microscope	115
	D. Formation of the Microscopic Image	115
	E. Microscopic Depth of Focus	116
III.	Properties of Microscopic Lens Systems: Bright Field Microscopy	117
	A. Objectives	117
	B. Eyepieces	119
	C. Microscopic Condensers	120
	D. Light Sources and Illumination	122
IV.	Phase Contrast Microscopy	123
	A. Principle and Image Formation	123
	B. Phase Optics	124
	C. Applications	124
V.	Fluorescence Microscopic Technique	125
	References	127

I. INTRODUCTION

The practical resolution of a morphological structure in biological preparations under the microscope does not depend entirely upon the quality of the optical instrument and the histotechnical perfection of the specimen. The nature of an object has a decisive influence on the visibility of the wanted structure and on the degree to which the fine details can be perceived. Chromosomes per se are not very much different from other biological microscopic objects. But chromosome work requires the application of a variety of light microscopic methods, each to degrees

111

varying from the most meticulous to the most cursory. This scale of variety is the reason that no fixed rules can be given, which satisfy all possible demands. The efficient use of microscopes in all fields of chromosome study calls for an understanding of the basis of the complex physics of the combination LIGHT + SPECIMEN + MICROSCOPE, thus enabling one to control the results and be aware of its inborn limitations. The attempt to influence the performance of the "set up" by empiricism and guess work was once justified as microscopic art.

This chapter, far from complete, tries to give a basic insight into the physical optics of the microscope and its technological realization. By understanding the scientific basis of his main tool, the student of chromosomes himself becomes able to adapt his microscope and modify his microscopic methods to his own desire without losing the wanted degree of accuracy, so necessary in communication with fellow workers in this field.

II. THEORY OF LIGHT MICROSCOPES

Let us first see how a simple lens can "magnify" or "reduce." Imagine that a lens projects an image of an object at infinity onto a screen. Under this condition, the image is sharp (focused) only if the screen is exactly in the image focal plane of the lens. The size of the image is smaller than the object. If the object moves toward the lens, then its image plane dissociates from the image focal plane and travels away from the lens. When the object has arrived in the object focal plane, its image plane has traveled into infinity. This is the complete reversal of the starting condition, but as the image moves toward infinity its image increases in size. When the object arrives in the focal plane, its image at infinity is infinitely large. The amount of increase in image size for any position of the object between infinity and focal plane depends on the focal length of the lens [for lenses of material of the same refractive index (n)], being greater for smaller focal lengths. When an object is closer to the lens than its focal distance, no real image can be formed on a screen; only a virtual image may be seen by the human eye. A real image is optically equivalent to an object.

A. Size of Image

To the microscopist, the actual size of the microscopic image is of most concern. The ratio between the size of the object and the size of the *real* image is called scale of image (linear magnification; i.e., $M:1$). This term is independent of the observer and distance of observation. Magnification (i.e., $M\times$), however, is defined by the visual angle under which the eye of the observer regards the object or the real image. The unit of magnification ($1\times$) exists only for viewing at the standard "least distance of distinct vision" ($= 250$ mm or 10 inches). Thus, a photomicrograph has a fixed scale of image, but it can be looked at under different magnifications.

An object (or real image) which can be comfortably looked at, at a certain distance from the eye, can actually be brought closer to the eye with the aid of a magnifying glass. The lens enables the eye to see the object as if it were at a farther distance, or were seen under a greater visual angle. This virtual image appears magnified in ratio to both visual angles.

B. NUMERICAL APERTURE AND LENS ABERRATIONS

It would seem that one could obtain any degree of desired magnification by putting strong lenses in front of the eye. We have seen that the obtainable amount of magnification with a lens is governed by its focal length. The necessary short focal length in high magnification demands a deep radius of lens curvature $[f = nr/(n-1)]$. High power lenses, as segments of spheres, can have only small diameters. Consequently, the reduced amount of light from the object transmitted to the pupil of the eye results in a dim image. A term describing the brightness of image is the "numerical aperture" (NA). It is derived as the mathematical product of the refractive index of the medium (n) between object and lens, and one half the sine of the angle subtending from the axial point of the object to the diameter of the lens: $NA = n(\sin\alpha/2)$. Besides this, simple lenses are not very well suited for microscopic work because lenses suffer from intrinsic inabilities to form perfect images. The chromatic and the spherical aberrations are the most offensive for microscopic work. The chromatic aberration is caused by the variation of the refractive index of the lens material for different wavelengths of light (colors). Thus, for every color of light different lengths of optical paths are present which cause a different focal plane for every color. The spherical aberration has its origin in the lateral extension of the microscopic object away from the optical axis and the curvature of the lens. For rays emanating at a distance from the optical axis, longitudinal differences in length of optical path exist, causing them to focus in different planes.

The aberrations can be overcome technically only by the use of lens systems, as utilized in modern microscopic objectives and eyepieces. Since technical remedies for the lens aberrations affect each other adversely, the improved lens systems can be designed only for one specific set of the following conditions.[1] The compound microscope is defined as an optical instrument which magnifies the angle of subtense of small objects, when all distances are under complete control: From the object at proper working distance, the objective forms a real, intermediate image at the fixed optical barrel length. The intermediate image is again magnified by the eye lens of the eyepiece and presented to the eye as if it were at the standard "least distance of distinct vision" as virtual image. The total magnification then equals the power of objective multiplied by the power of the eyepiece: $M = M_{obj} \cdot M_{ep}$.

As already mentioned, the biological microscopic object is not a point, nor is it optically homogeneous. Its finer microscopic structures are of a magnitude which influence penetrating waves of light by more than spectral absorption or transmission. Minute holes, edges, etc., act upon a traversing parallel front of light waves in such a manner that every point of the structure becomes the source of a new spherical wave. Overlapping of the waves originating from such diffracting object points causes interference. Interference gives rise to brightness in one direction and darkness in another. Brightnesses are the maxima and darknesses the minima of this wave motion.

Maxima obtained with white light are interference spectra. The angles which subtend between the direction of the trains of the orders of interference spectra or maxima ($\pm I_n$) and the nondeflected maximum progressing in the original direction of the light (0—order) depend on the distance (d) between two corresponding points in the diffracting object and on the wavelength of light:

$$\sin \theta_{\pm n} = I_n \cdot \lambda/d.$$

This means that the microscope can only form exact and true images of very small structures when *all* maxima of significant intensity are accepted by the numerical aperture of the objective.

---

[1] Corrections for aberrations of lens systems are only available as "best case" compromise. The designers of microscopes correct lens systems of their make only, to suit their own selected working distance and optical barrel length. Also it is their common practice to compensate any rest aberrations of the objectives with specific over- or undercorrection of their eyepieces. Hybrid microscopes of parts of different makes do not give the best performance, even if the screw threads match.

C. Resolving Power of the Microscope

The resolving power of a compound microscope is given as: the smallest distance between two diffracting points or lines which can be perceived as two. The resolving power can be deduced from the formula of the diffraction grating $d = \lambda/\sin\theta$ in which we substitute $\sin\theta$ with the familiar term of the numerical aperture: $NA = n(\sin\alpha/2)$.[2] Then we find $d = \lambda/NA$ as the general formula of the resolving power of the microscope, valid only for illumination by very narrow, axial pencils of parallel light. Under actual conditions of illumination with finite cones of parallel light, the formula changes to $d = \lambda/(Na_{obj} + NA_{illum})$. From this formula we can see how greatly the resolving power of the microscope is affected by the substage assembly (condenser and lamp). The condition of parallel illuminating light in the specimen plane is given only by two distinct principles of illumination: "axial critical" and Koehler's illumination. "Axial critical illumination," useful only for special spectral and microphotometric measurements, is achieved when the condenser projects a reduced, sharp image of the light source (*filament* of a lamp) into the specimen which is already sharply focused in the microscope. Koehler's illumination, for visual and photographic observations, is a little more complicated. A collecting lens projects an image of the light source onto the aperture diaphragm of the microscope condenser. The microscope condenser forms an image of a special second diaphragm, located at the lamp's collecting lens, into the already focused specimen under the microscope.

D. Formation of the Microscopic Image

At this point the formation of the microscopic image according to Abbe (1904) can be presented as follows. With the sharp image of the light source (or the special diaphragm) in the specimen plane, all wave fronts traverse parallel through the specimen. During the passage, orders of interference spectra are formed by diffraction in the structure of the object. The objective focuses all rays emerging from one point of the image of the lamp in one corresponding point in its image focal plane. In this plane a central image of the light source is formed surrounded by other images of the light source in a certain pattern, which is caused by and depends on the admitted orders of interference spectra from the specimen. From all these light source images, wave fronts are aiming at

---

[2] NA represents the maximum value for $\sin\theta$.

every point in the intermediate image plane. All these wave motions generate, by interference with each other, a real image in this plane. This intermediate image is further magnified for visual observation by the eye lens of the eyepiece in the manner of a magnifying glass, without any contribution to detail or resolution.[3]

For microscopic work requiring very high resolution (chromosome structure), it should be remembered that in regard to resolving power the wavelength of light is of the same importance as the numerical aperture of the optics.[4] The shorter the wavelength (UV;blue), the smaller the angular deviation of orders of maxima which can enter a lens with a given numerical aperture. The resolving power of an objective can be doubled with illumination of the proper degree of obliquity. According to the diffraction theory a grating can be resolved when the 0-order *and* one of the diffracted orders are admitted. By use of the "oblique critical illumination" (Abbe, 1904; Köhler, 1928; Langeron, 1925; Romeis, 1943; Spitta, 1920; Martin, 1955), these two orders may be brought into the objective, which otherwise would gather only the nondeviated axial 0-order.

E. Microscopic Depth of Focus

The depth of focus (D_v) to be expected from a chosen combination of eyepiece and objective is a term of practical importance as it relates to microscopic objects, which like chromosomes have a substantial thickness. The focal depth of a microscope is independent of the quality of lens systems and is determined solely by natural optical laws. The following formula is valid only for visual microscopic images *seen* at the standard (least distance of distinct vision) of 250 mm:

$$D_v = \frac{n}{NA \cdot M \cdot 0.25} + \frac{250}{M^2}, \text{ mm}$$

(n = refractive index of mounting medium)

This formula shows that D_v depends on the total magnification M and the numerical aperture (NA) of the objective. The depth of focus is smaller, the higher the total magnification. The D_v of oil-immersion systems ranges from 0.5 to 1.0 μ.

---

[3] Abbe's theory has been questioned by others, but it still forms the basis for correlation of the principles and performances of lenses in microscopes and the reliable interpretation of the images.

[4] Obtaining a shorter wavelength illumination with filters is less expensive than high NA objectives.

A shallow D_v is of use in the determination of the thickness of a structure. The latter is approximately equal to the distance between upper and lower focus, which can be read on the scale (in microns) at the fine adjustment of the microscope stand.

Intentional or inadvertent focusing on a series of focus planes of a "thick" object as routinely exercised under visual observation, creates in the observer's mind the impression of a greater depth of focus as given by the above formula. This condition, among others, however, does not apply in photomicrography, and as shown in the next chapter the operational photomicrographic depth of focus is more limited.

This concludes our excursion into the basic theory of light microscopes. The next step is to become familiar with the properties of actual microscopic lens systems.

III. PROPERTIES OF MICROSCOPIC LENS SYSTEMS: BRIGHT FIELD MICROSCOPY

A. OBJECTIVES

According to their correction, objectives can be grouped into four classes: monochromats, achromats, fluorites, and apochromats. Every class contains dry and immersion systems. In the latter, the space between specimen and front lens is filled with water, glycerol, or oil, each having a higher refractive index than air ($= 1$). This increases the numerical aperture of the system through removal of the total reflection at the cover glass/air border for the marginal orders of interference maxima. Immersion liquids ought to have the refractive index specified by the maker of the lens system. Objectives are identified by the linear magnification of the intermediate image at the specified optical tube length and the numerical aperture, which are engraved on them. Dry objectives are very sensitive to variations in the thickness of the cover slip. Some brands are engraved with the proper thickness and some dry systems are available with a correction mount, which enables the user to adjust for aberrant "cover slip" thicknesses. Most dry systems are corrected for a "cover slip" of 0.17 mm total thickness, which includes also the layer of mounting medium between specimen and cover slip. Actually a cover slip of 0.15 mm thickness should be used. However, objectives can be obtained corrected for use without cover slips. Dry objectives with especially long working distances for use in tissue culture work are available. Immersion systems are insensitive to variation of the thickness of the cover slips and are to to be preferred over dry systems of equal magnification for critical work. Some objectives can be obtained on special order with a correction for infinite optical barrel length, to be used with additional optical equipment (polarizing, spectroscopic, and photometric) in the optical tract of a microscope (Richards, 1950).

1. Monochromats

Monocromats belong in a group of photometric special objectives which are used to record the selective spectral absorption of thymonucleic acid in chromosomes in the shorter ultraviolet (Caspersson, 1950). Monochromats are corrected mainly for $\lambda = 2537$ Å and have to be used with quartz eyepieces and quartz condensers.

2. Achromats

Achromats are corrected for a small waveband in the yellow-green range of the spectrum (5460 Å) which is the light of maximum visibility for human eyes. These are the cheapest low NA objectives made and if properly used are excellent for all but the most critical work in chromosome studies. They exhibit overcorrection for blue and undercorrection for red light. Images containing these colors are formed away from the plane of the yellow-green images. Consequently, achromatic objectives form images which cause color margins to appear on objects. This is more predominant in the outer part of the field of view. These secondary color spectra do not disturb *visual observation* with quality achromats, as the eye is markedly less sensitive to red or blue light. But this is entirely different in photomicrographic data recording where some emulsions are highly sensitive to red or blue radiation (see chapter by Christenson, this volume). A photograph with panchromatic material of the lines of a stage micrometer will give information about the quality of correction of achromatic objectives, which should be used only with those eyepieces recommended by their manufacturer. Planachromats have the very valuable property of presenting a flat image over the whole field of view, but they are only corrected as achromats and have to be used with compensating eyepieces.

3. Fluorites

Fluorites are more effectively corrected than achromats. Their correction extends from the blue to the yellow spectral range with almost no appearance of color margins due to the secondary spectra. Compensating eye-pieces are generally required for fluorites. The systems have medium numerical apertures.

4. Apochromats

Apochromats are high NA lens systems which are corrected for all colors of the visible spectrum from violet to red, and thus do not show secondary spectra. There is still a slight difference in the magnification of images of the different colors, which is eliminated by the use of proper compensating eyepieces. The sometimes disturbing curvature of the microscopic image is corected in the planapochromats. Ultrafluars and reflecting objectives have color correction from short ultraviolet into the infrared range of the spectrum. They are special-purpose systems (Caspersson, 1950).

B. Eyepieces

For visual observation with the microscope, the real, intermediate image from the objective is viewed through the eyepiece, as one looks at an object with a magnifying glass.[5] Most eyepieces consist of two lenses. The upper one (eye lens) performs the services of a high quality magnifying glass. The lower lens (field lens) serves the purpose of converging all rays coming from the objective into the entrance aperture of the eye lens. This improves the brightness of the microscopic image and helps image definition through reduction and relocation of the intermediate image. When the eyepiece is in place, the intermediate image is positioned in the aperture of the eyepiece diaphragm. With Huygenian eyepieces made of simple lenses, no further improvement of the microscopic image can be expected. Compensating eyepieces, however, have this property, and are constructed with cemented lens systems in the eye lens and sometimes in the field lens. Eyepieces are to be used with the objectives for which they were designed.

Measuring eyepieces are Huygenian or compensating eyepieces with an adjustable eye lens. Reticles, etc., are put on the eyepiece diaphragm, and the eye lens is adjusted so that the divisions of the reticle are clearly perceivable.

---

[5] Excessive power of the eyepiece only dims the image. Total magnification should not go below the 500- or above the 1000-fold value of the numerical aperture of the objective.

C. MICROSCOPIC CONDENSERS

The purpose of the condenser is to provide adequate illumination to the specimen by filling the aperture of the objective with light. Thus, the condenser has to be an image-forming system and consequently possesses focal length and working distance like any other optical lens. Specimen-supporting layers which exceed 1.2 mm in thickness, as in tissue culture work, require long working distance condensers. Very commonly the condenser is not treated as an optical device, but rather, along with its diaphragm, is used only according to "romantic or autocratic feelings" of the "man in charge." Condensers are designed to receive light from a light source at 12 inches (30 cm) distance. A closer lamp requires an auxiliary lens at the rear of the condenser. With the lamp at 30 cm, the condenser forms a reduced real image in the specimen plane. The size of this image is controlled by the focal length of the condenser, and if formed from a source of sufficient diameter, it will fill the aperture of the objective fully with light. This results in an evenly illuminated field of view. The industry has equipped modern condensers with a removable front lens which allows the use of the same condenser with objectives from low to high power. The front lens should be out of the optical path for NA's lower than 0.3. Removing the front lens increases the focal length of the condensing system and increases the image size of the lamp to fill the larger aperture of low power, low NA objectives.

The purpose of the focusing adjustment of the condenser mount is solely to obtain a sharp image of the light source in the specimen, regardless of its size. It pays to keep in mind that the NA of the objective, thus its resolving power, is only fully effective if the NA of the illumination is equal to it, but never greater nor much smaller. Matching of the NA of a high NA condenser used with a lesser NA objective is the specific purpose of the condenser iris diaphragm. The calibration, once customary on this diaphragm, is in terms of the condenser NA. Reducing the opening of the diaphragm reduces the convergence of the illuminating beam and reduces the aperture of the condenser. Since the aperture of the diaphragm is imaged in the rear lens of the objective, where it can be seen after the eyepiece has been pulled,[6] it should be evident that this condenser diaphragm *dictates* the working NA and thus the resolving power of the entire microscope. The diaphragm should be closed only so much,

---

[6] This is seen only when microscope and condenser are properly focused on the same object plane.

so that the leaves are just visible in the rear lens. Occlusion of more than
¼ of the aperture of the objective will give bold contrast and the *delusion*
of a greater depth of focus accompanied by a serious, measurable loss
in resolution. Too large an opening will cause the specimen to be flooded
with light, introducing glare, reflections, etc., with subsequent loss of
definition in the image. If under ordinary circumstances[7] an objective
should require more "stopping down" than ⅓ of its aperture before the
maximum resolution of a good image is obtained, the objective is of no
value or the operator used the wrong eyepiece with it or his light source
is of too high an intensity.

The condenser diaphragm should not be handled carelessly, as it may
lead to erroneous conclusions about the structure of an object.

Like the objectives, condensers have a depth of focus which also varies
reciprocally to the NA in the following magnitude:

Condenser NA	0.25	0.3	0.4	0.5	0.65	0.8	0.95
Depth of focus (μ)	>10	5	3	2	1	0.5	0.3

The expected thickness of the object (determined from the average range
of measurements) would suggest a value of condenser NA. The wanted
resolution determines the NA of the objective.

Chromosome microscopy, in contrast to that with sectioned tissue specimens, in general requires relatively low working NA's of the condenser;
therefore, the nominal NA of the objective should not exceed the effective
NA of the condenser by more than 10%. The perfection to which the
necessary compromise can be worked out is a direct measure of the individual's experience in handling microscope and chromosome preparations.
Condensers for high resolution work also need correction for spherical
and chromatic aberration. These are available as aplanats, corrected about
the same as achromatic objectives and to be used with them, and fully
corrected achromatic-aplanatic condensers for more critical work. Condenser apertures of greater than NA 0.95 require an immersion medium
between slide and top lens; total reflection otherwise prevents the intended
purpose.

Condensers should be centered on the optical axis of the objective.
Checking of this is one of the justifiable times when the condenser dia-

---

[7] The allocation of tracks in autoradiographs is a special condition where little
resolution but bold contrast is needed. Thus the condenser diaphragm has to be
"stopped down" appropriately.

phragm should be almost fully closed. The intensity of the microscopic image should be controlled with neutral density filters in front of the condenser or at the lamp.

D. Light Sources and Illumination

The substage condenser can receive the light as daylight from a cloud-covered sky or as artificial light from a microscope lamp. The actual light source should never be a point source, as apertures and focal length and *areas* of lamp, condenser, and field-of-view are in a specific relationship to each other. There are a number of "illuminators" on the market, which are made only to sell. A decent lamp for serious microscopic work should have built into the housing a lamp-condensing + collector lens system followed by a Koehler iris diaphragm as well as integral heat filters and filter holders. Such a lamp could be used with Koehler's illumination, which satisfies every microscopic requirement for bright field, phase contrast, and general fluorescence microscopy. Koehler illumination can be obtained as follows. Put a specimen on the stage and focus on it with any available light using a 10:1, 0.4 NA objective. Position the lamp at 12 inches ($\sim$ 300 mm) from the condenser diaphragm and close it. Close the lamp's Koehler diaphragm to $7/8$, and after adjusting the mirror, try to form a sharp image of the actual light emitter (i.e., filament of the lamp) on the condenser diaphragm leaves by adjusting the lamp collector lens. Then open the condenser diaphragm about $2/3$. Now look in the microscope and, using the condenser focusing adjustment, try to get the image of the $7/8$-closed Koehler diaphragm sharply focused *into the specimen in microscopic focus.* (With a simple achromatic condenser color margins will appear around this image. The image is regarded as sharp if the edge of the image appears green.) Now open the Koehler diaphragm until the leaves just disappear from the field of view. Check adjustment of the condenser diaphragm for *maximum resolution,* not for bold contrast. On changing the objective, the openings of the Koehler diaphragm and the condenser diaphragm should be readjusted. Some present-day microscopes feature built-in lamps, which make it possible to achieve Koehler illumination very conveniently, thus saving valuable time.

In purchasing microscopic equipment it is worth remembering that manufacturers produce to sell and advertise to sell. The widely distributed sales information sheets are not the proper source of basic education in microscopy, as they will hardly provide the necessary information, i.e., whether the instrument will do for a certain purpose. The instruction manuals should be consulted for detailed information and they should be consulted for proper operation of the equipment and its maintenance.

The foregoing theories and facts give a basic picture of the light microscope, as operated with transmitted light, i.e., bright field microscopy. This method of operation is the standard one, and phase and fluorescence microscopy are only special modifications of the same basic principle, as we will see in the next sections.

IV. PHASE CONTRAST MICROSCOPY

A. PRINCIPLE AND IMAGE FORMATION

Phase contrast microscopy deals mainly with unstained objects (i.e., living chromosomes) which are barely visible with the bright field microscope. That we can see colorless objects at all with transmitted light depends on the formation of the microscopic image as a diffraction pattern by interference of wave trains. The wave motions originate from the same point in the object but are traveling in different zones of the angular cone of the objective. The contrast in the image depends mainly on the distribution of intensities between the axial undiffracted 0-order and the obliquely traveling interference maxima. The interference maxima are usually faintest, but they carry the valuable information. The oblique and axial wave trains can be in or out of phase. The phase relation between oblique and axial wave trains with ordinary objectives is determined by the residual aberrations of the combination of the mounted specimen with the lens system and by the chosen microscope focus. Thus, a chromosome may appear bright or dark depending on the focus. The phase contrast effect of Zernike (1935) is produced by modification of the phase and amplitude (intensity) relation between axial and oblique wave trains from each diffracting object point. This serves to improve the visibility of uncolored (low contrast) objects without loss of resolution. The variation in brightness from light to dark, as obtained with phase contrast, occurs on boundaries between regions of different refractive indices in the object, and the boundary halos represent essential physical boundaries in the object. Thus chromosomes and spindle apparatus are visualized by phase contrast as differential refractivities in the cell. The width of the marginal halo around chromosomes in squash preparations is proportional to the degree of mismatch in refractive indices between chromosome and medium.

B. PHASE OPTICS

Annular illumination is employed; thus, an annular diaphragm (phase annulus) is mounted within the condenser. This ring illumination prevents loss of resolution by intentionally suppressing the intensity in the axially traveling wave trains. A converging, hollow cone of light results, from which, after passage through the specimen, the undeviated rays enter the objective in a diverging hollow cone. All rays diffracted by the structures of the object travel separately inside or outside of this cone. In the rear aperture of the objective, the cross section of the cone forms a conjugate annulus. In this position the phase relation of the diffracted rays to the undeviated rays can be easily altered by a phase plate, as the nondeviated rays are strictly confined to the conjugate annulus. If the undeviated rays are selectively retarded by $\lambda/4$ with a thin dielectic film deposited on the annulus, "bright" (negative) phase contrast is obtained; if the diffracted rays are retarded, "dark" (positive) phase contrast results. "Dark" (positive) phase contrast shows the thicker or more refracting structures of the object darker on a bright background; "bright" phase contrast has the reverse effect. To improve the contrast, some phase plates have an additional partially transmitting deposit of metal over the conjugate annulus. The centering of the condenser annulus with respect to its conjugate annulus in the objective must be very accurate. In good constructions it is adjusted by centering of the diaphragm holder instead of moving the whole condenser. In place of the eyepiece a centering telescope is used to view the alignment. A number of phase contrast systems are available, but their discussion is beyond the scope of this chapter.

C. APPLICATIONS

The structural resolution achieved with phase equipment is slightly under that obtained with comparable bright field optics. Naturally, tissue culture work requires phase contrast optics corrected for long working distances.

Koehler-type illumination is the best for phase contrast work and is easily obtained in the usual way. The use of monochromatic light increases the contrast provided by the specimen. Strictly monochromatizing filters such as first-order interference filters with band passes around the maximum sensitivity of the human eye at 5660 Å should be used. As the human eye is more able to distinguish between degrees of dimness, low brightness of the field of view is favorable for usual work. Phase contrast microscopy has proven to be one of the most powerful tools in chromosome studies, and in routine work it is one of the methods of choice for its simplicity in handling of the material. It enables the direct visualization of mitotic divisions within the living cell and their photocinematographic recording as well as speedy chromosome counting and morphological evaluation. One should remember for cell physiology work, that the image one sees with phase contrast is caused only by varying degrees of differences in optical refractivities in the cell or its substructures. Amplitude objects (i.e., the DNA difference of contracted short arms in human chromosomes 17 and 18) consisting of varying degrees of optical density only, are classic bright field objects and not very well suited for phase objects.

V. FLUORESCENCE MICROSCOPIC TECHNIQUE

In chromosome studies, fluorescence microscopy has not been used as extensively as in other fields of biological research (Haitinger et al., 1959; Price and Schwartz, 1956) but it has been used to demonstrate the points of attack of mitotic poisons (Lettre, 1950) in vivo and tie-in points of certain chemicals into the chromosome structure, etc. (Werth, 1953; Kosenow, 1956; Stich, 1952; Dempsey and Basset, 1943; Strugger et al., 1953; Krooth et al., 1961). The fluorescein-labeled antibody technique (Price and Schwartz, 1956) and its applications promise usefulness in genetics. The extreme sensitivity of fluorescence microscopic methods and their promising aspects justify its discussion in a text on chromosome methodology at the present time.

Fluorescence microscopy deals with microscopic objects which, when irradiated with a light of one wavelength, reradiate light of a longer wavelength. The excitation is not confined to the ultraviolet range of the spectrum. The intensity yield of fluorescence for a given amount of fluorescing material is highest around the center of its maximum spectral absorption. In biological material primary fluorescence can be present or it can be introduced as secondary fluorescence by imbibition with fluorescing dyes (fluorochroming of chromosomes) or incorporation of biogenic compounds labeled with fluorescing material or supravital staining. The color phenomena are mostly mixed tints rather than strong pure colors. The concentration of the fluorescing substance, its physicochemical state, the nature of the material on or within it, the thickness of the specimen, the temperature, the mounting medium, and the energy of the exciting radiation are known factors which influence the fluorescence intensity, its color, and its duration. With these qualifications, fluorescence microscopy is a very valuable tool in the differentiation of tissue structures, and sometimes in demonstrating physiological or pathological changes in parts of the preserved or living cell.

The equipment to be used in a "darkroom" depends on the specific fluorescing compound to be used or studied, and is determined by the required wavelength of excitation (Kosenow, 1956; "Lamp Bulletin LD-1," 1950; "Super Pressure Mercury Lamps," 1959; "High Pressure Xenon Lamps," 1962; "Farb-und Filterglass," 1959; "Glass Color Filters," 1948). Excitation light should be of a wavelength as close as possible to the maximum of spectral absorption of the fluorescing compound. From the position of the absorption band, an "exciting light-isolating filter" is selected with the help of spectral transmission curves of filter glasses. The wave length of the band of fluorescence should be determined and another filter glass selected which has as little transmission as possible at the wavelength of excitation, but will transmit freely all light of the fluorescence. This latter filter is used over the eyepiece to block out the exciting light. This is absolutely necessary, as strong visible exciting light will mask the low intensity of fluorescence and, in case of excitation with invisible ultraviolet, prevent fluorescence within the eye and irritation of the eye by too much ultraviolet radiation. The exciting filter is used in front of the condenser of the microscope, and the blocking filter can be introduced at any convenient location above the specimen. The objective should not show autofluorescence. In biological work the shortest wavelength generally used is 3600 Å, which is very well transmitted by microscope condensers of glass. High NA types should be used, and water, glycerin, or paraffin oil can be used as immersion liquids. These are non-fluorescing and also useful as mounting media for the specimen on non-fluorescing glass slides with ordinary cover slips.

For some conditions it is advantageous to use the reflecting (cardidoid) condensers for dark field illumination in fluorescence work. The high obliquity of radiation leaving the condenser in a hollow cone prevents most of the exciting light from entering the objective; thus, very thin secondary filters can be used. The light source should be imaged by a relay lens directly onto the small central mirror. Thus, a very bright illumination with exciting light is obtained which is superior in intensity to the bright field illumination as ordinarily used.

The light source should be very rich in light of the exciting wavelength. The source should be strong, since much light is lost during passage through the exciter filters, and the fluorescence is proportional to the amount of excitation energy available. High pressure mercury, xenon, or carbon arc lamps are used. The problem in fluorescence microscopy is primarily to select a lamp which has maximum light emission exactly at the center of the absorption of the fluorescing material and to find a filter combination which on one side passes all the light of the excitation waveband, being opaque to all other light, and on the other side passes only all light of the fluorescence emission.

Generally "best case" compromises can be worked out, even if one has to employ such tricks as using the spectral visibility curve of the human eye for compensation of defects.

The foregoing section has been written to give a concise basic outline of the fluorescence microscopic technique, and the references given show the broad possibilities of this method which, properly adapted to chromosome research, could produce significant results.

In conclusion it becomes evident that the application of old methods to new objects or their adaptation to suit a particular need requires familiarity with the background of the methods. As Schopenhauer stated, the primary is to know the rule by understanding, before reasoning. This can be acquired by study, but a good deal of one's own thinking and enthusiasm have to go into it.

References

Microscopy

Abbe, E. (1904). "Gesammelte Abhandlungen." Fischer, Jena.
Caspersson, T. (1950). "Cell Growth and Cell Function." Norton, New York.
Köhler, A. (1928). "Handbuch der biologischen Arbeitsmethoden" (E. Abderhalden, ed.), Section II, Part 2, No. 6, pp. 1691-1978. Urban & Schwarzenberg, Berlin.
Langeron, M. (1925). "Précis de Microscopie." Masson, Paris.
Martin, L. C. (1955). *In* "Physical Techniques in Biological Research" (G. Oster and A. W. Pollister, eds.), Vol. I, pp. 326-375. Academic Press, New York.
Richards, B. W. (1950). When to use special microscopes. *In* "Biophysical Research Methods" (Uber, ed.), pp. 343-380. Wiley (Interscience), New York.
Romeis, B. (1943). "Taschenbuch der mikroskopischen Technik," 14th ed. Oldenbourg, Berlin.
Spitta, E. J. (1920). "Microscopy." Dutton, New York.

Phase Microscopy

Köhler, A., and Loos, W. (1941). Das Phasenkontrastverfahren und seine Anwendung in der Mikroskopie. *Naturwissenschaften* **29**, 48-61.
Zernike, F. (1935). *Z. Techn. Physik* **16**, 454 (a Reference in Köhler a. Loos [1941]).

Fluorescence Microscopy

Dempsey, E. W., and Basset, D. L. (1943). Observation on the fluorescence, birenfringence and histochemistry of the rat ovary during the productive cycle. *Endocrinology* **33**, 384-401.

"Farb-und Filterglass" #365/1959 (1959). Jenaer Glaswerk Schott and Gen. Mainz, Germany.

"Glass Color Filters" (1948). Corning Glass Works, Corning, New York.

Haitinger, M., Eisenbrand, J., and Werth, G. (1959). "Fluoreszenzmikroscopie." Akad. Verlagsgesellschaft, Leipzig.

"High Pressure Xenon Lamps" GmBH, #W957/3/D1K1/762 (1962). OSRAM, München, Germany.

Kosenow, W. (1956). Geschlechtsdiagnose mit Hilfe von Kernmerkmalen der Leukocyten. *Triangle Sandoz J. Med. Sci.* **2**, 321.

Krooth, R. S., Tobie, J. E., Tjio, J. H., and Goodman, H. C. (1961). Reaction of human sera with mammalian chromosomes shown by fluorescent antibody technique. *Science* **134**, 284-286.

"Lamp Bulletin LD-1" (1950). General Electric Lamp Department, Cleveland, Ohio.

Lettre, H. (1950). Über Mitosegifte. *Ergeb. Physiol. Biol. Chem. Exptl. Pharmakol.* **46**, 379.

Price, G., and Schwartz, S. (1956). *In* "Physical Techniques in Biological Reserch" (G. Osler and A. W. Pollister, eds.), Vol. III, p. 91. Academic Press, New York.

Stich, H. (1952). Trypaflavin und Ribonucleinsäure. *Naturwissenschaften* **38**, 435.

Strugger, S. P., Krebs, A. T., and Gierlach, Z. S. (1953). Investigations into the first effects of roentgen-rays in living protoplasm as studied with modern fluorochromes. *Am. J. Roentgenol. Radium Therapy Nucl. Med.* **70**, 365-375.

"Super Pressure Mercury Lamps" #W064/4/FKK1/659 (1959). OSRAM. GmbH, München, Germany.

Werth, G. (1953). Zur fluoreszenzmikroskopischen Darstellung von Desoxyribonucleinsäure u. d. Kernucleotide der Ascitestumorzellen der Maus. *Acta Histochem.* **10**, 209.

Suggested Reading

Barer, R. (1956). *In* "Physical Techniques in Biological Research" (G. Oster and A. W. Pollister, eds.), Vol. III, pp. 29-90. Academic Press, New York.

"Bausch & Lomb Interference Filters." (1960). Bausch & Lomb Optical Co., Rochester, New York.

Bennett, A. H., Jupnik, H., Osterberg, H., and Richards, O. W. (1951). "Phase Microscopy." Wiley, New York.

Conrady, A. E. (1957). "Applied Optics and Optical Design." Dover, New York.

Osterberg, H. (1952). "Colloque sur le contraste de phase et le contraste par interférences," pp. 227-234. Editions de la Revue d'Optique, Paris.

Wredden, J. H. (1948). "The Microscope." Grune & Stratton, New York.

Applied Photography in
Chromosome Studies

LEROY P. CHRISTENSON

*School of Dentistry, Dental Illustration Laboratory, University of Minnesota,
Minneapolis, Minnesota*

I. Introduction 129
   A. Limitations of Camera-Microscope 129
   B. Quality of Specimens for Photomicrography 130
II. Photomicrography 131
   A. Aligning the Camera-Microscope 131
   B. Determining Image Magnification 132
   C. Control of Glare 139
   D. Determining the Photographic Exposure 139
   E. Use of Filters 140
III. Photosensitive Materials and Processing 142
   A. Light-Sensitive Materials 142
   B. Darkroom Procedures 148
   Appendix 152
   References 152

I. INTRODUCTION

A. LIMITATIONS OF CAMERA-MICROSCOPE

Photographic records of microscopically observed chromosome patterns are a necessary part of laboratory procedures in human cytogenetic studies. For investigators engaged in these studies, a carefully prepared photomicrograph has significant value as a communication medium in the illustration of published reports, in the exchange of information between investigators, and as a visual aid in teaching. Such photomicrographs are the result of good microscopic technique and proper selection and processing of photographic materials. Careful attention to these details will give accurate and reliable photographic records of chromosome patterns and will reduce to a minimum the artifactual information of chromosomes appearing in an image as aberrations of density, size, or shape.

129

The technical limitations of image formation in a camera-microscope occasionally make it impossible to record all information of the three-dimensional chromosome on the two-dimensional plane of a photographic film. During visual examination of a specimen, manipulation of the fine focus adjustment permits the microscopist to concentrate upon specific points in the image and to interpret details which are enhanced through additional optical corrections introduced by the eye. Some of these details are those structures that travel down and away from the central plane of focus causing a "fading-off" of one or more arms of a chromosome, or structures that travel toward the objective lens, giving an appearance of thickness or darkness to the chromosome. When these anomalies of the chromosome image are observed, they should be described in detail to add value to the photomicrograph. Many of these important details are lost in the photographic recording because the photographic film is an untrained observer, recording with impartiality all defects and aberrations present in the projected image. An incorrect choice of film emulsion and processing technique can result in additional deletion of information from the recorded image of the chromosome pattern.

B. QUALITY OF SPECIMENS FOR PHOTOMICROGRAPHY

Because the ultimate goal in photomicrography of human chromosomes is to obtain a maximum of resolution, meticulous technique must be used in the preparation of the material to be photographed. Obviously, microscope slides and cover slips that have not been thoroughly cleaned or that are defective because of air bubbles, strain markings, or scratches should not be used, since these defects cause aberrations in the optical pathway for the image formation by the microscope optics.

Chromosomes to be photographed should be in a single plane of focus and individual chromosomes should be spread apart, since overlapping causes structural distortions. Occasionally, the preparation may require a gentle resquashing before the desired separation and spreading of chromosomes is achieved.

During visual screening, the quality of the staining reaction should be observed. Since stains used in chromosome studies are generally pale in color, any variations of technique in preparation or fixation of the specimen can result in a shift of the spectral absorption band of the stain reaction. Therefore, appropriate filters must be selected and inserted into the light path for better image contrast while maintaining maximum resolution of the image. When unusual corrections of the filter combinations are required to ensure proper image contrast, it is sometimes necessary to change to a photographic film with an emulsion more sensitive to the specific wavelength transmitted by the combination.

Specimens that are over-stained are difficult to photograph. A haze produced in the cellular debris surrounding the chromosome pattern causes a loss of contrast in the projected image which adversely affects the quality of the photomicrographic image.

II. PHOTOMICROGRAPHY

Whenever photomicrography is discussed, it is necessary to emphasize the importance of the microscope. The optical quality of a projected image is controlled by the microscope, whereas the camera functions only as a means of recording this image. The principles of microscopy are discussed in the chapter by Runge (this volume). Having achieved a thorough understanding of the microscope, we are ready to align the camera-microscope and to apply the principles of microscopy and photography to record the projected image.

A. ALIGNING THE CAMERA-MICROSCOPE

Good technique requires proper alignment of the lamp, the microscope, and the camera on the optical axis of the microscope. This can be done as follows (see Shillaber, 1944; Kodak Data Book, 1957):

a. Position the lamp about 15 inches from the microscope stage. Center the lamp filament in the center of the light-collecting lens of the lamp housing.

b. Partially close the diaphragm of the lamp collecting lens and focus an image of the lamp filament on the microscope mirror. Since the image should form a concentric circle with the mirror, carefully adjust the light source until the image and mirror coincide.

c. Close the substage diaphragm and adjust the focus of the lamp filament to center on the substage diaphragm. The image of the filament should fill the diameter of the substage diaphragm. If it does not, reposition the lamp and adjust the distance of the lamp housing.

d. Select a medium power objective and proper condenser elements.

e. Place a stained chromosome preparation on the microscope stage.

f. Open the substage diaphragm and focus on the specimen. Carefully adjust the substage mirror to direct the light to the specimen and into the objective.

g. Close the field diaphragm on the lamp condenser to its smallest opening and again carefully adjust the mirror to keep the light beam centered.

h. With the microscope in sharp focus, the substage diaphragm wide open, and the lamp condenser field diaphragm closed, rack the substage condenser up and down until a focused image of the edges of the field iris opening is in the plane of the specimen.

At this point, the requirements for Koehler Illumination have been established.

i. To center the condenser with the objective, open the lamp iris, close the condenser iris to give a 9/10ths cone of light, and replace the ocular with a pinhole eyepiece or cap. Now observe the rear focal plane of the objective where the image of the condenser iris will be seen. Adjust the condenser centering screws and make the image of the condenser aperture concentric with the rear aperture of the objective. This is necessary for each change of objectives.

j. Check step g and make any readjustment necessary to center the field diaphragm. At this point, the ocular should be in position.

k. To control glare in the image, the condenser diaphragm should be three quarters open. Then the lamp field diaphragm should be opened sufficiently to illuminate the area to be photographed—no more and no less.

l. Open the condenser diaphragm to its widest. While carefully observing the image of the specimen, gradually close the condenser diaphragm until there is a sudden increase in contrast restricted to the smallest object detail. The coarser details of the image may show a slight enhancement of the colors of the stain, a slight increase of depth of field, and a slight improvement of the flatness of field. This has provided the second step for the control of glare in the image. At this position, the diaphragm will be about $\frac{3}{4}$ to $\frac{2}{3}$ closed.

m. If the above steps have been carried out by use of the visual eyepiece, the focusing screen at the film plane of the camera should be checked to determine if the center of the image field is in the center of the film plane. If this condition does not exist, a comprehensive textbook on photomicrography should be consulted for more detailed instructions.

B. DETERMINING IMAGE MAGNIFICATION

After the alignment steps have been carried out, a suitable ocular is chosen, one designed with optical properties to match the requirements of the objective being used. To obtain the total magnification of objective $\times$ ocular, the distance of the camera film pane from the ocular eyepoint must be equal to the standard viewing distance, 250 mm. If the distance from ocular eyepoint to film plane is twice the standard viewing distance, the total magnification of objective $\times$ ocular will be doubled. Therefore it can be stated:

$$\text{magnification} = \text{objective} \times \text{ocular}$$

and:

magnification at film plane

$$= \text{objective} \cdot \text{ocular} \cdot \frac{\text{projection distance to film (mm)}}{250 \text{ mm (standard viewing distance)}}$$

For example:

$$\text{magnification} = 100 \cdot 10 \cdot \frac{350}{250}$$
$$= 1000 \cdot 1.4$$
$$= 1400$$

By measuring the distance between two lines in the projected image from a stage micrometer slide, it is possible to calibrate the magnification. Thus:

$$\text{magnification} = \frac{\text{measured distance in image field}}{\text{value of equal distance in object field}}$$

i.e., if two points in the object field are 0.1 mm apart, and their distance apart is 50 mm at the ground glass, then:

$$\frac{50 \text{ mm}}{0.1 \text{ mm}} = 500 \text{ magnification}$$

(See Shillaber, 1944; Kodak Data Book, 1957.)

When total magnification at the film plane has been determined, any prints of these images produced by contact printing of the negative will provide a 1:1 relation to the magnification. Consideration, therefore, must be given to the type of camera used for photomicrography, since the camera determines the film size which, in turn, limits the maximum size of the image (see Figs. 1 and 2).

Basically, there are two types of camera: a 35 mm camera using a roll film with a negative format of 24 $\times$ 36 mm, and the larger bellows camera using film sizes $3\frac{1}{4} \times 4\frac{1}{4}$ inches, 4 $\times$ 5 inches, or larger. The

35 mm camera imposes a limitation, even though it is more compact and allows up to 36 photographs to be taken on one roll of film. The limitation, most disregarded in the 35 mm camera, is the size of the recorded image on the 24 × 36 mm negative as compared with the 3¼ × 4¼ or 4 × 5 inch negative. In some 35 mm camera attachments

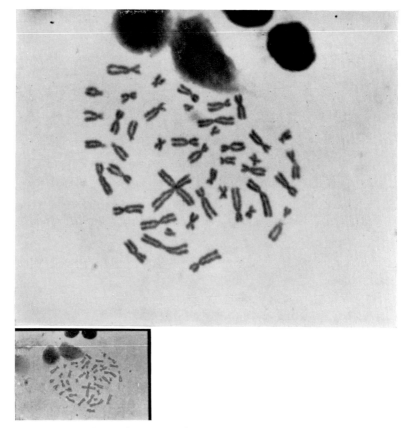

Fig. 1. Comparison of image size between 4 × 5 inch and 35 mm camera with high dry objective (contact prints).

A Feulgen-stained, air-dried metaphase plate was photographed with a 45 × apochromatic objective, 8 × photo-ocular and 1.5 × camera bellows extension factor on a Reichert MEF photomicroscope. The Reichert 35 mm camera attachment had a correction factor of 0.5 ×. Filters used for contrast were Wratten 58 + Wratten 22 (approximate band pass 560–600 mμ). A Kodak Wratten M plate developed in DK50 was used for the 4 × 5 inch camera. Afga IFF film developed in Edwal FG7 was used for the 35 mm camera.

for photomicrography, the eyepoint to film distance is limited by the physical construction of the unit. Some of these units have incorporated into their design a supplementary lens with a designation of $\frac{1}{3}$, 0.5 $\times$, or other identification number. Simply, this means that the film plane will be $\frac{1}{3}$ or 0.5 $\times$ the combined magnification of objective $\times$ ocular. If a

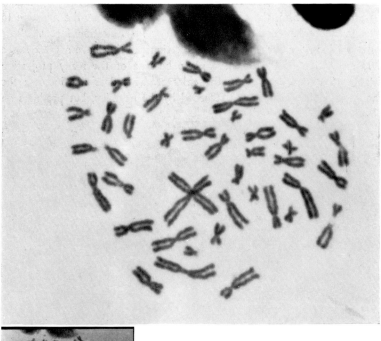

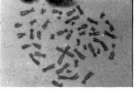

FIG. 2. Comparison of image size between 4 $\times$ 5 inch and 35 mm camera with oil immersion objective (contact prints).

The same metaphase plate as used in Fig. 1 was photographed with a 90 $\times$ apochromatic oil immersion objective, a 7.5 $\times$ ocular, and 1.5 $\times$ camera extension factor (0.5 $\times$ for the 35 mm camera).

A filter combination of Wratten No. 74 and Bausch and Lomb 546 interference filter used for 564 mμ wavelength. Film emulsions and developers were the same as for Fig. 1. Note the graying background of the 35 mm print indicating underexposure to this wavelength of light.

100 × oil immersion objective and a 10 × ocular are used for visual examination of the specimen, the supplementary lens in the 35 mm camera attachment reduces this magnification to 333 × or 500 × (⅓ · 1000 or 0.5 · 1000). However, on the larger bellows camera using larger size sheet film, the image can be photographed at the original 1000 × when the bellows is at 250 mm from the eye point.

With 35 mm film, therefore, it is necessary to subject the negative to photographic enlargement to regain the lost magnification factor. Those prints produced by enlargement or projection printing have a great range in magnification of the negative plane because of the many projection distances that can be used in the enlarger. This does not increase the magnification in the image as recorded by the negative, but produces an

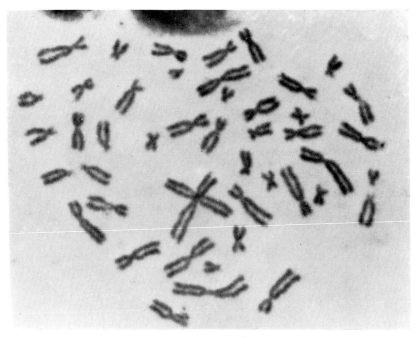

FIG. 3. Enlarged print (approximately 3 ×) from the 35 mm negative used for contact print in Fig. 2.

The negative was treated for 15 seconds in Victor Intensifier to give increased printing density. Enlargement was made on multigrade paper with No. 3 printing filter (Kodak Polycontrast). Compare image quality of this figure with 4 × 5 inch contact print in Fig. 2.

enlargement only of the object magnification that was established in the negative (see Fig. 3).

For clarity, it is suggested that prints of photomicrographs be identified with the number of diameters of primary magnification. The current practice is to use the symbol $\times$ either before or after the numerical value, i.e., $\times$ 1000 or 1000 $\times$. If image size has been altered by projection printing, the amount of the enlargement should be a separate notation.

Large size images of chromosomes are convenient in the construction of karyograms and are produced by projection printing. In order to produce a given image size in photographic prints, negatives made in a bellows camera require fewer diameters of enlargement than the negatives from a 35 mm camera. An additional advantage of larger size negatives is the possibility of making simple contact prints for publication.

Depth of Focus. In a photomicrographic print, the depth of focus is determined by the standard viewing distance, the NA of the objective, and the image size in the print. This differs from the depth of focus observed during visual microscopic examination where the natural accommodation of the eye causes it to see greater depth than can be recorded on a photographic plate.

The image projected by a lens system to the photographic image plane is in the form of cone shaped bundles of light. The size of the cross section area of these cones (circle of confusion) at the plane of intersect with the film plane determines the sharpness of the image point. If the cross section area is too large, the image point has a fuzzy or unsharp appearance. It is, therefore, out of focus or not within the depth of focus of the lens. Furthermore, when viewing any photographic print, the angular resolution of the eye must be taken into consideration.

Therefore, when viewing a photomicrographic print at the standard viewing distance of 250 mm, if the size of an image point corresponding to 1° of angular arc appears to become fuzzy, we can evaluate the depth of focus (Michel, 1940) by the expression:

$$\text{depth of focus (DF)} = \frac{1}{14} \cdot \frac{1}{NA \cdot SI} \cdot (1 + \frac{1}{SI}), \text{ mm}$$

where NA is numerical aperture of the objective and SI (scale of image) is image size in the final photographic print; i.e., if NA = 1.2 and SI = 2 mm, then the above expression becomes:

A

B

138

$$DF = \frac{1}{14} \cdot \frac{1}{1.2 \cdot 2} \left(1 + \frac{1}{2}\right), \text{mm}$$

$$= \frac{1}{22.4}$$

$$= 0.044 \text{ mm}$$

or if the NA = 0.8 and SI = 2 mm,

$$DF = \frac{1}{14} \cdot \frac{1}{0.8 \cdot 2} \left(1 + \frac{1}{2}\right), \text{mm}$$

$$= \frac{3}{448}$$

$$= 0.067 \text{ mm}$$

From the above it can be observed that if the NA is constant and the SI in the photographic print is increased by enlargement, the value of the denominator increases and the resultant value for depth of focus decreases.

C. Control of Glare

Glare in the microscopic image may arise from several sources; i.e., a maladjustment of microscope tube length, a light source that is too large, an improperly prepared specimen or poor microscopic slide, a condenser not matched to the objective, or an improper adjustment of the condenser and/or the condenser diaphragm. The image of the specimen is brought into sharp focus at the film plane. If glare is present, steps k and l of the section on aligning the camera-microscope should be rechecked.

In some cases a neutral density filter must be used in the light beam to reduce the intensity, but do not use excessive closure of the condenser diaphragm for control of light intensity (see Fig. 4).

D. Determining the Photographic Exposure

The exposure time for a particular photographic emulsion can be determined by a trial and error method or by use of a photoelectric measur-

---

FIG. 4. Degraded image caused by excessive closure of substage diaphragm. Filter combination was Wratten 58 and Wratten 22 and photograph was made with a Wratten M plate. A: 45 × apochromatic objective, 8 × photo-ocular, and 1.5 × extension factor (enlarged 1.4 × by projection printing). B: 90 × apochromatic oil immersion objective, 8 × photo-ocular, and 1.5 × extension factor (enlarged 1.4 ×).

ing device. If a photoelectric device is used, consult the operating instructions to determine the image intensity and the appropriate calculations necessary for adequate exposure. If the exposure determination is made by trial and error, several photos are taken and the final results determine the best time interval. This will establish a standard exposure, at a standard NA, and a standard magnification. Any changes made to account for a new set of conditions will use the following (see Kodak Data Book, 1957):

$$\frac{\text{new exposure}}{\text{standard exposure}} = \left(\frac{\text{standard NA}}{\text{new NA}}\right)^2 \times \left(\frac{\text{new magnification}}{\text{standard magnification}}\right)^2$$

If it is necessary or desirable to change films, the following formula can be used:

$$\text{exposure time} = \text{exposure with standard film} \times \left(\frac{\text{standard speed}}{\text{new speed}}\right)$$

When colored filters are used to give monochromatic light for better resolution or to give more contrast to the image, a filter factor must be established. This factor is supplied by the manufacturer and specified according to the spectral sensitivity of the film emulsion:

$$\text{standard exposure} \times \text{filter factor} = \text{new exposure time}$$

E. Use of Filters

In photomicrography, filters are optical devices which modify the quality of the light beam used for illumination. The filter types can be of optically polished solid glass, dyed gelatin cemented between optically flat glass plates (Wratten type filters), or evaporated metallic film on glass plates (interference band filters). The latter provides a narrow band width transmission which allows a nearly monochromatic light to pass through the microscope optics. This is valuable in high resolution work. The solid glass and dyed gelatin filters provide a wider transmission. Tables giving transmission characteristics of solid glass filters can be found in the "Handbook of Chemistry and Physics" (1957-1958, Chemical Rubber Publishing Co., Cleveland, Ohio), "Jenaer Glaswerk Schott und Gen., Mainz" (1959, Mainz, Germany), or "Corning Glass Company Color Filters" (1962, Corning, N. Y.). Tables of transmission characteristics for Wratten filters are published by Eastman Kodak Co. under the title, "Wratten Light Filters."

1. Wratten Light Filters

The primary purposes of these filters are to provide approximately monochromatic light, to control the color band of the illumination source in order to obtain better performance from the microscope optics, and to regulate contrast in specimens, particularly stained specimens.

The staining of tissue preparations for chromosome studies adds dye particles to the chromosomes, increasing the contrast for better visual examination and creating a light filtering effect. Since the stain or staining reaction imparts a color to the chromosome, this "dye screen" will have specific spectral band absorption characteristics and the transmitted light may not be compatible with the spectral sensitivity curve of the photographic film. That is, the color image of the specimen (chromosome) could occur in the spectral region of highest sensitivity for the film; so, a suitable contrast for visual examination would not have enough contrast for photographic examination. By filtering the light beam, with filters which have a band pass isolated to the region of the peak absorption band of the specimen, greater contrast is added to the photographic image. As a rule, use a filter or filter combination with a visual color in contrast to the color of the specimen; i.e., yellow-orange against blue or green against red.

Stained preparation	Filter color
Violet	Yellow
Purple	Green
Blue	Red
Green	Red
Yellow	Blue
Red	Green
Brownish	Blue

Wratten M filters for microscopy can be used singly or in pairs. The book, *Wratten Light Filters* (Eastman Kodak Co., Rochester, N. Y.), gives the spectral transmission curves for these filters.

Giemsa stain and Wright stain produce light blue to blue in the chromosomes; the red filter of a Wratten No. 25 (orange-red color) or a Wratten No. 29 (pure red) should be used. Feulgen stain produces reddish-purple chromosomes which requires a Wratten No. 58 (green) and a Wratten No. 22 (orange) for a dominant wavelength of 575 mμ. Fuchsin stains chromosomes violet and requires a Wratten No. 15 (strong yellow). Chromosomes stained with orcein are reddish in color and require a

Wratten No. 58 (green) or a Wratten No. 15 (strong yellow) plus a
Wratten No. 45 (blue) which gives a dominant wavelength of approximately 525 mμ. Such variations in wavelengths indicate that Neofluar or
apochromatic objectives are needed to give proper resolution of detail.

III. PHOTOSENSITIVE MATERIALS AND PROCESSING

The chromosome preparation is photographed with a photosensitive film
and the resulting negative is printed on photosensitive paper to obtain the
positive print. The final choice of film to be used will depend upon the
quality of the chromosome preparation as imaged in the microscope. This
writer has used almost exclusively the Kodak Wratten "M" plate and
the bellows camera for all photomicrography, with development in Kodak
DK-50 or D-42 developer according to directions packaged with the film.
This gives a standardization procedure for developing and printing the
negatives. If the specimen demands, changes can be made to Panatomic-X,
Tri-X Pan, or Royal Pan films.

The black and white 35 mm films that are used are in the low and
medium speed range, having extra-fine and fine grain emulsions. Development is carried out in the recommended fine grain developers or by using
one of the several special liquid concentrate fine grain developers. If
negatives from the low speed films are too low in contrast, they can be
given a short redevelopment in an intensifier solution (Kodak or Victor)
which permits projection printing on Polycontrast No. 3 paper. All large
negatives from the bellows camera are contact printed on No. 1, 2, or 3
contact paper. This, of course, depends on the density of the negative.
Since each of these materials, film and paper, has special characteristics,
it is necessary to understand the following terms so that the best choice
can be made for making the negative and the final positive print.

A. LIGHT-SENSITIVE MATERIALS

1. Photographic Film

Photographic film is the medium upon which the photographic image
is recorded. The sheet or roll of film is made up of an emulsion of silver
halide salts in gelatin spread very thinly on a clear acetate base. When
exposed in a camera, the emulsion is so affected by light that a latent or
invisible image is produced. This image becomes visible only after treatment with a chemical bath or developer. The silver halides are affected

in proportion to the intensity of the light striking them. The brighter the light, the thicker the layer of exposed halides; the weaker the light, the thinner the layer of exposed halides. Development will show the converted black metallic silver to be heaviest in the areas exposed to the brighter light and thinnest in the areas exposed to weaker light.

Certain characteristics are incorporated into film emulsions to make it more suitable for a specific problem. Silver halides (mainly silver bromides) are mixed with gelatin and spread as a thin layer on a base material, such as a glass plate, or clear acetate (as in roll film and cut sheet film). Because silver bromide is sensitive mainly to blue and ultraviolet light, special dyes are mixed with the emulsion to provide sensitivity to other wavelengths as well as to increase over-all sensitivity (film speed). The back of the film base is coated with a light-absorbing dye to prevent extremely strong rays of light from scattering and reflecting when passing through the emulsion and clear base.

1. *Film speed* is the measure of a film's sensitivity to a known amount of light. This is referred to as its ASA number. The larger the ASA number, the faster (more sensitive) the film. The ASA number is a guide to correct exposure with exposure-computing devices and also provides an accurate comparison of one film with another. As an example, a film with an ASA rating of 25 will require 4 times as much exposure as a film with an ASA rating of 100.

Films are more sensitive to blue light. Daylight contains a higher percentage of blue than any other spectral color, so most films have been assigned two ASA speed numbers: a higher number indicating speed to daylight and a lower number indicating speed to tungsten light. Film manufacturers have reduced this inequality, so many films now have one composite ASA number which is valid for either daylight or tungsten illumination.

2. *Color sensitivity* of the emulsion allows colored objects to be recorded in black and white tones. Silver halides are sensitive to blue and ultraviolet light but are insensitive to other colors. Emulsions are altered to make them sensitive to other wavelengths, thus enabling them to record colored objects in various shades of gray. Because various photographic emulsions differ in their response to light they can be classified as:

(a) Blue-sensitive (called "ordinary" or "non-color-sensitized") materials which are responsive only to blue-violet and ultraviolet regions of the spectrum;

(b) Orthochromatic materials, sensitive to green, blue, and ultraviolet;

(c) Panchromatic, sensitive to red and all other colors including ultra-violet, are divided into: (1) type B panchromatic which has a relatively higher green sensitivity and most nearly approximates the color sensitivity of the human eye; and (2) type C panchromatic with a relatively high red-green sensitivity.

Color sensitivity has an important effect both in the handling of the material and the results obtained.

3. *Film grain* is a mottled appearance characteristic of every negative when viewed under high magnification. This is caused by apparent clumping of silver grains. Graininess is inherent in every emulsion. Similar types of emulsion increase in graininess as emulsion speeds increase. At equal gamma (gray scale ratio), normal developers produce almost equal graininess with a given film. Special fine-grain developers will produce a lower grain with some loss of emulsion speed and contrast. Over-all graininess increases with density; therefore, over-exposure and over-development must be avoided.

4. *Contrast* is the degree of difference between lightest and darkest densities which a film can produce. A film of low contrast will produce the greatest difference between white and black. It will have more gray tones between the whitest and blackest part of the negative. Films of high contrast will produce the opposite. Subject contrast is the degree of difference between brightest and darkest part of object being photographed and can be reduced or increased by proper choice of emulsion contrast.

5. The ability of a film to record the brightest and darkest portions of a subject plus the gray tones in between is a measure of its *latitude*. Films with higher exposure index ratings have a longer exposure latitude scale and possess greater capabilities for recording differences in object luminance as density differences. These density differences in the negative reproduce as a long range of gray tones in the positive print.

6. *Resolving power* is expressed in the number of lines per millimeter that can be distinguished separately in a photographic image. It depends on the brightness scale of the subject, the degree of development of the film, and, especially, on the amount of exposure given the film. Resolution falls off at very high and very low exposure values. Ability of negative materials to reproduce geometrically definable edges is a measure of sharpness, which determines the degree of definition which can be obtained in a negative.

With an understanding of these terms, it is possible to make a choice of the right emulsion from the listings in Table I of most commonly available films.

Table I

SOME COMPARATIVE CHARACTERISTICS OF KODAK SHEET FILMS AND PLATES[a]

Film Type	Color sensitivity	Speed	Contrast	Resolving power
Plate				
Wratten "M"	Pan B	Medium	High	Very high
Tri X Pan	Pan C	High	Low	High
Panchromatic	Pan B	Medium	Low	Medium
Super Ortho	Ortho	Medium	Medium	High
Sheet Films				
Contrast Process Pan	Pan B	Medium	Very high	Very high
Panatomic-X	Pan C	Medium	Medium	High
Royal Pan	Pan C	High	Medium	Medium
Contrast Process Ortho	Ortho	Medium	Very high	Very high
Royal Ortho	Ortho	High	Medium	Medium

[a] From Kodak Data Book (1957).

The listing of films of one manufacturer is not intended to suggest that these are the only films available. Negative emulsions manufactured by Agfa, Ansco, Dupont, or Ilford, which compare with those listed in Table I will have about the same contrast and resolving power. It is necessary for the photomicrographer to consult the technical information supplied by the film manufacturer in order to establish the characteristics of the emulsion and the recommended processing procedures best suited to his particular needs.

For those microscopists desiring to photograph with 35 mm films, the following films are listed:

Low-to-medium speed; extra-fine grain; low-to-medium contrast
    Adox KB-14 and KB-17
    Agfa: Isopan IFF
    Ansco Versapan (listed as high speed by manufacturer)
    Ilford Pan F
    Kodak Panatomic-X
Medium speed; fine grain; medium-to-good contrast
    Adox KB-21
    Agfa: Isopan IF
    Ilford FP3
    Kodak Plus-X Panchromatic
High speed; normal grain; good-to-high contrast
    Agfa Isopan: ISS (normal grain)
    Agfa Isopan: ISU (reasonable grain)
    Ansco Super Hypan (gradation control through processing)
    Ilford HP-3 (medium grain, medium contrast)
    Kodak Tri-X

High contrast films (variable speed and lines of resolving power)
 Agfa Isopan Record [rated at ASA 600–1250 with normal contrast subjects and
   at higher ASA for subjects of low contrast; resolution is 75 lines per millimeter (see Agfa Technical Data Sheet, 20A, May, 1963].
 Kodak High Contrast Copy (formerly called Microfile)

Here again, the manufacturer's technical information should be consulted, since considerable care must be exercised in the processing of these
films in order to preserve the characteristics of fine grain size and contrast
gradation.

Even though the listings of 35 mm films contains many "brand" names,
there are fewer emulsion types from which a choice can be made than
there are in the sheet films. For some investigators using 35 mm cameras,
this has not been a serious disadvantage since they have obtained good
results when using the low and medium speed emulsions. These films
have good latitude range and record the lightest to darkest features of
the chromosome image.

High contrast emulsions do not have capabilities for producing a long
range of gray tones, although the appearance of edge sharpness of the
chromosome in the negative image gives a false impression that the film
emulsion has recorded faithfully all the subtle qualities of the projected
image. This image distortion is compounded to an even greater extent
by printing the negative on hard contrast (No. 4) or extra-hard contrast
(No. 6 or document line copy) printing paper, which results in photographic prints having characteristics of India ink drawings.

Color positive films, although not normally used for publication in
chromosome studies, should be listed because of their possible use for
projection transparencies of chromosome patterns and other stained specimen photomicrography. The important consideration is that the color
balance of the film emulsion match the color temperature of the light
source. Almost all microscope illuminators employ a tungsten bulb with
a filament temperature range of 2900°K to 3600°K, depending on the
voltage applied to the lamp from the variable voltage (AC) transformer.
Color films best suited for use under these light source conditions are
listed in Table II.

If the voltage to the light source cannot be regulated to reach the temperature of the film's color balance, special light balancing filters must
be used.

Of the films listed, Kodachrome II film has a fine grain and softer
gradation (contrast). Ektachrome, Type B (E-3) has a medium grain

and a higher image contrast. High Speed Ektachrome, Type B, has a larger grain and extended gradation scale. Anscochrome Tungsten 100 has a medium-fine grain with a medium range contrast and more warm color tones.

Table II
COLOR BALANCE AND ASA RATING OF COLOR FILMS FOR PHOTOMICROGRAPHY

Film	Color balance (°K)	Speed (ASA value)
Anscochrome, 100 (Tungsten)	3200	100
Ektachrome, Type B (E-3)	3200	32
High Speed Ektachrome, Type B	3200	125
Kodachrome II, Professional Type A	3400	40

2. Photographic Papers

Photographic papers have some of the same complex characteristics as photographic film; therefore, only a limited discussion is presented.

a. Physical Properties. Printing paper emulsion consists of light-sensitive silver halides in gelatin and special agents to control printing speed, grade, and image tone. The halides used are silver chloride and silver bromide. Silver chloride is less sensitive to light and is used in slower-speed papers. Special dyes regulate sensitivity to various parts of the spectrum and control printing speed relationships between grades of paper.

b. Exposure Scale. The exposure scale of the paper indicates the time necessary to obtain gradations in shading from light to dark and varies with the type of paper used.

c. Scale Index. Printing papers are generally graded from 0–5 to indicate the type of negative that can be successfully printed with each grade of paper. This number is called a scale index. For example, a negative with a high density scale will be reproduced best on a paper with a high scale index. The following data (see Kodak Data Book, 1960) will aid in matching negative density to paper grade.

Paper grade	Scale index	Density scale of negative
0	1.7	1.40 or higher
1	1.5	1.2–1.4
2	1.3	1.0–1.2
3	1.1	0.8–1.0
4	0.9	0.6–0.8
5	0.7	0.6 or lower

Papers differ greatly in sensitivity to light or the amount of exposure required in printing; papers for contact printing are slower than papers used for enlargements. A numerical rating of speed indicates relative exposure required when shifting from one paper to another within the same scale.

d. Development Latitude. Development latitude is the ability of a paper to produce an acceptable print if: (a) the image occurs too rapidly and development is stopped before the recommended development time; or (b) an image is not dense enough after recommended development time has elapsed and development is continued beyond the normal time.

If proper paper is chosen for the negative and proper exposure time is used, it should not be necessary to "juggle" development times in order to obtain a satisfactory print.

Prints have less contrast with overexposure and underdevelopment and greater contrast with underexposure and overdevelopment.

e. Paper Contrast. A negative printed on No. 1 and No. 2 grades of the same type paper will have the same maximum density, but the print on No. 2 has more contrast because a No. 2 paper reaches its maximum density more rapidly.

f. Multi-Grade Papers. These are special emulsion papers designed to give the same range of contrast as single-grade papers, but the desired contrast or grade of paper is achieved by exposure through a special set of filters.

B. DARKROOM PROCEDURES

The following is only a brief discussion of chemicals, steps for processing the negative, and steps for making the paper positive print.

1. Chemicals for Processing of Film and Paper

a. Developers. These convert the latent silver image to a visible image and are composed of the following substances:

(1) Reducing agents, hydroquinone and Metol or Elon, reduce the exposed halide to metallic silver. Hydroquinone works very slowly and produces good contrast. Metol or Elon are fast acting and work in the shadow areas.

(2) Accelerators produce an alkaline state for the reduction of silver halides. They energize the reducing agent and swell the emulsion to allow better penetration. Na_2CO_3 is used in medium-contrast devel-

opers, NaOH in high-contrast developers, and borax in low-contrast, fine-grain developers.

(3) A preservative, usually sodium sulfite, is added to prevent oxidation of reducing agents by dissolved O_2 in the solution.

(4) A restrainer (KBr) is added to prevent "overworking" of reducing agents and to prevent reduction of unexposed silver halides.

b. Short Stop. A bath consisting of 1¼ parts of 28% acetic acid per 32 parts of water is used after development to stop the developer action, neutralize its alkalinity on the film or paper, and prepare emulsions for the acid fixing bath.

c. Hypo or Fixing Bath. This is a combination of chemicals to stabilize the reduced silver image and preserve the negative or positive print by converting the unexposed silver to a soluble complex. This combination is:

(1) Sodium thiosulfate (hypo) to dissolve the unexposed halides. (ammonium thiosulfate plus sodium thiosulfate constitutes the newer rapid liquid fixing baths.)

(2) 28% Acetic acid to complete neutralization of alkaline developing bath.

(3) Sodium sulfite is added as a preservative. Acetic acid plus hypo causes free sulfur to be released. Sodium sulfite combines with this free sulfur to form more thiosulfate.

(4) Potassium alum toughens and hardens the emulsion which has undergone swelling during the development period.

Standard developing temperature is 68° F, although effective development can be accomplished in a range 60–75° F. With low temperature, the developer action is slower and the time of development is longer. With high temperatures, the developer action is faster and the development time is reduced. It is important to have all processing solutions at the same temperature. Variations in bath temperatures cause unevenness in the emulsion which results in reticulation patterns and changes the grain size.

2. Steps in Processing Exposed Photographic Films

(a) Load tank with film. (*Do not* touch emulsion with fingers! Handle by edges only.)

(b) Turn on lights and measure developer temperature.

(c) Set timer according to requirements of developer and temperature.

(d) Start timer and immediately begin pouring developer into tank.

(e) Begin agitation of film. First bounce tank sharply several times to dislodge possible air bubbles on film surface. Then gently rock or vibrate tank to keep solution in motion. Continuous or intermittent agitation may be used. If intermittent, agitate for at least 10 seconds every minute.

(f) When developing time expires, pour off developer as rapidly as possible.

(g) Immediately pour in short stop bath and agitate for one minute.

(h) Pour off short stop bath and drain (do not let excess acetic acid carry over to hypo). Add hypo fixing and agitate for one full minute. Agitate every 2 or 3 minutes until recommended time has elapsed.

(i) Pour off hypo and open tank to begin washing cycle.

(j) Wash film in running water for approximately 5 minutes.

(k) Soak for 5–10 minutes in recommended hypo eliminator.

(l) Rewash for final 5 minutes.

(m) Add wetting agent, "Photo-Flo," to wash water in tank. Soak film for 60 seconds, then remove and hang to dry. Surplus water and calcium scum (if any) can be removed by wiping gently with a damp photo-sponge or chamois cloth. Drying should be done in a dust-free room.

(n) Wipe up spilled chemicals immediately and clean equipment thoroughly.

Keep a Tidy and Uncontaminated Work Area.

3. Steps for Printing the Positive Print

a. Exposure-contact

(1) Contact printing is best done on any commercial printing box. (Glass top should be spotlessly clean.)

(2) Place dust-free negative on glass with emulsion side up.

(3) Place printing paper (grade chosen according to estimate of negative value) on negative, emulsion side down (negative emulsion face to face with paper emulsion).

(4) Close platen and expose to light. (Time is determined by trial and error or previous experience.)

b. Enlarging. Enlarging uses a reverse type camera with a lens, bellows, film holder, and light source at the film plane.

(1) The dust-free negative is placed in the film carrier and inserted into the enlarger, emulsion side down.

(2) The light source is turned on and the image projected onto an easel paper holder.

(3) The image is sharply focused by moving the lens and bellows up and down.

(4) Image size is controlled by moving the complete enlarger assembly away or toward the easel paper holder.

(5) After focus and image size are adjusted, the enlarger light is turned off.

(6) Proper grade of enlarging paper is placed in the easel with emulsion side up.

(7) Enlarger is switched on and proper time of exposure is given.

c. Developing

(1) Take paper from printing easel; mark on back side the paper grade and seconds of exposure for future reference. Use soft lead pencil but do not press too hard. Then quickly immerse print in developer with emulsion side up by using a continuous motion to slide the paper under the surface of the developer. Developing solutions should be used according to directions at 68° F.

(2) Develop for exactly $1\frac{1}{2}$ minutes; keep this time constant. If print is too light, there is not enough exposure. If print is too black, there is too much exposure.

(3) Rock tray gently during development.

(4) After $1\frac{1}{2}$ minutes, print may be passed through running water, then into short stop for at least 30 seconds.

(5) Take print from short stop, allow to drain a few seconds, then place in fixing bath for 10–15 minutes. Keep prints moving from time to time to ensure complete fixation.

(6) Remove from hypo and wash in running water for 10 minutes. It is best to use a print washer designed for this purpose.

(7) Place prints in hypo eliminator bath for 10 minutes (or time recommended by manufacturer).

(8) Place prints back into print washer for another 5 minutes.

(9) Remove and drain excess water. Squeeze onto polished drying tins or electric drying machine, or place in blotter roll to complete drying and finishing of print.

APPENDIX

Material	Source
A. *Supplies*	
Roll and sheet films	Agfa, Inc., Rockleigh, N. J.
Contact printing paper	Ansco Products, Binghamton, N. Y.
Bromide enlarging paper	Eastman Kodak Co., Rochester, N. Y.
Variable contrast papers	E. I. DuPont de Nemours Photo Products, Wilmington, Del.
Processing chemicals	Ilford, Inc., New York 23, N. Y.
B. *Darkroom Equipment*	
Roll film daylight processing tank	
Nikor #35	Burleigh Brooks, Inc., Englewood, N. J.
Kodak Day Load	Eastman Kodak Co., Rochester, N. Y.
Ansco, #JN232	Ansco Products, Binghamton, N. Y.
G. E. Mechanical Interval Timer	General Electric Corp., X-Ray Division, Milwaukee, Wis.
Daylight developing cut film tanks	
F-R Adjustable Cut Film	The F-R Corp., Bronx 51, N. Y.
Stainless Steel (light tight cover and cut film hangers)	
Calumet Model 44 or 45	Calumet Mfg. Co. Chicago 26, Ill.
or Fisher IT4512	Oscar Fisher Co., Inc. Newburgh, N. Y.
or Leedahl NA303DL	Leedahl, Inc. Chicago 8, Ill.

References

Kodak Data Book (1960). "Kodak Photographic Papers." Eastman Kodak Co., Rochester, New York.

Kodak Data Book (1957). "Photography through the Microscope." Eastman Kodak Co., Rochester, New York.

Michel, K. (July 1940). "Grundzuege der Mikrophotographie," Sonderheft 4. Zeiss-Werke, Jena.

Shillaber, C. P. (1944). "Photomicrography in Practice and Theory." Wiley, New York.

Additional Readings

Gurr, E. (1962). "Staining Practical and Theoretical." Williams & Wilkins, Baltimore, Maryland.

Henney, K., and Dudley, B. (1939). "Handbook of Photography." Wittlesey House, New York.

James, T. H., and Higgins, G. C. (1948). "Fundamentals of Photographic Theory." Wiley, New York.

Kodak Data Book (1944). "Photomicrography: An Introduction to Photomicrography with the Microscope." Eastman Kodak Co., Rochester, New York.

Kodak Data Book (1960). "Negative Making for the Professional Photographer." Eastman Kodak Co., Rochester, New York.

Kodak Data Book (1960). "Processing Chemicals and Formulas for Black and White." Eastman Kodak Co., Rochester, New York.

Kodak Data Book (1960). "Kodak Films." Eastman Kodak Co., Rochester, New York.

Kodak Data Book (1961). "Kodak Master Darkroom Guide for Black and White." Eastman Kodak Co., Rochester, New York.

Lester, H. M. (1960). "Photo-Lab Index," Morgan and Morgan, New York.

Longmore, T. A. (1955). "Medical Photography," The Focal Press, London.

Mack, J. E., and Martin, J. J. (1940). "The Photographic Process," McGraw-Hill, New York.

Neblette, C. B. (1962). "Photography. Its Materials and Processes." D. Van Nostrand and Co., Inc., Princeton, New Jersey.

Identification of Chromosomes

KLAUS PATAU

Department of Medical Genetics, University of Wisconsin, Madison, Wisconsin

I.	Morphological Identification in the Absence of Special Markers	155
II.	Markers and Other Aids to Chromosome Identification	166
III.	Nomenclature	173
IV.	The Human Complement	177
	References	185

I. MORPHOLOGICAL IDENTIFICATION IN THE ABSENCE OF SPECIAL MARKERS

Individual chromosomes can be characterized by the length of their two arms or by their total length and arm ratio, i.e., the length of the long arm divided by that of the short one (instead of the arm ratio, the centromere index is sometimes used, i.e., the length of the short arm divided by the total chromosome length). Unfortunately, these quantities are given to considerable variation even between homologs of the same nucleus. It is not uncommon for one member of a recognizably homologous pair to be appreciably less contracted and correspondingly thinner than the other. In favorable material, a coefficient of length variation of about 5.3% with a lower fiducial limit of 4.4% ($P = 0.05$) has been found. This is probably close to the irreducible minimum.[1] Since there is

---

[1] Let x_1 and x_2 be the lengths of two homologous chromosomes in the same cell. The coefficient of variation is then:

$$100 \sqrt{ 2n \sum_n (x_1 - x_2)^2 } / \sum_n (x_1 + x_2)$$

wherein n, the number of degrees of freedom, is the number of measured pairs of homologs. Patau (1960) computed this coefficient from published measurements by Rothfels and Siminovitch (1958) on chromosome 1 of the rhesus monkey (10 df) and from published measurements by Levan and Hsu (1959) on chromosome 1 of man (10 df)—in both cases the coefficient of variation was 5.8%. From my own measurement on eight pairs each of chromosomes 4 and 5 of man (see below) the value 4.5% was obtained, which does not differ significantly from 5.8%. The best over-all estimate is 5.3% with 36 df.

also some variation in contraction between arms of the same chromosome, the arm ratio, too, is far from constant. Length variation exists undoubtedly *in vivo* but may be further increased during preparation. For instance, in slides obtained by the air-drying method, chromosomes at the periphery of a spread tend to be somewhat larger than their homologous partners in the middle.

In view of the unavoidable length variation, it is essential to take the relative degree of contraction into account rather than to base chromosome identification on length only. Indeed, length measurements are not a useful aid in the identification of homologs in individual cells since length differences that are large enough to be significant are also large enough to be recognized without measurements. However, hope dies hard that length measurements might put chromosome identification on a more objective basis. For this reason, a discussion of measurements and their evaluation may be appropriate (see also Patau, 1960).

Chromosome measurements are usually done on highly enlarged photographic prints or camera lucida drawings. Photographs have the disadvantage that chromosomes lying at different distances from the optical axis of the microscope are likely to be imaged at somewhat different magnifications. In the case of camera lucida drawings, this error source can be avoided by drawing each chromosome in the middle of the field. Unless sister chromatids are very closely associated, as in prophase chromosomes, both chromatids should be measured along their individual axes and the results averaged. The centromere region, more or less achromatic and poorly defined in its extension, poses a problem. If it is included in the measurements, i.e., if in Fig. 1 (top left) AC and CE are regarded as arm lengths, these lengths will obviously not be proportional to the deoxyribonucleic acid (DNA) contents of the arms. For certain purposes, it is important to approximate such a proportionality by restricting the measurements to regions such as AB and DE in Fig. 1. Because of the irregular tapering-off of the arms toward the centromere, the choice of the points B and D is obviously somewhat arbitrary, but it is clear that in Fig. 1 the arm ratio AB/DE = 3.20 is more likely than the ratio AC/CE = 2.66 to reflect the relative gene contents of the two arms. However, if such genetic implications are irrelevant for the purpose at hand, it might be better to measure AC and CE, avoiding the use of the poorly defined points B and D. The results may be more reproducible.

In the light microscope, a chromosome shows no sharp outline but a diffraction fringe, and where we locate the points A end E (Fig. 1)

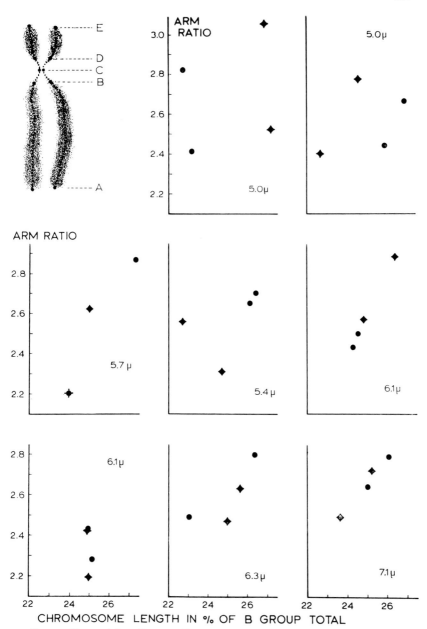

FIG. 1. Upper left: diagram illustrating chromosome length measurements; rest: partial karyograms of B chromosomes from eight metaphases (circles and diamonds: chromosomes 4 and 5, respectively, as identified by autoradiography).

within this fringe is somewhat arbitrary. In high-contrast photographs, a chromosome may have a well-defined outline, but this is illusory since the outline can be made to shift by varying the photographic technique. Photography or camera lucida—the uncertainty resulting from the limited resolving power of the microscope is the same and it is substantial enough to render measurements of objects as small as the short arms of acrocentric chromosomes wholly meaningless.

It should be obvious from the foregoing that systematic differences between the measurements obtained by different investigators are to be expected. However, if the work is done carefully and in a consistent manner, repeated measurements by the same investigator on the same chromosome will show, if this is not too small, much less variation than there is in the average between homologous chromosomes of the same cell. It is the real length variation of chromosomes rather than the inaccuracy of measurement that limits the usefulness of chromosome measurements.

Patau (1960) pointed out that for certain purposes it is practical to plot chromosomes as points in a rectangular coordinate system, using as abscissa and ordinate the two arm lengths expressed as per cent of the nuclear total. Instead of the arm lengths, other parameters, e.g., the total chromosome length (again expressed as per cent) and the arm ratio, may be used. For such an array of points the term "karyogram" was proposed. A "partial karyogram" would represent the chromosomes of a selected group rather than of the whole complement.

In a karyogram, two points will be the closer to each other the more similar in length and arm ratio the two chromosomes are. This, however, does not justify interpreting every pair of associated points that appear fairly well separated from all other points as representing homologous chromosomes. Fortuitous pairs are far from rare even in purely random distributions of points. To support the claim of having identified several pairs of homologs by means of measurements, it is necessary to show that a similar pattern of pairs reoccurs in karyograms derived from different cells.

The partial karyograms of the two pairs of B chromosomes from eight cells in Fig. 1 will serve to illustrate this point. It has recently become possible to distinguish these pairs by means of autoradiography with tritiated thymidine (see below) in many, though not in all cells. The present eight cells were selected for showing the autoradiographic patterns characterizing the two B pairs 4 and 5 with such clarity that the identification of each chromosome was beyond doubt. However, let us for the moment consider, one by one, the eight karyograms as if nothing were known but the locations of the four points. In several of these karyograms, fairly well separated pairs will be seen, but any temptation to interpret these as pairs of homologs should disappear when it is noticed how incompatible the relative positions of the two pairs are in different karyograms. The obviously random nature of these point patterns justifies in itself the conclusion that these length measurements cannot distinguish between chromosomes 4 and 5. The conclusion is fully confirmed by the results of the autoradiographic identification of these chromosomes.

Even less justified than the interpretation of pairs of points in a single karyogram as representing pairs of homologs is the belief that the method of simply pairing off chromosomes by length will lead to the identification of homologous chromosomes. The method is usually applied to groups of chromosomes with similar arm ratios or to acrocentric chromosomes. It consists in setting apart the two largest (or the two smallest) chromosomes as one pair, the next two largest (or smallest) as a second pair, and so forth without any evidence that the mean length difference between successive nonhomologous chromosomes is large enough relative to the inherent chromosome variation (with a coefficient of variation of about 5%—see p. 155) to make this procedure meaningful. If homology of the paired chromosomes is not assumed, the method lacks purpose; if it is assumed, it is apt to be misleading.

Patau (1960) in his criticism of the pairing-off method also pointed out the absurdity of attempting to establish the significance of the mean length difference between pairs by a statistical test based on the same length values that were used to separate the pairs in the first place. The data represented by the karyograms of Fig. 1 provide a good example. Let us again assume that the chromosomes 4 and 5 had not been identified by autoradiography. Applying the pairing off method, we call in each cell the pair of the two largest chromosomes "4" and that of the two smallest "5." The difference between the mean lengths of "4" and "5" has inevitably the same sign in all cells. Not surprisingly, if the t-test is applied to the mean of the eight differences, 0.45 ± 0.08 μ, the deviation of the mean from zero appears formally highly significant ($t_7 = 5.6$; $P = 0.0008$). Obviously, this result of a hopelessly biased procedure is void of any biological meaning. When the chromosomes are correctly identified and now the mean of the eight length differences (4–5) is computed, it proves to be insignificant: 0.06 ± 0.16 μ [the analogous mean difference (4–5) of arm ratios is also insignificant: 0.019 ± 0.058].

Small wonder that in five of eight cells the pairing off method leads to errors of identification (see Fig. 1) .

The number of cells in which the pairing off method proved more or less misleading might easily have been higher. The frequency with which that method is likely to lead its user astray depends of course on the difference between the true mean lengths of the two chromosome pairs concerned and on the true coefficient of length variation, which is about 5% in favorable material. Assume for instance the difference between "true" lengths to be also equal to 5%. It can then easily be shown that the expected frequency of at least partial failure of the pairing off method exceeds 42%.[2] Even if the above difference were as large as 10%, i.e., twice as large as the coefficient of variation, the expected frequency of at least partial failure of the method would still exceed 15%.

Lejeune (1964) has tried a statistical approach to circumvent the obstacles that hamper the identification of individual chromosomes from certain groups, above all the C group (see below), which are made up of a number of similar pairs. He entered the points representing the chromosomes of a given group from 50 male and 50 female cells into one partial karyogram and then employed a photographic out-of-focus technique to demonstrate certain concentrations of points. These concentrations he interpreted as the mean locations of the chromosomes in the karyogram. He stressed that he had found in the C group eight such concentrations corresponding to seven autosome pairs and one or two X chromosomes. Patau (1964) raised several objections. In the first place, there is no evidence that would rule out random density variation as origin of these concentrations. Secondly, autoradiographic studies have shown (see below) that at least one X chromosome in the female is a medium-sized rather than a large C chromosome, but in Lejeune's karyogram there is only one X location marked and this represents the longest C chromosome. Thirdly, Patau pointed out (1964, p. 50) that two chromo-

---

[2] Let on the average the chromosome pair W be larger than the pair Z. Let w_1, w_2 and z_1, z_2 be the respective lengths as measured in one cell. The pairing off method would be completely successful only if $w_1 \geqslant z_1$, $w_1 \geqslant z_2$, $w_2 \geqslant z_1$, and $w_2 \geqslant z_2$. The events $w_1 \geqslant z_1$ and $w_2 \geqslant z_2$ are independent of each other, but the other two events are not independent of these. However, the probability of complete success must be smaller than the probability of obtaining $w_1 \geqslant z_1$ and $w_2 \geqslant z_2$. This probability is equal to the square of $p(w_1 \geqslant z_1)$, and this can easily be computed under the reasonable assumption of an approximately normal distribution. The probability of at least partial failure is therefore larger than $1 - p^2(w_1 \geqslant z_1)$, which in the above example turns out to be 0.42.

somes whose locations are too close to each other in the karyogram cannot produce two peaks in the density distribution.

Patau understated his case when he named as critical distance of the two locations the standard deviation of a single-chromosome distribution. Actually, the distance between the means of two normal distributions must be about 2.2 times the standard deviation before any hint of bimodality will appear in the combined distribution and considerably more before the peaks will be pronounced enough to cause significant concentrations of points in Lejeune's scatterdiagram. A distance equal to 2.6 times the standard deviation would probably still be insufficient (Fig. 2).

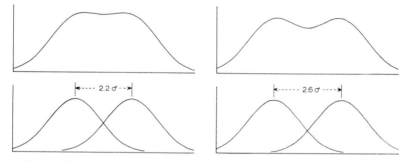

Fig. 2. Two examples of a combined distribution being more or less bimodal, depending on the difference of the means of the two component distributions (see text).

Unfortunately, Lejeune did not publish standard deviations, but he did state that the (mean) difference between the homologs of chromosomes 1 and 2 was 5% and 5.7%, respectively. It can be shown that the expected difference between homologs is equal to $2\,\sigma/\sqrt{\pi}$ if the distribution is normal with standard deviation σ. Hence, we estimate $s = 5.35 \times \sqrt{\pi/2} = 4.7\%$ as coefficient of variation, which is in very good agreement with the estimates obtained from measurements by other authors (p. 155). It follows that two chromosomes with about equal arm ratios must differ in length by considerably more than $2.2 \times 4.7 = 10\%$ if each is to produce a significant point concentration in the karyogram. It will be seen from Lejeune's (1964) Fig. 5 that at least the chromosomes 10 and 8 and also 6 and X are very far from fulfilling this condition. Probably all neighboring chromosomes are too close to each other to produce significant point concentrations, but the lack of information on the variation of the centromere index makes a more definite conclusion impossible. At any rate, some of the concentrations in the C group are undoubtedly, the rest probably, fortuitous.

Homologous chromosome arms, although usually differing in length, are presumed to have identical DNA contents and practically identical dye contents in Feulgen-stained slides. It would be a major advance in chromosome identification if these dye contents could be measured accurately enough to bring the coefficient of variation of the measurements greatly below the level, 5% or so, of the coefficient of length variation. Unless the gain in accuracy is great, one might as well stay with length measurements. At present, it is doubtful whether any amount of laborious refinements of the microspectrophotometric method could make it feasible to determine the Feulgen dye content of single chromosomes with sufficient accuracy to make the effort worth while.

Even if not used for DNA measurements, the presumed constancy of the Feulgen dye content is important for purposes of chromosome identification insofar as recognizable differences in the intensity of the Feulgen staining of different chromosomes in the same cell can safely be interpreted as signs of different degrees of chromosome contraction. For instance, two chromosomes of equal length and arm ratio cannot be homologous if they differ in Feulgen density. On the other hand, two similar chromosomes of different length may be homologous if the shorter one appears also more darkly stained. Unfortunately, orcein is a much less reliable indicator of the relative degrees of chromosome contraction than the Feulgen dye. Orcein-stained mitoses often show more intense staining in some parts than in others. Thus it may happen that homologous chromosomes have recognizably different dye contents. This does not occur in Feulgen slides. Orcein's lack of consistent uniformity of staining is probably shared by most dyes that have been used in human cytogenetics, especially those that do not leave the cytoplasm entirely unstained. It appears that a moderate reinforcement of Feulgen staining by orcein does not introduce any noticeable nonuniformity.

The superiority of Feulgen staining, with or without reinforcement by orcein, can readily be seen in squash preparations. However, most work is now being done with air-dried preparations, and in these the chromosomes are so large that the Feulgen staining becomes very pale. A more intense staining can be obtained by giving the stained slides only the briefest of rinses with water (without SO_2) followed by another air drying. Thereafter, they are permanently mounted. The excess dye thus retained can hardly be claimed to represent the Feulgen reaction *sensu strictu,* but the staining appears to be uniform. These slides seem to fade more rapidly than ordinary Feulgen slides.

It cannot be stressed too emphatically that any decision to deny or to assert the homology of two chromosomes must be based on a comparison of the masses, or rather DNA contents, of the corresponding chromosome arms. This involves an assessment of relative degrees of contraction and a judgement as to whether or not differential contraction compensates for observed differences in the lengths of the arms. Ideally, such comparisons should be done in the microscope rather than in photographs since the photographic process is apt to misrepresent the relative dye contents of chromosomes. In photographs, chromosomes all too often are given a much higher contrast than they had in the microscope. An increase in contrast facilitates the reproduction of chromosomes in print, but it interferes with identification since it exaggerates differences in contraction. Also, even minute nonuniformities of the illumination in the microscope or in the enlarger can cause the chromosomes in certain areas of a cell to appear thicker than those in other areas. Although the cutting out of chromosomes from a photograph is undoubtedly helpful in that it permits comparison of chromosomes side by side, it will be well to keep in mind that photographs can be misleading—the more so the more the contrast is increased.

The easiest way to obtain impressive looking pictures of chromosomes is phase contrast photography, but for critical work this cannot be recommended since it does not lead to a reliable representation of chromosome masses. Figure 3 will illustrate the point. In the chromosomes of the diploid cell, photographed with bright field optics, homologous arms

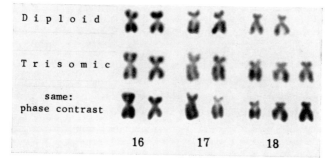

FIG. 3. The E chromosomes from a diploid and from an 18 trisomic cell of a mosaic (unpublished). Blood culture; Feulgen-orcein-squash preparation. Note image deterioration as a result of change from bright field to phase contrast optics.

appear to have the same mass, and the most striking difference between chromosomes 17 and 18 lies in the smaller mass of the short arm of 18 relative to that of 17. In the chromosomes of the trisomic cell, the situation is no less clear in the bright field photograph. There are three chromosomes 18 that match well and are clearly distinguished from the two chromosomes 17 by the smaller mass of their short arms. Minor differences in length are compensated by inverse differences in density, especially in the two chromosomes 17. However, in the phase contrast photograph of the same chromosomes all this does not hold true any more, with the result that a reliable identification of the chromosomes 17 and 18 has become impossible.

How far the identification of homologous chromosomes by length and arm ratio, with due allowance for differences in contraction, can be carried depends to a great deal on the quality of the slide and on finding a cell in which the chromosomes in question are particularly well displayed. They should show similar degrees of contraction not only within the arms but also in the centromere region, and there should be no overlapping of arms. Since cells in which all chromosomes are equally well laid out are extremely rare, the complete analysis of the chromosome complement of a given individual will usually entail the detailed study of certain chromosomes in some cells, of others in other cells, and so forth. In special cases it may be necessary to look at many cells in order to find one in which the chromosomes in question are displayed with the exceptional clarity that may be needed to solve the problem at hand. A very few cells of this kind may suffice to establish a firm conclusion, whereas the mere piling up of ambiguous observations never does.

Many authors have stated that they identify chromosomes not only by the lengths of their arms, but take other features into account as well. What these are is not always explained. One such feature, indeed one of great importance, is of course the relative degree of contraction of chromosomes. Then there are secondary constrictions, satellites, certain characteristics of the Y, and under special circumstances a peculiar appearance of one X chromosome in the female. However, most autosomes at metaphase appear to lack any special features, any "markers," that could be demonstrated by means of the presently available techniques to be more than random irregularities of coiling. It cannot be said too emphatically that in the case of chromosomes for which no significant special feature has been established, attempts at identification must rely on the lengths of arms and on their degrees of contraction and on nothing else. Nothing can be more misleading than to let oneself be impressed by ill-defined similarities in appearance of certain chromosomes unless these similarities recur in other cells with sufficient regularity to show that they are not fortuitous. Consider for instance the B chromosomes in Fig. 4 which seem to form two distinct pairs. However, the chromatids of the first two B chromosomes are not only longer but appear also somewhat thinner than those of the last two. The length difference can therefore not be taken as evidence for a difference in mass. The longer B chromosomes further show an overlapping of chromatids which may be a coincidence but may also be related to the lesser rigidity of the thinner chromatids. Lastly, no such constellation of B pairs was seen in other cells. It is concluded that these pairs are probably fortuitous. The conclusion is further supported by the demonstration (p. 159) that chromosomes 4 and 5 have practically the same mean length. As in this case, it is generally important to base conclusions about the homology or nonhomology of certain chromosomes on an analysis of defined features and not on vague impressions.

A method of chromosome identification that involves, as it must if it is to be efficient, an assessment of relative masses or DNA contents of chromosome arms rather than a comparison of their lengths alone depends obviously on the investigator's skill, that is, on his experience and on his innate ability "to see." It is a subjective method, but it is not as subjective as it might seem. At the microscope, good cytologists usually agree on what can be seen. If they disagree it is likely to be about a question of interpretation. Assume for instance two cytologists who both find that three given chromosomes from a diploid cell, W_1, W_2, and Z, appear to have the same arm ratio, that W_1 and W_2 appear to be equally long, that Z is shorter than these by about 5%, and that there are no recognizable differences of contraction between the three chromosomes. One cytologist points out that even two homologous chromosomes would differ in length by 5% if one were more contracted than the other so that its mean DNA content per unit chromatid length exceeded that of the other by 5%. This cytologist does not believe that such a small difference in contraction could be ascertained by eye, especially since chromatids are fairly irregular structures. He concludes that it is not justified to assert that W_1 and W_2 are homologous rather than W_1 and Z or W_2 and Z. If the other cytologist wishes to disagree, he obviously can do that only by claiming, rightly or wrongly, the ability to detect such a small difference in contraction. One sometimes wonders whether all authors who go far in identifying pairs of presumed homologs in difficult groups have quite realized what remarkable feats of discernment they are by implication claiming.

II. MARKERS AND OTHER AIDS TO CHROMOSOME IDENTIFICATION

The first markers discovered were satellites at the short arms of acrocentric chromosomes. In the Denver Report (1960) the definition of the chromosomes 13, 14, 15 (D group) and 21, 22 (G group) was based on the presence or absence and on the size of satellites. It was an unfortunate choice: very soon it became clear that all of these chromosomes have satellites, although this may not be true in all persons. Usually the number of visibly satellited acrocentrics is well below ten, but it is by no means clear whether the apparent absence of a satellite reflects a real absence or merely such a small size as to make it invisible in the light microscope. Very small satellites occur that are just recognizable in the technically best mitoses but invisible in all others of the same slide. Some persons have an unusually large satellite at a G or a D chromosome, and a chromosome thus marked can be traced in a pedigree (for an example see Cooper and Hirschhorn, 1962). In general, it is evident that homologous chromosomes often differ in the size of their satellites; indeed, there is nothing to dispel the suspicion that any two nonhomologous acrocentric chromosomes may be every bit as likely to have equal-sized satellites as any two homologous ones. At present, to make any use whatsoever of satellites cannot be justified when attempting to identify homologous acrocentrics.

Secondary constrictions[3] other than the stems of satellites are splendid markers, if they can be made to manifest themselves with sufficient regularity. Since in this respect ordinary preparations of human chromosomes are found wanting, there is an obvious need for special methods that would increase the frequency of manifestation of secondary constrictions. Several such methods have been described. Kaback et al. (1964) showed that under their conditions of leucocyte culture (which include omission of thymine from the medium TC-199 and removal of polymorphonuclear leucocytes) the addition of 5-bromodeoxyuridine (in a final concentration of 200 μg/ml of culture) causes a considerable increase both in the frequency and in the degree of manifestation of the secondary constrictions in the chromosomes 1 and C' (see below). These are about the only constrictions (Fig. 4) that can even without special measures be seen in more

---

[3] The term is here used without regard to the, at present quite doubtful, nature of these structures and in spite of the fact that even their appearance need not be that of a constriction (see below).

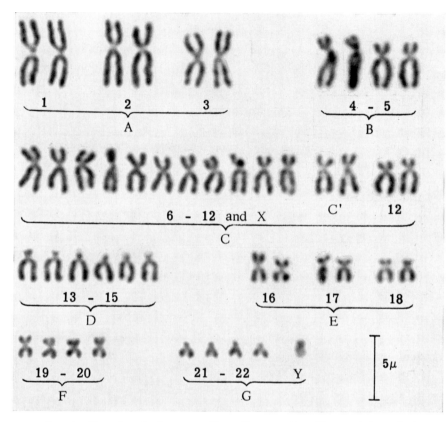

FIG. 4. Normal male karyotype (from Patau, 1964, with permission of the University of Michigan Press). Blood culture; Feulgen-orcein-squash preparation. Note secondary constrictions in first chromosome 1 and both chromosomes C'.

than a negligible minority of cells (however, the frequency of manifestation of secondary constrictions may fluctuate greatly from culture to culture). It might be worth while to explore whether 5-bromodeoxyuridine could be incorporated without disadvantage into a leucocyte culture routine. For most cytogenetic purposes, a small amount of induced chromatid breakage would hardly matter. How much of this is to be expected is not clear: the authors merely state that "no gross chromosomal rearrangements or alterations in number had occurred. . . ."

To date, the above appears to be the only publication that deals with the enhancement of secondary constrictions in leucocyte cultures. Sasaki and Makino (1963) were successful in producing very clear secondary constrictions in tissue cultures derived from legally aborted embryos. They ascribed their success to the use of a calcium-free medium, but since Inhorn's attempts to duplicate their results failed both in tissue cultures and in leucocyte cultures (1964), it would seem that some unknown conditions other than the absence of calcium also played a role. In Sasaki and Makino's photographs, which show excessive contrast (phase?), the secondary constrictions appear as achromatic gaps. Quite a few of these "constrictions" may represent fortuitous irregularities, but at least those described for the chromosomes 1, C', 16, and Y are undoubtedly significant. The ones in the chromosomes 1 and C' are identical with those mentioned above.

Saksela and Moorhead (1962) also used tissue cultures derived from human embryos, but instead of modifying the culture conditions they tried to determine which fixative and which drying-on procedure would serve best to enhance secondary constrictions. They succeeded in getting a high frequency of manifestation not so much of constrictions in the literal sense but of "understained" (the authors used preferably Giemsa but also orcein), fuzzy, puff-like structures. The most prominent of these are located in the chromosomes 1, C', 16, and Y and are, in spite of their different appearance, undoubtedly identical with the secondary constrictions obtained independently, though published later, by Sasaki and Makino (1963). Saksela and Moorhead (1962) describe one more puff and several constrictions of more ordinary appearance, but these structures are perhaps still somewhat problematic. Saksela and Moorhead's study is of particular interest in that they show that the conditions which induce a puff-like appearance of secondary constrictions also induce a strangely fuzzy appearance of one X chromosome in a high proportion of normal female metaphases but no such alteration in male cells. The authors conclude that the partially despiralized or "negatively heteropycnotic" X is the one that forms the sex chromatin body and is late labeling (see below) in autoradiographs.

What the conditions are that bring on these desirable results is far from clear. Saksela and Moorhead (1962) fared best by fixing the cells with a 1:1 mixture of methyl alcohol and acetic acid and by "flaming" the slides as a part of the drying-on procedure. However, when Inhorn and Therman tried this method on cells both from tissue cultures and from leucocyte cultures they had no success at all (1964). On the other hand, Dr. R. I. DeMars is obtaining (by a somewhat different method) results, both in regard to secondary constrictions and to the fuzzy X, that compare well with those reported by Saksela and Moorhead (cf. Fig. 5). In case a reader should fail to succeed with Saksela and Moorhead's (1962) recipe, he might wish to try Dr. DeMars' method. This has not yet been published. I am greatly obliged to Dr. DeMars for the following information and his permission to insert it here. His method pertains to fibroblast cultures.

Cells from a maximum density population are trypsinized. Aliquots of the cell suspension are inoculated into culture dishes containing cover slips so that there are about 100–150 cells per square millimeter of cover

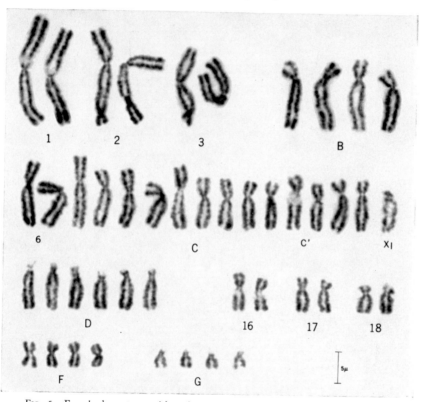

FIG. 5. Female karyotype with a long-arm telocentric X (Salonius and Opitz, 1964). Fibroblast culture and preparation by Dr. DeMars (see text); orcein. Note secondary constrictions in chromosomes 1, C', and 16, and the "fuzzy" appearance of the abnormal X (marked X_l, this chromosome is also late replicating in autoradiographs).

slip surface. Usually on the second day of subculture many divisions are present. Colchicine (0.05 µg/ml) is added for 30–60 minutes. The monolayers of cells are then gently washed once with 0.17% NaCl, kept for 30 minutes in fresh 0.17% NaCl, and fixed in 1:3 acetic alcohol (ethanol). Before the drying-on of the cells, the cover slips are transferred for 10–20 minutes to 50% acetic acid at room temperature. Single cover slips, with the cells on the upper side and covered by a layer of 50% acetic acid, are then put on ordinary microscope slides and waffed about 4–5 inches above a Bunsen flame until only a small droplet of acid remains on top. This is removed by absorbent paper, the cover slip is slipped off the slide, and its lower side blotted dry. Generally, there is a good supply of technically excellent mitoses in some areas of the cover slip while other areas are unusable.

The large "puffs" in the two chromosomes 1 and in one C' of Fig. 5 appear almost achromatic even in this orcein-stained preparation. In Feulgen-stained slides such "puffs" show no recognizable coloration. The appearance of the same constrictions in ordinary preparations, also Feulgen-stained, confirms that these regions have at most a very low DNA content as compared with isopycnotic segments of equal length.

Secondary constrictions vary much more in length than other chromosome regions. In the case of C', in which this variation is especially pronounced, Patau et al. (1961) stressed that the isopycnotic segments of the two chromosomes C' of the same cell always match no matter how much their secondary constrictions may differ in length. This fact is of crucial importance for any attempt to identify a chromosome C' whose secondary constriction is not clearly visible. In Fig. 5, for instance, there is only one immediately recognizable C'. The chromosome marked in this karyotype as its partner was selected not so much because it shows an indication of a constriction at the right location—this could be fortuitous—but because it matches C' extremely well in the isopycnotic segments, i.e., the short arm and the region between the secondary constriction and the end of the long arm. The length difference of the two chromosomes practically equals the length of the secondary constriction in the longer C'.

An altogether new approach to the problem of chromosome identification makes use of the fact that in autoradiographs based on the incorporation of tritiated thymidine different chromosomes often have recognizably different labeling patterns. For a description of the method see the article by Schmid in this volume. Suffice it here to say that all subsequent references to autoradiography will imply that the tritiated thymidine was present in the culture medium from a certain time until fixation. "Relatively heavy label" is then synonymous with "relatively late termination of DNA synthesis."

Probably, no two nonhomologous chromosomes have the same average labeling pattern, but such differences are to a considerable extent blurred by a great deal of variation. Because of this, homologous autosomes of the same cell show usually some and occasionally striking differences in labeling. These may be differences in the total amount of label, or in its distribution along the chromosome, or in both. This variation poses a serious problem in the case of nonhomologous but morphologically not distinguishable chromosomes. The investigator who finds a few cells in which chromosomes with similar labeling patterns seem to occur in pairs may have been lucky and perceptive enough to hit upon and to recognize the true average patterns. However, unless the similarities and differences are more striking than they often are, there may remain some doubt whether he was not mislead into a faulty pairing off by encountering cells in which the labeling patterns of nonhomologous chromosomes happened to be similar. There is obviously a need for more objective methods, but since these have to be tailored according to circumstances, a few general remarks must suffice here.

The information one wishes to extract from autoradiographs concerns average labeling patterns of specific chromosomes. This is a statistical problem that may not always be solvable. However, such difficulties may be overcome by finding a suitable marker chromosome. For instance, Patau et al. (1964a) made use of a telocentric chromosome D_1 as well as an isochromosome derived from the long arm of D_1 to show that on the average the pair D_1 synthesizes DNA later than the other two D pairs (Fig. 6A). Employing a marker chromosome may turn an exceedingly difficult statistical problem into an almost trivial one, but it is still a statistical problem and must be treated as such if one's conclusions are to be reliable. For instance, in a case of G/G translocation mongolism (Patau et al., 1964b), carrier cells were available that had two G chromosomes and the translocation chromosome. The latter could be distinguished from the F chromosomes by being more symmetrical and somewhat larger. In all but three autoradiographs of 22 mitoses, the translocation chromosome had clearly more label than the two single G chromosomes combined. If the translocation had been of the type 21/22, this would have been expected to occur in 11 of 22 cells (or even less

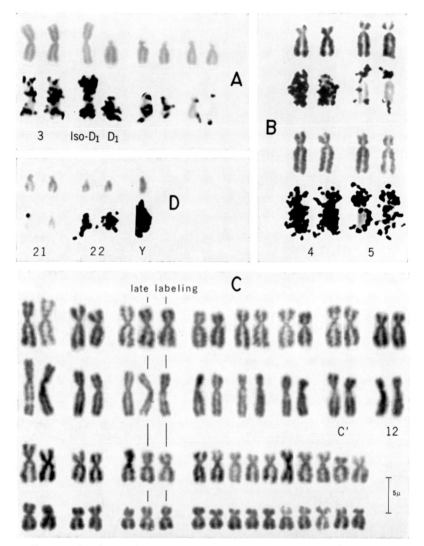

FIG. 6. Identification by means of autoradiography (Patau *et al.*, 1964b). A, B, D: characteristic labeling patterns of indicated chromosomes (Iso-D$_1$: iso-chromosome derived from long arm of D$_1$). C: the C chromosomes from four metaphases of an XXXY patient (unpublished). Two X chromosomes identified by being "late labeling," the third X may be the one to left of these.

frequently if the deletion of short-arm material had noticeably decreased the amount of label). The difference from 19/22 is highly significant ($P = 0.0004$), and it is concluded that the translocation chromosome consisted of the long arm of two mongolism chromosomes and that these on the average are later replicating than the other G pair. It might be difficult to derive a methodologically as satisfactory result as the above from autoradiographs of mitoses from a trisomic mongoloid, in other words, in the absence of a marker chromosome. This does in no way rule out the possibility that a judicious selection of cells in which autoradiographic patterns appear to be especially regular may turn out to be an effective short cut to correct results. However, at present there is no assurance that this rather intuitive approach can be trusted.

In the systematic discussion of the identification of specific chromosomes, autoradiographic results, with one exception, will be used only to the extent that they are in my opinion established beyond reasonable doubt and that they are useful for the characterization of chromosomes that cannot be reliably identified by morphological criteria. A similarly conservative policy will be followed in regard to secondary constrictions.

III. NOMENCLATURE

In 1960, a study group convened at Denver "to attempt the formulation of a common system of nomenclature." The ensuing Denver Report (1960) was widely accepted as authoritative but met with considerable criticism by Patau (1961) who pointed out numerous inconsistencies. Recently, the Denver Report was superseded by the London Report (1963) issued by a similar group which included most of the members of the Denver group. The new report is a much more cautious document, and while some may feel that it contains less than might have been said, it is not open to the objections leveled against the Denver Report. The system of chromosome numbers and of letters for chromosome groups as described below is in full accord with the London Report.

The human complement was divided into the same seven groups independently by the authors of the Denver Report (1960) and by Patau (1960). Within most groups it is difficult or impossible to identify individual chromosomes, but there is rarely any doubt to which group a given chromosome belongs. Autosomes, or pairs of homologous autosomes, that can be identified are designated by numbers which as much as possible have been assigned so that the smaller of two chromosomes has the larger number. About this principle there has been general agreement since 1960. A chromosome group may be designated either by the smallest and the largest chromosome number occurring in it (Denver Report, 1960; London Report, 1963) or by a capital letter (Patau, 1960; London Report, 1963). Thus "group 13–15" is synonymous with "D group." The letter symbols have the advantage of brevity. It is certainly clumsy to speak of "a chromosome of group 13–15" or of "a translocation (13–15)/(21–22)" when the same can be expressed by "a D chromosome" or "a D/G translocation." When a symbol for a translocation chromosome is to be inscribed into a karyotype or the photograph of a mitosis, brevity becomes a necessity.[4]

It is embarrassingly trite to say that any nomenclature, let alone a scientific one, should be free of ambiguities and that a scientific publication should not leave the reader guessing about the meaning of terms and symbols, yet these principles have been neglected in human cyto-genetics on a scale for which it would be difficult to find a parallel in more mature branches of science. Thus it is plainly misleading when of two authors one, without qualification, speaks of 13 trisomy and the other, also without qualification, of 15 trisomy although both refer to the same chromosome and are perfectly aware that there is no evidence to show to which of the three pairs of its group this chromosome belongs. It is also misleading when in a karyotype two chromosomes are given the same number unless the author wants to claim that these chromosomes are in fact homologous or unless he states specifically that no such claim is intended. In the latter case, one wonders which purpose these numbers are meant to serve. It is assuredly not a scientific purpose.

The reader is entitled to know what an author means. It is therefore, and not for the first time, recommended that numbers or the symbols X and Y be ascribed to individual chromosomes only if the author is reasonably certain that he has identified them correctly. It follows that not all karyotypes can be labeled in the same way. For instance, if the pairs 21 and 22 are clearly distinguished, these chromosomes should be arranged in pairs and these should be given individual numbers; if not, the four chromosomes should be mounted equidistally and labeled G or

---

[4] Some authors are using Latin numbers for these same groups. This is not only in conflict with priority (such numbers have been used previously for a variety of group systems, none identical with the present one) but also has a practical disadvantage. To speak of a "C chromosome" is unambiguous, to speak of a "III chromosome" invites confusion with a chromosome 3.

21–22 as in Figs. 4 and 5. The use of preprinted forms for mounting karyotypes is also not practical for another reason. Chromosomes from different cells may have very different sizes, and a form that accommodates large chromosomes will waste a great deal of space in the case of small chromosomes. It may not be amiss to remind authors that space in publications is expensive and that editors appreciate an arrangement of the chromosomes of a karyotype that fills a rectangular area as completely as possible.

It has been proposed to label each chromosome or chromosome pair by both its number and its group symbol. This is redundant. The purpose of group symbols is only to designate chromosomes whose individual number is not known.

Individual chromosomes may be identified cytologically by at least three different criteria, to wit, by the lengths of their two arms with due allowance for differences in contraction, by secondary constrictions, and by autoradiographic labeling patterns. In addition, chromosomes may be identified, though in a very different sense, by phenotype, as for instance in cases of autosomal trisomy in which the presence of a certain syndrome specifies the extra chromosome even though the microscope may not yet have disclosed more than the group to which this chromosome belongs. This multiplicity of criteria used for identifying chromosomes can and did lead to confusing inconsistencies of nomenclature of which chromosome 21 furnishes probably the best example.

According to the oldest and still cytologically meaningful and widely accepted definition, 21 is the larger pair of G chromosomes (in practically all published karyotypes in which a larger and a smaller G pair can be distinguished, these are marked 21 and 22, respectively; see also Hungerford, 1964). There never had been any evidence that this is the mongolism chromosome; in fact, this seems now increasingly unlikely. However, at the time of the Denver convention it had appeared possible to base a new definition of 21 on the presence of satellites, and it appeared further that by this definition the mongolism chromosome would be 21. All this, of course, became meaningless when it was found that satellites occur at all G chromosomes. Rather than openly to drop an obsolete claim, some authors preferred to turn it into a definition of 21 by phenotype. In violation of priority, 21 was now to designate the chromosome that, in triplicate, causes mongolism. Unfortunately, many authors who speak of mongolism as of "21 trisomy" do not even explain whether they are merely using the phenotypical definition or whether they are making a claim concerning the cytological identity of the mongolism chromosome. There is only one antidote to this and similar instances of confusion: adherence to reasonable rules of priority. The word "reasonable" needs elaboration.

It would not be reasonable to sacrifice a generally accepted nomenclature to priority. It is therefore proposed that considerations of priority be applied only to questions that have been left unanswered by the London Report (1963), and that in such cases the oldest usage be adopted that is compatible with it. It would also not be reasonable to let priority stand in the way of real improvements of a given nomenclature, but it is certainly in keeping with scientific tradition to expect of authors who wish to bypass priority that they explain why they find this necessary.

Realistically, the London Report does not claim that all chromosomes can be identified, but it retains the numbers 1–22 and the symbols X and Y to be used as it becomes possible to identify individual chromosomes in karyotypes by any means available, including secondary constrictions and autoradiographs. However, the Report stipulates that the numbers should be given "as nearly as possible" according to length in descending order. This rule can and should be followed even if two or more pairs of the same group are first identified by a criterion other than length, for once they have been identified they also can be measured and then be numbered according to their mean lengths. It is in the interest of an unambiguous nomenclature that in such cases the identified chromosomes be given symbols other than numbers until the length relations have been clarified.

To ascribe a number to certain chromosomes according to phenotype and to others according to microscopic criteria is so incongruous as to invite the kind of confusion that has evolved around the mongolism chromosome. It is also a disservice to human cytogenetics to obscure semantically a neither unimportant nor unsolvable problem—how to identify by cytological means a phenotypically defined chromosome—by giving the chromosome one of the numbers that ordinarily designate chromosomes in karyotypes. Obviously, a chromosome for which as yet only a definition by phenotype exists ought to be given a symbol other than one of these numbers. Therman *et al.* (1961) proposed to use for this purpose the group symbol with a suffix. For instance, D_1 would represent the D chromosome responsible for the first syndrome that was found to be caused by trisomy for a D chromosome; G_1 (or possibly G_M) would stand for the mongolism chromosome.

IV. THE HUMAN COMPLEMENT

Group A: Chromosomes 1–3. The three pairs can easily be distinguished. In one arm of *chromosome 1,* a secondary constriction close to the centromere can often be seen in ordinary slides (Fig. 4) and with high frequency as result of special methods (p. 166, Fig. 5). This secondary constriction can serve to distinguish one arm from the other. In the Denver Report, chromosome 1 was listed as having an arm ratio of about 1.1, but this value is too biased to have any meaning (see Patau, 1960, p. 263). On the other hand, *chromosome 3* clearly has unequal arms, and this makes it possible to distinguish this chromosome fairly reliably from similar sized isochromosomes (in photographs, taken before autoradiography, of 16 cells in which I thought it possible to distinguish the chromosomes 3 from an isochromosome derived from the long arm of D_1, autoradiography revealed the distinction to be correct in 14 and erroneous in two cells—unpublished). At least in the case of isochromosomes derived from the long arms of an X or of D_1, that distinction is made very easy by autoradiography since both these isochromosomes have typically very little label around the centromere when the distal regions are already heavily labeled. In the same cells, the chromosomes 3 have on the average much less label and display this in a quite different pattern, as typically shown in the present Fig. 6A and also in Fig. 6 of Schmid (1963).

Group B: Chromosomes 4–5. Autoradiography of metaphases from a *cri-du-chat* patient (Patau *et al.,* 1964a and unpublished) made a reliable determination of the labeling pattern of the B chromosomes possible since the partially deleted short arm (as first described by Lejeune *et al.,* 1963) served as marker for one of the four B chromosomes. In about 21 of 26 cells, these chromosomes showed differences in labeling that separated two pairs from each other, with the deletion chromosome always belonging to the less heavily labeled pair. The labeling patterns having been established (see below), eight cells from several persons with a normal B group were selected for showing these autoradiographic patterns with special clarity as well as for having all B chromosomes well displayed. These were measured as reported on p. 159. The observed mean differences in length and arm ratio ($0.06 \pm 0.16\,\mu$ and 0.019 ± 0.058, respectively) are so insignificant that all hope of ever being able to distinguish 4 and 5 by length and/or by arm ratio must be given up. Indeed, we may never know which of the two pairs is on the average slightly larger: to find this out would probably require too large a number of measurements to be worth the effort. It is therefore proposed to base the definition of these chromosomes entirely on the autoradiographic patterns.

Definition of chromosomes 4 and 5: On the average, 4 as a whole terminates DNA synthesis considerably later than 5; the distal region of the long arm of 4 probably terminates it slightly later than the rest of the chromosome; in 5 the short arm terminates DNA synthesis appreciably later than the rest (cf. Fig. 6B).

Variation obscures the labeling pattern within 4 very often, that within 5 sometimes. Sometimes, too, does the over-all amount of label in a chromosome 5 approach that in a chromosome 4 of the same cell, but in such cases the labeling patterns within chromosomes may still suffice for identification. I have never seen a chromosome 5 exceeding a chromosome 4 of the same cell in over-all labeling: this is probably a rare event.

Both the foregoing definition and the remarks about variation apply about equally well to metaphases that have only a light or medium amount of over-all label as to those that are, within the limits of the usable, heavily labeled. The differences seen between a, b, and c in Fig. 7 of Schmid (1963) have in my opinion little to do with the nucleus having been in an "early," "intermediate," or "late" stage of DNA synthesis, but represent selected deviates from the average pattern: Schmid's Fig. 7b comes close to the latter, Fig. 7a differs from it in that in both chromosomes 5 there is somewhat more label in the long than in the short arm, whereas his Fig. 7c is so atypical that one can but guess that the lower pair (because of the label in the long arm) represents 4, which in Figs. a and b occupies the higher position.

According to the definition proposed here, the *cri-du-chat* chromosome is derived from a chromosome 5. The deleted segment of the short arm is on the average relatively heavily labeled when observed in the normal partner. The normal chromosome 5 and the *cri-du-chat* chromosome appear to have the same average labeling pattern in their long arms.

Group C: Autosomes 6–12 and At Least One X Chromosome. It will be best to discuss first the one chromosome in this group that can be identified by a well-established secondary constriction, which is none too rarely visible even in ordinary slides (Fig. 4) and can be produced with a high frequency of manifestation by special methods (see p. 166). Since in previously published karyotypes this autosome had been given any of the numbers from 7 through 10, not to speak of the symbol X, Patau (1961) proposed to escape this confusion by calling it "C'." Most authors now designate it by the number 9. Unfortunately, they also apply this number to the ninth largest of the presumed autosome pairs in metaphases in which the secondary constriction of C' is not visible. This is evidently based on the observation that a C' with a visible constriction occupies more or less the ninth place and on the assumption that the manifestation of the secondary constriction has no effect on the length of C'. This assumption, however, is quite unjustified as pointed out above (p. 170) : without a visible secondary constriction, C' usually does not rank the ninth place (Fig. 5). The interchangeable use of two unrelated definitions of chromosome 9, by secondary constriction or by length, has resulted in the number 9 being applied to different chromosomes depending on the manifestation of the secondary constriction. It would seem best to retain the unambiguous symbol C'.[5]

Once both chromosomes C' are recognized, they can often be used to separate pair 12, which has the smallest short arms, from the rest of the C group (Figs. 4 and 6C). Sometimes, it may be possible to identify pair 6, but I cannot go along with assertions that in first-rate slides this identification can usually be made. As a rule, there are still other possible partners for the presumed chromosomes 6, and as long as such other possibilities exist one ought not to claim an identification. Perhaps the identification of C chromosomes can occasionally be carried still further, but I have yet to see the karyotype in which there is only one plausible way of pairing off all 15 or 16 C chromosomes. The criticism by Patau (1960, 1961) of earlier claims that all C chromosomes had been identified is in my opinion still valid and relevant, but it need not be reviewed here since the discovery of the late-replicating X (German, 1962; Gilbert et al., 1962; Morishima et al., 1962) has made a direct test of such claims possible. So did the discovery by Saksela and Moorhead (1962) that certain methods of preparation will cause the late-labeling X to betray its identity by a peculiarly fuzzy appearance (see Fig. 5).

---

[5] Schmid (1963) accepts "Sasaki and Makino's finding of two (C) pairs . . . having heterochromatic bands near the proximal ends of the long arm" (in my opinion, this claim is insufficiently documented) and relates it to de la Chapelle's (1961) conclusion that there are two pairs of constricted C chromosomes. However, the two chromosomes of this kind in de la Chapelle's Fig. 3 agree very well in the lengths of the short arm and of the isopycnotic region of the long arm. They are clearly two chromosomes C' illustrating the magnitude of the length differences that can result from the length variation of the secondary constriction.

It soon became obvious that the late-replicating X is on the average definitely one of the medium-sized rather than one of the largest C chromosomes (Fig. 6C), although in nearly all published karyotypes in which the X chromosomes are "identified" both belong to the largest C chromosomes (they still do—but then, what are facts compared with tradition). It is clear then that the pairing off method in the hands of practically everybody who tried it, identified at least one X chromosome in the female karyotype wrongly. It is in the nature of that method as applied to the C group that a wrong identification of a single chromosome by necessity will throw off the identification of at least one other chromosome and more likely of several. One might have thought that this debacle would have discredited the method. But no, it has still been used in all seriousness to show that at least the non-late-replicating X is one of the longest C chromosomes. Thus a method that originally failed quite consistently to reveal a length difference between X chromosomes of the same metaphase is now called upon to prove that a sizeable difference exists. Actually, in my experience it is not at all difficult to find in such cases a non-late-replicating C of about equal size that will match the late-replicating X chromosome or chromosomes well enough (Fig. 6C). This is hardly conclusive, but certainly no less so than the kind of "evidence" upon which the assertion is based that the two types of X chromosomes differ in average length.

There is still another assertion that is sometimes mentioned as a well-known fact, but for which there is no evidence. It is the claim that the X, or at least the late-replicating X, varies more in length than similar autosomes. Boyes (1961) has reported an above-normal length variation for the X chromosome of the house fly. The so-called evidence for this also holding true in man rests entirely upon the reliability of the pairing off method being perfect, which in the C group it obviously is not. Then there is the observation that occasionally the late-replicating X is among the largest or among the smallest C chromosomes, which again proves nothing unless it can be shown that this goes beyond the length variation found in autosomes. There is no reason to think that it does. The coefficient of length variation had been estimated to be 5.3% in large chromosomes (p. 155), and there is no basis for assuming that this relative standard deviation is any smaller in medium-sized chromosomes. Let the chromosome length in the C group range from 4.2 to 5.6%, a range given by two of the contributors of Table II in the Denver Report (1960). Assume further, plausibly, that chromosome length variation is approximately normal. It can then easily be computed that a single autosome with a mean length from the middle of the range would be larger than at least one member of the largest C pair in about 5.7% of cases and would equally often be smaller than at least one member of the smallest C pair. There is nothing to indicate that the length variation of an X chromosome amounts to more than that.

Patau (1960) developed a method by means of which an unbiased estimate of the length and arm ratio of the X can be computed from measurements of the C chromosomes in a sufficient number of male and female cells. This method rests upon the assumption, still tenable though unproved, that the average length of all X chromosomes in males and females is the same. The actual computation was based on too small a sample, but it is noteworthy that the obtained estimates agreed fairly well with later autoradiographic results both in regard to length and to arm ratio.

Group D: Chromosomes 13–15. These chromosomes, although at best medium-sized, are sometimes called the "large" acrocentrics in contradistinction to the small acrocentrics of the G group. The short arms of the D chromosomes are on the average somewhat larger than those of the G chromosomes, but are otherwise of similar appearance. It will be pointed out below that in regard to the short G arms there is a great deal of polymorphism among normal persons. It will be prudent to take the possibility seriously of this holding true for the short D arms also. In view of this, it would seem inadvisable to base the identification of D chromosomes even in part upon the appearance of their short arms. The length of their long arms, at least when taken by itself, is an equally useless criterion. From the six sets of measurements given in Table II of the Denver Report, the mean length difference between the two longest pairs of D chromosomes is computed as 5.4% of their mean length; the corresponding value for the two shortest pairs is 4.6%. Considering that these differences must have a standard deviation of about $5.3 \sqrt{2} = 7.5\%$, it should be clear that any pairing off of D chromosomes according to the length of the long arm is an exercise in futility. It might be added that an unbiased determination of these differences, if it were possible, would probably yield still smaller values.

The chromosome D_1 is phenotypically defined by the well-known trisomy syndrome. It has recently become possible to identify this chromosome also cytologically by means of autoradiography with tritiated thymidine: D_1 is on the average the latest replicating of the D chromosomes, except that the centromere region is fairly early labeling. The evidence is conclusive, identical results having been obtained in studies on two D_1 trisomics (Yunis *et al.*, 1964b), on a familial case of nonhomologous D_1/D translocation (Yunis *et al.*, 1964a), on another D_1 translocation (Giannelli, 1964), and on the two D_1 marker chromosomes mentioned above (p. 171). These studies further indicated that the other two D pairs also differ from each other in their average labeling patterns, one being very early replicating. It should now be possible, with proper statistical precautions, to obtain unbiased estimates of the mean lengths of the three D pairs as identified by autoradiography and on this basis to define the pairs 13 through 15. The symbol D_1 would then become superfluous.

Group E: Chromosomes 16–18. Chromosome 16 is very easily identified. Saksela and Moorhead (1962) and, independently, Sasaki and Makino (1963) detected a secondary constriction in its long arm near the centromere (see Fig. 5). Heritable polymorphism for this chromosome in phenotypically normal persons has been reported, but significant differences between the two chromosomes 16 are in my experience not exactly common.

The pairs 17 and 18 are very similar. The long arm of 17 is slightly larger than that of 18, but this is a much less reliable criterion of distinction than the size of the short arm, which is considerably smaller in 18 than in 17 (see also the relevant remarks on p. 164). Having by now seen quite a few trisomic metaphases which by this criterion showed conclusively three chromosomes 18 (as for instance in Fig. 3) and having never seen one with three unmistakable chromosomes 17, I have come to regard the question of trisomy 17 or 18 as settled. However, Yunis *et al.* (1964c) have used the fact that 18 is the latest replicating of the E chromosomes to confirm by autoradiography that the chromosome responsible for the well-known trisomy syndrome is indeed 18.

Group F: Chromosomes 19–20. The two pairs are so similar that a reliable distinction between them according to size may be impossible.

Group G: Autosomes 21–22 and the Y Chromosomes. All are acrocentric. In most suitable metaphases, the Y can readily be distinguished from the G autosomes by one or the other of the following criteria. They are listed more or less in order of descending usefullness.

(i) The chromatids of the Y tend to remain associated throughout their length when those of the G (and other) autosomes start, under the influence of colchicine or the like, to fall apart except at the centromere (Fig. 4).

(ii) The Y has a secondary constriction which was discovered independently by Saksela and Moorhead (1962) and by Sasaki and Makino (1963), both groups of authors having used a special method. In ordinary slides, this constriction is rarely seen really well, but it seems to manifest itself in an irregular outline which often is diagnostic for this chromosome, especially in dried-on preparations. In a normal, full-sized Y, the secondary constriction is located in the middle of the long arm.

(iii) At least in Feulgen squash preparations, the distal half of the normal metaphase Y is often negatively heteropycnotic, appearing faded and diffuse in striking contradistinction to the ends of the long arms of autosomal G chromosomes (Fig. 4).

(iv) The centromere region, including the short arms, of the Y tends to be more compact and thicker than the same region in G autosomes (Fig. 4). It is probably for this reason that the metaphase Y has been called (positively) heteropycnotic.

(v) Not having satellites, the Y never participates in the so-called satellite association that is so common among autosomal G and D acrocentrics.

The full-sized Y exceeds the G autosomes somewhat in length, although possibly not in DNA content, but shorter Y chromosomes are quite common among what seem to be phenotypically normal males. Even the deletion of practically the whole distal half of the long arm does not seem to have a recognizable effect upon the phenotype. At any rate, selection against certain classes of partial Y chromosome deletion must have been weak to make the substantial amount of Y polymorphism possible that has been noted by many cytogeneticists. Because of this, the identification of the Y should not even in part be based on its length unless the size of the Y in the male under investigation has already been established.

A high degree of polymorphism in normal populations exists also in regard to the G autosomes. This is well known as far as the satellites go, but undoubtedly it also holds true for the whole short arms and probably even for small proximal regions of the long arm. Some persons have two well-defined G pairs: 21 having a somewhat larger long arm than 22 and a far from negligible short arm as compared with the extremely tiny short arm of 22 (Fig. 6D). In most persons such a clear separation into two pairs is lacking (the G autosomes of Figs. 4 and 5 fall into this category), and it does not even seem that the size difference between the long arms is consistently present. Certainly there is very considerable variation between normal persons in regard to the size of the short arm in different G autosomes. In one person, I have even seen two G chromosomes with larger long arms carrying smaller short arms than the other pair. In view of this polymorphism, it is hardly surprising that as yet no metaphase has been found that would conclusively show whether the mongolism chromosome belongs to the smaller or larger G pair. The most suggestive pictures, published (e.g., Barnicot *et al.,* 1963, Plate 2) or unpublished, of the G group of mongoloids still add up to no more than an impression that the extra chromosome belongs to the smaller pair.

There is of course the disturbing question of whether, even in cases of two morphologically well distinguished G pairs as described above as 21 and 22, these are always pairs of homologs. This question can be answered by collecting two kinds of evidence. One consists of G bivalents in the spermatogenesis of males with a large and a small G pair. I know to date of only one usable case of this kind: Fig. 1 in the paper by Ford and Hamerton (1956) shows the two smallest G autosomes forming one bivalent, the two largest the other. The second kind of potentially decisive evidence consists of autoradiographs of the chromosomes of persons who have morphologically well distinguished G pairs. Figure 6D is the only useful picture of this kind I have as yet been able to obtain, but this is so exceptionally clear that the distribution of label seems unlikely to be merely a statistical fluke. It would thus appear that, in persons whose G chromosomes form two clear pairs 21 and 22 as described above, these are indeed pairs of homologs and that the smaller pair 22 is late replicating relative to 21.

Whether this tentative conclusion should prove correct or not, autoradiography could probably be relied upon to establish homology in the case of insufficient morphological separation of G pairs. If the smaller G pair should indeed be late replicating, mongolism would represent 22 trisomy, since the mongolism chromosome was late replicating in the case discussed above (p. 171). The cytological identity of the mongolism chromosome is not likely to remain in doubt for long.

Addendum

Since this article went to press, I have seen unpublished results by Dr. J. J. Yunis that go far toward showing that the mongolism chromosome is indeed No. 22. His evidence strongly supports the above tentative conclusion that 22 is relatively late replicating, and it confirms that the mongolism chromosome is late replicating.

Acknowledgments

Work reported herein was supported by grant no. HD 00338 from the National Institutes of Health, U. S. Public Health Service. This is paper No. 1001 from the Genetics Division, University of Wisconsin.

References

Barnicot, N. A., Ellis, J. R., and Penrose, L. S. (1963). Translocation and trisomic mongol sibs. *Ann. Human Genet. (London)* **26**, 279–285.

Boyes, J. W. (1961). Human X-chromosome arm ratios and percentages of total complement length. *Am. J. Human Genet.* **13**, 104–105.

Cooper, H. L., and Hirschhorn, K. (1962). Enlarged satellites as a familial chromosome marker. *Am. J. Human Genet.* **14**, 107–124.

de la Chapelle, A. (1961). Constrictions in normal human chromosomes. *Lancet* II, 460–462.

Denver Report (1960). A proposed standard system of nomenclature of human mitotic chromosomes. *Lancet* I, 1063–1065.

Ford, C. E., and Hamerton, J. L. (1956). The chromosomes of man. *Nature* **178**, 1020–1023.

German, J. L. (1962). DNA synthesis in human chromosomes. *Trans. N.Y. Acad. Sci.* **24**, 395–407.

Giannelli, F. (1964). Deoxyribonucleic-acid replication pattern of trisomy D_1. *Lancet* II, 1068.

Gilbert, C. W., Muldal, S., Lajtha, L. G., and Rowley, J. (1962). Time-sequence of human chromosome duplication. *Nature* **195**, 869–873.

Hungerford, D. A. (1964). Observations on the morphology and behaviour of normal human chromosomes. *In* "Mammalian Cytogenetics and Related Problems in Radiobiology," pp. 133–155. Macmillan (Pergamon), New York.

Inhorn, S. L. (1964). Personal communication.

Inhorn, S. L., and Therman, E. (1964). Personal communication.

Kaback, M. M., Saksela, E., and Mellman, W. J. (1964). The effect of 5-bromode-oxyuridine on human chromosomes. *Exptl. Cell Res.* **34**, 182–186.

Lejeune, J. (1964). *In* "Somatic Cell Genetics," 4th Macy Conf. Genet. (R. S. Krooth, ed.). Univ. of Michigan Press, Ann Arbor, Michigan.

Lejeune, J., Lafourcade, J., Berger, R., Vialatte, J., Boeswillwald, M., Seringe, P., and Turpin, R. (1963). Trois cas de délétion partielle du bras court d'un chromosome 5. *Compt. Rend.* **257**, 3098-3102.

Levan, A., and Hsu, T. C. (1959). The human idiogram. *Hereditas* **45**, 665–674.

London Report (1963). The London Conference on the normal human karyotype. *Cytogenetics* **2**, 264–268.

Morishima, A., Grumbach, M. M., and Taylor, J. H. (1962). Asynchronous duplication of human chromosomes and the origin of sex chromatin. *Proc. Natl. Acad. Sci. U.S.* **48**, 756–763.

Patau, K. (1960). The identification of individual chromosomes, especially in man. *Am. J. Human Genet.* **12**, 250–276.

Patau, K. (1961). Chromosome identification and the Denver Report. *Lancet* **I**, 933–934.

Patau, K. (1964). *In:* "Somatic Cell Genetics," 4th Macy Conf. Genet. (R. S. Krooth, ed.). Univ. of Michigan Press, Ann Arbor, Michigan.

Patau, K., Therman, E., and Inhorn, S. L. (1964a). The identification of certain clinically important autosomes by autoradiography with tritiated thymidine. *Abstr. Ann. Meeting Am. Soc. Human Genet.* p. 20.

Patau, K., Inhorn, S. L., and Therman, E. (1964b). Unpublished data.

Patau, K., Therman, E., Inhorn, S. L., Smith, D. W., and Ruess, A. L. (1961). Partial-trisomy syndromes. II. An insertion as cause of the OFD syndrome in mother and daughter. *Chromosoma* (*Berlin*) **12**, 573–584.

Rothfels, K. H., and Siminovitch, L. (1958). The chromosome complement of the rhesus monkey (Macaca mulatta) determined in kidney cells cultivated in vitro. *Chromosoma* (*Berlin*) **9**, 163–175.

Salonius, A. L., and Opitz, J. M. (1964). Unpublished data.

Sasaki, M. S., and Makino, S. (1963). The demonstration of secondary constrictions in human chromosomes by means of a new technique. *Am. J. Human Genet.* **15**, 24–33.

Saksela, E., and Moorhead, P. S. (1962). Enhancement of secondary constrictions and the heterochromatic X in human cells. *Cytogenetics* **1**, 225–244.

Schmid, W. (1963). DNA replication patterns of human chromosomes. *Cytogenetics* **2**, 175–193.

Therman, E., Patau, K., Smith, D. W., and DeMars, R. I. (1961). The D trisomy syndrome and XO gonadal dysgenesis in two sisters. *Am. J. Human Genet.* **13**, 193–204.

Yunis, J. J., Alter, M., Hook, E. B., and Mayer, M. (1964a). Familial D ∼ D translocation. Report of a pedigree and DNA replication analysis. *New England J. Med.* **271**, 1133–1137.

Yunis, J. J., Hook, E. B., and Mayer, M. (1964b). Deoxyribonucleic-acid replication pattern of trisomy D_1. *Lancet* **II**, 935–937.

Yunis, J. J., Hook, E. B., and Mayer, M. (1964c). Deoxyribosenucleic-acid replication pattern of trisomy 18. *Lancet* **II**, 286–287.

Human Chromosomes in Disease

JORGE J. YUNIS

*Medical Genetics Laboratory, Department of Laboratory Medicine,
University of Minnesota, Minneapolis, Minnesota*

I.	Introduction	187
II.	Sex Chromosomal Abnormalities	189
	A. Klinefelter's Syndrome	189
	B. Turner's Syndrome	194
	C. XO/XY Mosaicism	200
	D. True Hermaphroditism	200
	E. Trisomy, Tetrasomy, and Pentasomy X	204
	F. Y Chromosome Abnormalities	207
III.	Autosomal Chromosome Abnormalities	209
	A. Trisomy G_1, Trisomy 21, Mongolism, or Down's Syndrome	210
	B. Trisomy 18 Syndrome	219
	C. Trisomy D_1 Syndrome	222
	D. Triploidy	228
	E. Tetraploidy and Octoploidy	229
	F. Other Autosomal Congenital Abnormalities	229
IV.	Chromosomes in Malignant Diseases	230
	A. Malignant Tumors and Acute Leukemias	231
	B. Chronic Myelogenous Leukemia	231
	C. Waldenström Macroglobulinemia	232
V.	Diseases with a Normal Chromosome Complement	233
VI.	Conclusion	233
	References	235

I. INTRODUCTION

Tjio and Levan (1956), definitely established that human somatic cells normally have 46 chromosomes. Their use of colchicine and hypotonic solution treatment of cells grown in culture was quickly adopted by other workers. The biological and clinical significance of this technique became apparent when Lejeune *et al.* (1959) demonstrated a specific chromosomal abnormality in mongolism, and this finding was followed by the study of chromosome patterns in a variety of clinical disorders. The significance of previous studies on the sex chromatin in cases of Turner's (Polani *et al.*, 1954; Wilkins *et al.*, 1954) and Klinefelter's syndromes (Bradbury *et al.*, 1956; Plunkett and Barr, 1956) was demonstrated when it was shown that sex chromatin-negative Turner's syndrome has an XO sex chromosome constitution (Ford *et al.*, 1959b) and sex chromatin-positive Klinefelter's syndrome has an XXY sex complement (Jacobs and Strong, 1959). It was soon realized that in the diploid somatic cells the number of sex chromatin bodies is one less than the number of X chromosomes present. On the basis of this observation, large-scale screening of buccal smears has been performed in an attempt to estimate the incidence of X chromosomal anomalies in newborns and institutionalized patients.

Within a few years an extraordinarily wide range of X chromosomal abnormalities have been discovered. It appears that this is in part due to the fact that although all viable zygotes seem to require at least one X chromosome, the genetic expression of any additional X chromosome material is quite small (Lyon, 1962; Grumbach *et al.*, 1963). Autosomal chromosome abnormalities have also been documented in a small number of chromosomes. The relative scarcity of abnormalities is probably related to a deleterious effect of autosomal trisomies and monosomies upon development (Patau, 1963a).

Large-scale screening studies suggest that approximately 0.4–0.6% of all live-born Caucasians (Maclean *et al.*, 1964; Marden *et al.*, 1964) bear a chromosomal abnormality. The true incidence of chromosomal aberrations will not be known until a systematic and detailed chromosome analysis is done on a large number of newborns. Although the information derived from such a study would be invaluable, the effort and time involved in accumulating a large enough sample would be considerable.

It should be borne in mind that most of the case reports and large-scale screening data have involved Caucasian populations. Therefore, the incidence figures may not be applicable to other ethnic groups. It is well known, for instance, that elevated maternal age is associated with an increased incidence of the various trisomies known in man, and non-Caucasian mothers generally bear children at a younger age. Similarly, environmental influences such as exposure to radiation, socioeconomic factors, or disease in the parents may play a less obvious but significant role in the frequency of chromosomal abnormalities.

Knowledge contributed by human cytogenetics may be of value in the general field of genetics: chromosome and sex chromatin studies are being used in the evaluation of homotransplantation barriers (Peer, 1958; Woodruff and Lennox, 1959); in the study of dosage compensation as implicated in Lyon's (1962) hypothesis; in the study of drug effect (Chèvremont, 1961) and radiation (Bender and Gooch, 1963) on mitosis; in the study of chromosome mapping (Lindsten, 1963); and in the study of mammalian cell genetics in tissue culture (Moorhead, 1962).

The field of human cytogenetics has grown so rapidly in the last few years that only a brief survey of the significant data can be accomplished in this chapter. Cytogenetics as it pertains to clinical problems will be emphasized, and variations of the main chromosome genotypes will be stressed because these patterns provide knowledge of fundamental biological significance.

II. SEX CHROMOSOMAL ABNORMALITIES

At the early stages of the human chromosome study, it was hoped that sex chromosomal aberrations would sharply define disease entities such as Turner's syndrome, Klinefelter's syndrome, and true hermaphroditism. The last few years of investigation in this field have revealed such an impressive array of genotypes and phenotypes for each of the clinical entities mentioned that some confusion has arisen. The data collected are vast, not always comparable or acceptable, and still incomplete. Nevertheless, enough cases have been reported to support some tentative conclusions concerning the role of the X and Y chromosomes in certain sex anomalies.

As the sex chromosomes behave differently from autosomes (see Barr's chapter), it is important to consider their phenotypic effects separately. Like autosomal chromosome aberrations, sex chromosomal abnormalities can be either numerical or structural, and this is important to remember when studying the phenotypic effects that they produce.

The clinical entities studied and the examples given have been selected to illustrate general principles.

A. KLINEFELTER'S SYNDROME

In 1942, Klinefelter *et al.* described a syndrome in postpubertal males consisting of: small testes with tubular hyalinization (testicular dysgenesis), azoospermia, gynecomastia, high concentrations of urinary gonadotropins, and low concentrations of urinary 17-keto steroids. Several years later, Bradbury *et al.* (1956) and Plunkett and Barr (1956) noted chromatin-positive nuclei in the tissues of such patients, and Jacobs and

Strong (1959) reported a case of chromatin-positive Klinefelter's syndrome with 47 chromosomes and an XXY sex chromosome complement. Since then, all patients reported with bilateral testicular dysgenesis and primary micro-orchidism, associated with sex chromatin-positive nuclei, have had an XXY sex chromosome complement (Fig. 1) or one of its variants.[1]

The most constant clinical observation in adult males with Klinefelter's syndrome is *primary micro-orchidism*. Other frequent but not invariable findings have been gynecomastia, diminished abdominal and facial hair, oligospermy, infertility, small phallus, small prostate, mental deficiency, psychiatric disorders, and eunuchoid habitus. The syndrome appears to be at least three to six times more common among mentally subnormal males than among those of average intelligence (Kaplan, 1961), and accounts for approximately 10 per 1000 institutionalized mentally defective males (Maclean *et al.*, 1962; Ferguson-Smith, 1958).

Although some cases with normal spermatogenesis have been noted and an exceptional case has been presumed to be fertile (Warburg, 1963), sterility is the rule. Thus, it is not surprising that Ferguson-Smith *et al.* (1957) found 3% of all males attending an infertility clinic and 11% of patients with extreme oligospermy or azoospermia to be chromatin positive.

The clinical findings in prepubertal patients are more variable. As some of the findings in the adult appear to be due to testicular failure, the syndrome is not readily apparent in children. However, in many children, micro-orchidism or small phallus may become apparent at an early age. Mental retardation, if it develops, is conspicuous before puberty (Ferguson-Smith, 1959).

1. Chromosome Patterns in Klinefelter's Syndrome

a. XXY Sex Complement. The frequency of chromatin-positive male newborns is 1.96–3.10 per 1000 (Caucasian) live births (Maclean *et al.*, 1964; Marden *et al.*, 1964). The XXY pattern would appear to be frequent, but no statistically significant figures are available on the proportion

---

[1] A variety of genotypes have been described in cases of Klinefelter's syndrome, among which have been found XXY/XX and XXY/XY mosaics, and XXY cases with additional X chromosomes. Regardless of the chromosome constitution, it is presumed that the common denominator of all cases, XXY, is basically responsible for the development of testicular dysgenesis.

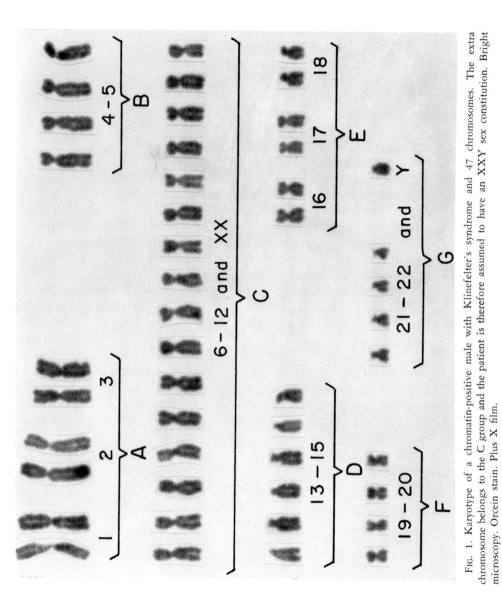

Fig. 1. Karyotype of a chromatin-positive male with Klinefelter's syndrome and 47 chromosomes. The extra chromosome belongs to the C group and the patient is therefore assumed to have an XXY sex constitution. Bright microscopy. Orcein stain. Plus X film.

which have an XXY karyotype, an XXY mosaic pattern, or XXXY or XXXXY sex complement.

Histological analyses of the testes of postpubertal patients with Klinefelter's syndrome have shown an apparent marked increase in Leydig cells which are frequently clumped together. Most of the seminiferous tubules are hyalinized and small (so-called "ghost" tubules) without elastic fibers, although occasional immature tubules lined exclusively by Sertoli cells are seen. In addition, rare tubules have spermatogenesis, accounting for the presence of a low number of spermatozoids in the semen of some patients.

Before puberty, the testicular picture is more variable. Grumbach (1961) mentioned a chromatin-positive premature boy whose testes were normal. Also, a 3-month-old chromatin-positive boy was found to have a small phallus, normal sized testes, and unremarkable testicular histology (personal observation). Deoxyribonucleic acid (DNA) replication study of leucocyte cells showed 47 chromosomes with late-replicating X and Y chromosomes, such as found with XXY cells.[2] Two 10-month-old boys with positive buccal smears lacked germ cells but the tubules were of normal size (Grumbach, 1961). Older children may show immature tubules with a normal number of Leydig cells (Ferguson-Smith, 1959), but by puberty the tubules become sclerosed. The testicular material, regardless of the age of the patient, has been found to possess sex chromatin bodies and its examination is important in ambiguous cases.

The usual explanation for the occurrence of cases with XXY karyotype is meiotic nondisjunction. Studies using deutan color blindness and the Xg[a] blood type as markers have shown that, in most cases, both X's come from the mother (Nowakowski et al., 1959; Frøland et al., 1963; Ferguson-Smith et al., 1964). A few cases of paternal nondisjunction have also been described (Ferguson-Smith et al., 1964). Maternal age has been found to be slightly elevated above the mean (Ferguson-Smith et al., 1964).

b. XXXY and XXXXY Klinefelter's Syndrome. It is well known that each sex chromatin mass represents a highly condensed and at least partly inactivated X chromosome, and the number of chromatin masses is one less than the total of X chromosomes. The presence of extra X chromosomes in patients with Klinefelter's syndrome increases the severity

---

[2] It is well known that X chromosomes in excess of one and the Y chromosome manifest late DNA replication (German, 1962; Schmid, 1963).

of the testicular lesion and the incidence and degree of mental retardation. Therefore, individuals with an XXXY sex complement are more affected than those with an XXY sex chromosome constitution but less involved than those with an XXXXY pattern, and there are no specific somatic defects that would enable one to diagnose the XXXY pattern clinically. On the other hand, patients with an XXXXY genotype show additional features that perhaps warrant clinical differentiation as a distinct entity. Patients with an XXXXY genotype present a marked degree of mental retardation, genital hypoplasia, and numerous skeletal anomalies of which the most constant has been proximal radial-ulnar synostosis. Hypertelorism, strabismus, epicanthic folds, and mongoloid slanting of the palpebral tissues have been found in several patients (Scherz and Roeckel, 1963). High arched palate or cleft palate, simian lines, and clinodactyly have also been noted in about half the reported patients. It is interesting that there is a high incidence of genital anomalies aside from micro-orchidism: undescended testes, small penis, and underdeveloped testicles have been seen frequently. Testicular biopsy has shown hypoplastic tubules without spermatogenesis in three patients, aged 7, 8, and 21 years (Fraccaro *et al.*, 1960a; Miller *et al.*, 1961; Von Anders *et al.*, 1960) and a normal testicular picture in a patient $7\frac{1}{2}$ months old (Barr *et al.*, 1962).

As to the origin of XXXXY or XXXY individuals, it is believed that they are generally the product of a double nondisjunction that may have occurred during oogenesis. If nondisjunction occurs during the first meiotic division and again during the second meiotic division, a gamete with an XXXX or XXX sex complement may be formed, depending on whether all four X chromosomes segregate together or whether only three do so. Fertilization with a normal sperm will then produce an XXXXY or XXXY (or XXXXX or XXXX) zygote.

c. Mosaicism. Several patients with Klinefelter's syndrome have been found to have two or more chromosomally distinct cell populations. In each of these individuals one of the cell populations generally has an XXY, XXXY, or XXXXY sex chromosome constitution. As examples of mosaicism in Klinefelter's syndrome, the following are cited: XY/XXY (Sandberg, 1961); XX/XXY (Ford *et al.*, 1959c); XXY/XXxY[3] (Crawfurd, 1961); XXXY/XXXXY, XY/XXY/XXYY (Maclean *et al.*, 1962); XXXY/XXXXY/XXXXYY (Gilbert-Dreyfus *et al.*, 1963). It appears that the clinical expression of these Klinefelter mosaics

---

[3] x = Presumed deletion of an X chromosome segment.

depends on the type of sex constitution present at a critical time of development. The patient described by Barr *et al.* (1962) with XY/XXXY mosaicism illustrates this point, since the patient was mentally deficient but had normal testes and secondary sexual characteristics. In this case it is presumed that the normal XY cells were mostly responsible for the differentiation of the gonads and the XXXY cells in some way affected the development of the central nervous system. Thus, it is theoretically possible to find, for example, an XY/XXY mosaic who is phenotypically normal, provided the XY cells exerted the predominant genetic effect. It is important to bear this possibility in mind when trying to predict the development of testicular dysgenesis and the mental status of newborn males with sex chromatin-positive buccal smears. This is particularly noteworthy because many newborn males with chromatin-positive buccal smears are mosaics (Maclean *et al.,* 1964; Marden *et al.,* 1964).[4]

2. Testicular Tubules Failure with Normal Sex Complement

Before chromosome analysis was available, many cases were diagnosed as Klinefelter's syndrome on the basis of clinical findings, although their sex chromatin patterns were male. These cases were known as examples of chromatin-negative Klinefelter's syndrome. Clinically and histologically they are much more variable than the cases of Klinefelter's syndrome as defined above and include patients with infectious or traumatic orchitis, radiation-induced testicular atrophy, cryptorchidism, idiopathic testicular atrophy, and germinal-cell aplasia or Del Castillo's (Del Castillo *et al.,* 1947) syndrome (Segal and Nelson, 1957; Stewart *et al.,* 1959; Ferguson-Smith *et al.,* 1960b, 1963).

B. TURNER'S SYNDROME

In 1938, Turner described a syndrome in postpubertal females consisting of sexual infantilism, short stature, webbed neck, and cubitus valgus. Albright *et al.* (1942) showed that these patients had an elevated urinary excretion of gonadotropins, and Wilkins and Fleischmann (1944) described "streak" gonads devoid of ovarian follicles in such cases. Polani *et al.* (1954) and Wilkins *et al.* (1954) demonstrated that most cases are chromatin negative, and Ford *et al.* (1959b) described an XO karyotype in a patient affected with Turner's syndrome.

Clinical and laboratory evaluation of these patients has shown that

---

[4] It should also be noted that a sex chromatin-negative buccal smear does not necessarily rule out Klinefelter's syndrome because an XXY pattern may be found elsewhere in the body (Sandberg, 1961).

many additional abnormalities occur frequently but not invariably in this syndrome (Polani, 1961, 1962; Lemli and Smith, 1963; Lindsten, 1963). This variation in phenotype has led to some confusion concerning the nomenclature. Since the most ubiquitous features are short stature, gonadal dysgenesis,[5] and an X monosomy[6] or partial loss of X chromosomal material, all patients with these features are classified here as instances of Turner's syndrome. Cases with streak gonads and sexual infantilism, but of normal or high stature and normal female or male sex chromosome complement will be referred to as examples of "pure gonadal dysgenesis" (Polani, 1961).

The diagnosis of Turner's syndrome is usually more evident after puberty, owing to primary amenorrhea and sexual infantilism. In female children, unexplained short stature, congenital lymphedema, low birth weight, and other associated anomalies suggest the diagnosis, and a chromatin-negative buccal smear is confirmative, although a positive buccal smear does not exclude the possibility, since mosaicism or structural abnormality of the X chromosome may be present.

In most cases the histological pattern of the dysgenetic gonad found in Turner's syndrome consists of wavy connective tissue, absence of follicles, and sometimes large clear "hilus cells" (streak gonads). The presence of gonadal dysgenesis is frequently presumed from impalpable adnexae, elevated follicle stimulating hormone (FSH) levels, and sexual infantilism.

Occasionally, ovarian development and menstruation are noted (Lindsten and Tillinger, 1962; Bahner et al., 1960; Greenblatt, 1958).

Turner's syndrome appears to be one of the rarer chromosomal anomalies, occurring in 0.4 per 1000 female births (Maclean et al., 1964). If no major congenital defect is present, the life's span is presumably normal.

1. Chromosome Patterns in Turner's Syndrome

a. X Monosomy. Patients with an XO sex complement appear to make up the largest proportion of cases with Turner's syndrome (Lindsten,

---

[5] Gonadal dysgenesis is defined here as an undifferentiated gonad, as seen in cases of XO Turner's syndrome and "pure gonadal dysgenesis." If definite follicles and ova are seen in an otherwise undifferentiated gonad, the term ovarian dysgenesis should be used.

[6] Individuals bearing 45 normal chromosomes with only one sex (X) chromosome are said to have an X monosomy or an XO sex constitution. Individuals having more than one cell population, one of which has an XO sex complement, are called XO mosaics.

1963). Furthermore, they appear to be more severely affected clinically than other cases. Coarctation of the aorta, neck webbing, epicanthic folds, and congenital lymphedema have been reported as occurring more frequently in this group (Lindsten, 1963).

The mechanism of formation of the XO sex constitution is speculative. Use of deutan color blindness (Ferguson-Smith and Johnston, 1960; Lennox, 1961) and the Xg^a blood type as markers (Lindsten, 1963) has shown that most of the cases which could be analyzed had an X of maternal origin. Nevertheless, since matings that would reveal a paternally derived X chromosome are rare, the data are inconclusive (Lindsten, 1963; Patau, 1963a). Because parental age is not increased (Lindsten, 1963; Boyer *et al.*, 1961) and Turner's syndrome is rarer than Klinefelter's syndrome, a loss of a sex chromosome between fertilization and completion of the first cleavage has been suggested as a possible explanation (Patau, 1963a).

b. XO/XX Mosaicism. Many patients with Turner's syndrome have two different cell populations, one an XO sex constitution, and the other a normal XX sex complement. Such individuals are called XO/XX mosaics. The two cell population types may appear in every tissue of the body or only in certain ones. Because of this difference in cell population distribution, the study of chromosomes or sex chromatin in a single tissue does not necessarily give a complete answer.

Presumptive evidence for mosaicism lies in a discrepancy between sex chromatin pattern and karyotype, or through observing a low percentage of chromatin-positive nuclei in phenotypic females. Furthermore, it is possible to find no sex chromatin bodies in one tissue of a patient with XO/XX mosaicism (Ford, 1960; Fraccaro *et al.*, 1960b) so that cases of "chromatin-negative" Turner's syndrome do not necessarily have an X monosomy or XO karyotype. The clinical spectrum of XO/XX mosaicism is wide and may vary from cases quite typical of Turner's syndrome with many associated anomalies (Lindsten, 1963; de la Chapelle, 1962) to cases with normal gonads and normal stature (Harnden, 1964).

Cases reported as having either a typical XO or an XX sex complement with the characteristic phenotype of Turner's syndrome might actually be XO/XX mosaics. Two of the patients studied on the author's laboratory are illustrative. The first one, a typical Turner's syndrome with 23% sex chromatin masses in buccal smear (normal for females is 20–40%) also had a vaginal smear that revealed 21% sex chromatin masses. Twenty metaphase plates analyzed from blood and skin cultures showed that most of the cells had 46 chromosomes and an XX sex chromosome complement.

A careful analysis of 100 mitoses from a repeat blood sample 3 months later revealed that 11% of the cells had 45 chromosomes and a missing chromosome in the C group. DNA replication studies using tritiated thymidine conspicuously demonstrated the absence of a late-replicating X chromosome in almost all the cells with 45 chromosomes (Fig. 2).

The study of mosaicism might meet with technical difficulties since approximately 3–8% of metaphase plates from blood or marrow preparations show broken cells with an artificial number. Technical difficulties thus may make it impossible to detect a small but clinically significant aberrant cell population.

The second patient studied was another clinically typical case of Turner's syndrome in whom 2% of sex chromatin masses were observed in repeated buccal smears, and the blood revealed an XO sex chromosome constitution in the 25 metaphase plates studied. Because the finding of 2% sex chromatin masses is likely to be associated with cells bearing two X chromosomes, a skin culture was performed. Twelve of 20 metaphase plates were found to have a normal chromosome constitution while 8 had 45 chromosomes with an absent X chromosome.

Sometimes, cases of mosaicism are strongly suspected but careful studies fail to detect it, e.g., the exceptional XO chromatin-negative female of short stature who gave birth to a normal child. Chromosome studies from blood, marrow, and skin failed to show mosaicism (Bahner et al., 1960).

The usually accepted explanation for XO/XX mosaicism is loss of an X chromosome during cleavage in the early embryo. Difference in clinical patterns may be related to the time of loss and the particular tissues involved.

c. Isochromosome X. Some cases of Turner's syndrome exhibit a large metacentric chromosome that resembles an extra No. 3 chromosome. Such cases appear to lack one of the normal X chromosomes. The extra and large metacentric chromosome has been assumed to be an isochromosome for the long arm of the "missing" X chromosome.

Of 56 cases of Turner's syndrome reported by Lindsten (1963), two had such an isochromosome and nine others were X isochromosome X/XO mosaics. In those cases of an isochromosome X which are not mosaics, it would seem that all chromatin bodies are large, suggesting that the isochromosome forms the sex chromatin body. DNA replication patterns of the isochromosome appear to confirm this (Lindsten, 1963).[7]

---

[7] It is known that one of the two X chromosomes in a normal female remains condensed in interphase somatic nuclei (sex chromatin body) and shows a very

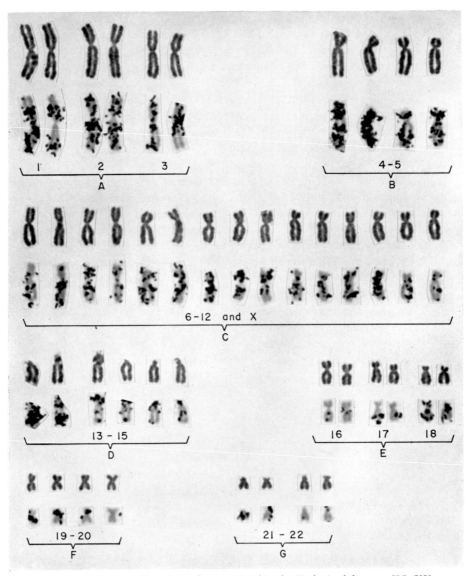

Fig. 2. Composite karyogram from an XO blood cell obtained from an XO/XX mosaic patient and exposed to tritiated thymidine for 5 hours. In each chromosome group the upper and lower rows represent chromosomes before and after autoradiography, respectively. Note the presence of 45 chromosomes and the absence of a late-replicating X chromosome. Other cells from this individual had 46 chromosomes and a typical late-replicating X, as observed in the group C of Fig. 12.

Preliminary evidence suggests that the isochromosome is of paternal origin. Studies of deutan color blindness and Xg[a] blood type imply that these genes are located on the short arm of the X chromosome (Lindsten, 1963).

d. Partial Loss of an X Chromosome. Presumed partial deletion of an X chromosome segment has been reported in a few patients with Turner's syndrome. Some have been reported to have a deletion of the short arm (Jacobs *et al.,* 1961) and others possibly of the long arm (Jacobs *et al.,* 1960), but the latter could conceivably be deletion of both the short and long arm, requiring a minimum of three chromosome breaks for its formation. Although there could be genes related to ovarian differentiation and body height in both the short and long arms of the X chromosome, it is possible that absence of the short arm of an X chromosome could well be the common denominator in all cases of Turner's syndrome.

e. Ring X Chromosome. The association of ring X chromosome and ovarian dysgenesis has been implicated in at least one instance (Lindsten and Tillinger, 1962; Lindsten, 1963). This chromosome seems to be formed by simple deletion of parts of both the short and long arms of the X chromosome with a subsequent fusion of the chromatid ends.

2. Ullrich's Syndrome

Polani (1961, 1962) has reported women with neck webbing and other anomalies often seen in Turner's syndrome, but with normal ovarian function, secondary sex characteristics, and presumably normal ovaries. These women have been chromatin positive and have normal XX karyotypes. However, the possibility of undetected mosaicism and subclinical ovarian dysgenesis still remains. It is still not clear whether these cases of Ullrich's syndrome are at one end of the cytogenetic and clinical spectrum of Turner's syndrome or whether they represent examples of a separate clinical entity.

3. Pure Gonadal Dysgenesis

Instances of pure gonadal dysgenesis are occasionally called Turner's syndrome because patients exhibit sexual infantilism, primary amenorrhea,

---

late DNA replication pattern. In accord with the Lyon (1962) hypothesis, it is thought that this peculiar behavior of the X chromosome appears early in embryogenesis and is a random process which X forms the sex chromatin body. In individuals possessing a normal X and an isochromosome for the long arms of an X chromosome, only the isochromosome X seems to be late replicating and to form the sex chromatin body, since the inactivation of the normal X presumably would leave active an isochromosome X unbalanced in genetic material and probably lethal for the cell.

and "streak" gonads. These cases are usually of eunuchoid habitus, tall, slender, and with an increased arm span. Cubitus valgus appears to be the only somatic anomaly of Turner's syndrome often seen in this disorder, but may be secondary to eunuchoidism. Occasionally these patients have an enlarged clitoris.

The sex chromosome complement can be XX (Jacobs *et al.*, 1961) or XY (Harnden and Stewart, 1959; de Grouchy *et al.*, 1960).

Jones *et al.* (1963) proposed a unified theory to explain the presence of streak gonads in a variety of conditions. They hypothesized that germinal follicles migrate into the primitive gonad at an early stage and that streak gonads result when this migration *does not* occur. Absence of an X chromosome; a genetic mutation; or toxic, endocrinological, or infectious agents may possibly produce streak gonads by inhibiting migration.

Individuals with an XY karyotype could be expected to differentiate along phenotypically female lines if the gonad became dysgenetic at an early state. This is consistent with Jost's (1958) observations of female phenotypic differentiation in male rabbits castrated before the 20th day of gestation.

C. XO/XY Mosaicism

Because XO cells lead to the presence of undifferentiated gonads and female sexual characteristics, and XY cells lead to the formation of testicular and Wolffian structures, the combination of XO and XY cells is bound to produce different phenotypic effects, depending on the distribution of XO and XY cells and the time of appearance of the XO clones.

In fact, the clinical spectrum produced by the XO/XY mosaicism appears to show more variability than any other chromosomal abnormality and has been described in phenotypic females (Jacobs *et al.*, 1961; Judge *et al.*, 1962; Jones *et al.*, 1963), phenotypic males (de la Chapelle and Hortling, 1963); and in individuals with ambiguous external genitalia (Hirschhorn *et al.*, 1960; Ferrier *et al.*, 1962; Yunis, 1964a; see Fig. 3).

Clinically, a patient with XO/XY mosaicism may appear as an example of female Turner's syndrome (Jacobs *et al.*, 1961; Jones *et al.*, 1963), pure gonadal dysgenesis (Judge *et al.*, 1962), or male pseudohermaphroditism (Ferrier *et al.*, 1962; Yunis, J. J., personal observation of three patients).

D. True Hermaphroditism

True hermaphrodites are individuals who possess definite testicular and ovarian structures. These structures may be combined in one gonad

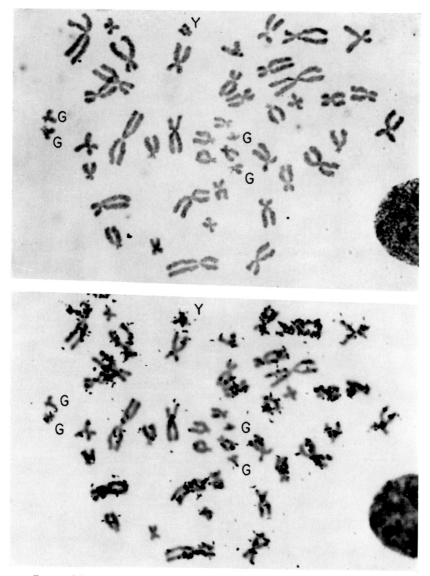

Fig. 3. Metaphase plates from an XO/XY mosaic individual. The cells began uptake of tritiated thymidine less than 5 hours before reaching metaphase and were photographed before and after autoradiography.

Fig. 3A. A cell with 46 chromosomes and an XY sex constitution. Note the typical late replication of the Y chromosome.

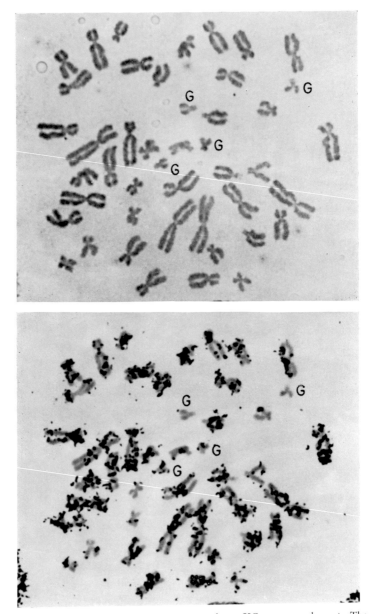

Fig. 3B. A cell with 45 chromosomes and an XO sex complement. The Y chromosome is absent.

(ovotestis) or else appear in separate gonads as ovary and testis.

True hermaphrodites usually have ambiguous external genitalia which may vary sufficiently so that some are raised as females (Sasaki and Makino, 1960), although most, because of the prominent penile structure, are brought up as boys. Patients reared as males frequently have perineal hypospadias and a bifid scrotum with undescended gonads and there may be no difficulty until adolescence, when pubertal changes conflict with the sex of rearing.

With the introduction of sex chromatin analysis into the study of sex anomalies, it was found that the great majority of cases of true hermaphroditism are chromatin positive (Grumbach and Barr, 1958).

On a temporary basis, true hermaphrodites will be classified here according to their genotype. Comprehensive reviews of true and pseudo hermaphroditism have appeared (Overzier, 1963; Polani, 1962).

1. XX True Hermaphrodites

At least 14 instances of true hermaphroditism with a chromatin-positive XX sex chromosome constitution have been reported (Hungerford *et al.*, 1959; Harnden and Armstrong, 1959; Ferguson-Smith *et al.*, 1960a; de Assis, *et al.*, 1960; Sasaki and Makino, 1960; German *et al.*, 1962; Solomon and Green, 1963; Yunis, J. J., personal observation of one case; Rosenberg *et al.*, 1963).

In some of these patients only one tissue was studied, and generally the number of mitoses analyzed was not enough to detect mosaicism with cells containing a Y chromosome (Fraccaro *et al.*, 1962). Furthermore, in the patients reported by Ferguson-Smith *et al.* (1960a) and German *et al.* (1962), a mosaicism was suspected but not proved.

Because of the small number of chromosome studies on patients with true hermaphroditism, it is still difficult to say how often an XX sex constitution is found. The family described by Rosenberg *et al.* (1963), with three true hermaphrodite siblings bearing an XX sex constitution, is thus far the best evidence in favor of the development of testicular tissue in the absence of a Y chromosome.

2. XX/XY True Hermaphrodites

A very interesting patient bearing an XX/XY mosaicism has been recently described by Gartler *et al.* (1962). On the basis of the chromosome studies and blood group findings, the authors postulated that their case arose through double fertilization and fusion of two egg nuclei. A second instance of XX/XY mosaicism presumed to be due to double fertilization of an egg possessing two dissimilar nuclei was described by Zuelzer *et al.* (1964). In this patient the external genitalia were typically male except for a slight gynecomastia. Biopsy of the two gonads revealed only normal testicular tissue.

3. XX/XXY True Hermaphrodite

A true hermaphrodite 4-year-old infant, bearing an XX/XXY mosaicism, has been observed by Turpin *et al.* (1962). The patient had ambiguous external genitalia with testis on the left portion of the scrotum and ovary at the level of the right internal inguinal ring. It is interesting to remember that the same genotype (XX/XXY) has been observed in two patients with Klinefelter's syndrome (Ford *et al.*, 1959c; Hayward, 1960). It is likely that the difference in phenotypic effects produced depended on the time of production and distribution of XX and XXY cells.

4. XX/XXY/XXYYY True Hermaphrodite

Fraccaro *et al.* (1962) described a 3-week-old infant with ambiguous external genitalia and abdominal gonads consisting of a right primitive testis and a left ovotestis. The sex chromatin was positive and the sex constitution XX/XXY/XXYYY.

5. XO/XY Mosaicism

Patients with unilateral testis and streak gonad are not considered here as true hermaphrodites, even though they may have ambiguous genitalia. The streak gonad is really an undifferentiated gonad although it has the appearance of ovarian stroma. As the somatic expression of "neutral" sex in mammals is female (Jost, 1958; Wells and Fralick, 1951; Raynaud and Frilley, 1947), patients with streak gonads (such as XO Turner's syndrome and XY or XX pure gonadal dysgenesis) have infantile female secondary sexual characteristics. Patients with an XO/XY mosaicism may also have streak gonads and Müllerian duct structures but the presence of XY cells in most cases differentiates one gonad or part of both into a testicular structure and develops Wolffian ducts. Thus, patients with testicular structures and streak gonads are regarded here not as true hermaphrodites but as a special type of male pseudohermaphrodite (Fig. 3).

E. Trisomy, Tetrasomy, and Pentasomy X

It is now well established that the presence of extra X chromosomes is not only compatible with life, but produces a mild phenotypic effect when compared with the autosomal polysomies. Females bearing up to five X chromosomes have been found.

1. Trisomy

a. Trisomy X. Since the original description of Jacobs *et al.* (1959) at least 38 cases of trisomy X have been reported (Day *et al.*, 1963a). In contrast to any other trisomy known in man, triplo X females do not show a reasonably constant phenotype. Some individuals may be phenotypically normal (Close, 1963) but most cases have had some sexual disturbance and/or mental deficiency (Fraser *et al.*, 1960; Maclean *et al.*, 1962; Johnston *et al.*, 1961). The sexual disturbances vary from amenorrhea and sterility to menstrual disorders of milder type. Deficient ovarian follicles have been found in the ovaries of several cases (Johnston *et al.*, 1961; Jacobs *et al.*, 1959; Uchida *et al.*, 1962b), but a number of patients have normal ovarian function and some have had children (Fraser *et al.*, 1960; Stewart and Sanderson, 1960; Barr, 1961; Day *et al.*, 1963a). None of the offspring of triplo X females are known to have chromosomal abnormalities, when theoretically about 50% might be expected to have an extra X chromosome, provided all germ cells had an XXX constitution and meiotic segregation took place without incident. The lack of clinical or chromosomal abnormalities in these children suggests that gametes with two X chromosomes are selected against.

Most adult patients with XXX karyotypes have been found by screening mental institutions so that an observational bias has been introduced in most reports. Approximately 4 per 1000 of institutionalized females bear a trisomy X (Maclean *et al.*, 1962; Day *et al.*, 1963a), whereas the incidence in newborns has been reported to be as high as 1.2 per 1000 births (Maclean *et al.*, 1964). The difference between these rates is said to be statistically significant so that there actually is a true increased frequency of mental deficiency in trisomy X. Triplo X females among schizophrenics have also been noted (Raphael and Shaw, 1963).

b. Mosaicism and Trisomy X. XXX/XX, XXX/XO, XXX/XX/XO and other cases of mosaicism have been reported (Day *et al.*, 1963a). A larger number of cases and a detailed description of patients are needed before an evaluation of findings becomes meaningful.

c. Partial Trisomy X.[8] A case of presumed familial partial trisomy X

---

[8] The term partial trisomy is used in this chapter to indicate the presence of an extra chromosome segment in addition to an essentially normal diploid complement (Patau, 1964).

has also been reported by Yunis and Gorlin (1963). Five of 11 members from three generations of this family showed a conspicuous extra chromosomal material in one of the No. 1 chromosomes, without displaying phenotypic effect.

   d. Double Trisomies. Some individuals with triplo X complement have also been found bearing an extra autosome. Both XXX trisomy 18 (Uchida and Bowman, 1961; Ricci and Borgatti, 1963) and XXX trisomy G_1 (Yunis *et al.*, 1964b; Day *et al.*, 1963b) have been described (Fig. 4). In these cases the phenotypic expression of the patients has been that of the extra autosome involved. This is in accordance with the mild and variable expression of the extra X chromosome found in cases of simple trisomy X.

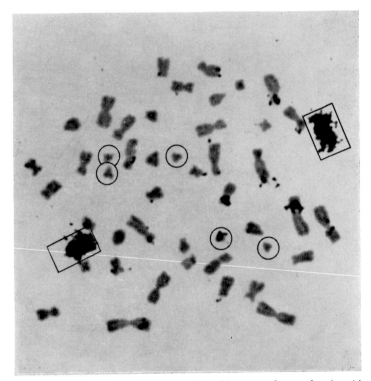

FIG. 4. DNA replication pattern of a cultured leucocyte from a female with 48 chromosomes and XXX-G_1 trisomy. The cell began incorporation of tritiated thymidine approximately 4 hours before reaching metaphase. Inside the rectangles there are two late, heavily labeled X chromosomes as seen in individuals with three X chromosomes. Notice also the presence of five G chromosomes inside the circles.

2. Tetrasomy and Pentasomy X

Very few females with more than three X chromosomes have been reported. Mental retardation has been prominent in all of them, suggesting that each extra X chromosome contributes to mental deficiency. Cases of this type include two women with XXXX pattern (Carr *et al.*, 1961) and a girl with an XXXXX chromosome constitution. In this girl, up to four sex chromatin bodies were found in buccal smear nuclei and up to three "drumsticks" in the polymorphonuclear cells (Kesaree and Woolley, 1963). Tritiated thymidine studies showed four of the five X's to have late DNA replication (Grumbach *et al.*, 1963).

F. Y Chromosome Abnormalities

The Y chromosome is the bearer of masculinizing factors. Until the description of XX true hermaphrodites, it was thought that the presence of testis was always Y induced. As a matter of fact, in all conditions other than XX true hermaphrodites, the Y chromosome appears to be directly responsible for the differentiation of testis. A classic example of this is the XXXXY Klinefelter's syndrome in which testicular structure is present despite the excessive number of X chromosomes.

After the work of Ohno and Makino (1961) and the studies of DNA replication of chromosomes (Schmid, 1963), it may be presumed that the Y chromosome behaves to a great extent like the X chromosome that forms the sex chromatin body. Aside from inducing testicular differentiation of the primitive gonad, the human Y chromosome seems significant only for housing the gene for hairy ears and even this has been debated.

A series of numerical and structural Y chromosome abnormalities have been observed and it has been found that while an excess of Y chromosomes does not appreciably produce phenotypic effect, humans may be sensitive to the partial or complete loss of Y chromosome material. It can be presumed that the loss of the Y chromosome by an XY fertilized egg would result in a female Turner's, the loss of a Y chromosome in some cells of an XY embryo may produce one of the phenotypes described under XO/XY mosaicism, and the loss of a Y chromosome segment might be associated with decreased differentiation of male sexual characteristics.

1. Numerical Aberrations

An extra Y chromosome has been observed in a fertile and phenotypically normal individual (Sandberg *et al.*, 1961) and in a patient with Klinefelter's syndrome (Carr *et al.*, 1961). Other numerical aberrations involving the Y chromosome are the following: XXXYY (Bray and Josephine, 1963), XO/XYY (Jacobs *et al.*, 1961; Cooper *et al.*, 1962), and XX/XXY/XXYYY (Fraccaro *et al.*, 1962).

2. *Structural Abnormalities*

It is well known that the Y chromosome has shown a great polymorphism in size and a long Y chromosome can be found without demonstrable phenotypic effect and as a specific feature among males of certain

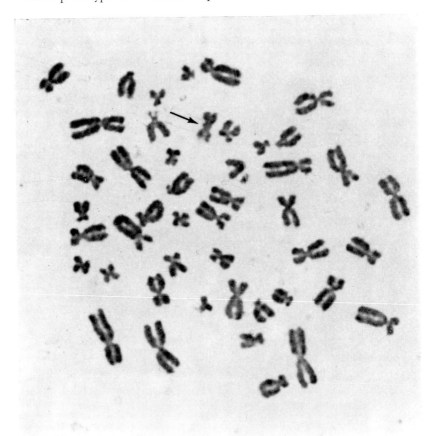

FIG. 5. Metaphase plate obtained from an XO/XY ~ Y mosaic individual. The cell shows 46 chromosomes with a Y ~ Y translocation chromosome indicated by arrow. Bright microscopy. Orcein stain. Plus X film.

families (Bender and Gooch, 1961; de la Chapelle *et al.*, 1963; Yunis, J. J., personal observations).

A presumed Y isochromosome (Klevit *et al.*, 1963) and a Y ~ Y translocation (personal observation) have also been observed. The patient with the Y ~ Y translocation was a 4-week-old infant with ambiguous external genitalia and abdominal testes. Blood karyotyping revealed 89% XO cells and 11% XY ~ Y cells (Fig. 5).

Presumed deletion of a sizable chromosome segment of the long arm of the Y chromosome has been reported in a few instances. Vaharu *et al.* (1961) described a $4\frac{1}{2}$-year-old girl with enlarged phallus, "gonadal dysgenesis," and partly fused labia. The karyogram of the patient showed 45 chromosomes plus a fragment interpreted as a severely deleted Y chromosome. Conen *et al.* (1961) also reported a patient with partial loss of Y chromosomal material in some cells. Despite this deletion and the presence of an XO karyotype in other cells in the same individual, some testicular differentiation was present.

A familial small Y chromosome has been recently observed by Yunis (1964a). The chromosome was present in 3 generations, showed a late DNA replication and its long arm was about 3/5 of the length of the long arm of the G chromosomes. No apparent phenotypic effect was associated with this finding.

III. AUTOSOMAL CHROMOSOME ABNORMALITIES

It is noteworthy that of the 22 pairs of autosomes, trisomy for only D_1, 18, and G_1 chromosomes are definitely known to be compatible with life and no viable autosomal monosomy has yet been observed.

In contrast to the autosomes, addition of extra X chromosomes or an X monosomy produces mild phenotypic effects (see Section II). This has been attributed to the heteropyknosis and late DNA replication of all X chromosomes in excess of one at an early period of embryogenesis. It is presumed that late-replicating X chromosomes are in a highly condensed state in interphase nuclei of somatic cells and have very little gene expression. An analogy to this phenomenon may be presumed for the Y chromosomes since they show heteropyknosis in early prophase, have late DNA replication, and the addition of extra Y chromosomes produces no measurable phenotypic effects.

Recently, Yunis (1964b) studied the DNA replication pattern of the autosomes implicated in trisomies D_1, 18, and G_1; partial trisomies D_1,

18, G_1, and C; and partial deletion of the short arm of an 18 chromosome. Because the chromosomes or chromosome segments involved in all the viable chromosomal abnormalities tested have been found to have largely late replicating DNA, it is postulated that these chromosomes or chromosome segments are not as deleterious as early replicating ones, when present in excess or defect, because late replicating DNA may be an expression of complete or partial metabolic gene inactivation[9] (Yunis, 1965).

A. Trisomy G_1, Trisomy 21, Mongolism, or Down's Syndrome

In 1866, Langdon-Down described a group of English mental defectives who strongly resembled each other, and because they all had certain "oriental" features, he named the condition mongolism. The most frequent findings besides mental retardation include: short stature, brachycephaly, flat occiput, epicanthic folds, oblique palpebral fissures, and hypertelorism. In addition, strabismus, nystagmus, cataract, furrowed tongue, irregular abnormal teeth, narrow high palate, a short nose, abnormal ear lobes, short neck, short broad hands, short incurved fifth finger, clinodactyly, a gap between great and second toe, protuberant abdomen, and hypotonicity are also noted. Longevity is diminished in these patients by the frequent association of congenital heart lesions (especially septal and atrioventricular canal defects), duodenal atresia, frequent pulmonary infections, and leukemia. The dermatoglyphics of the hands in mongolism frequently reveal simian lines, a high axial triradius, an increased number of ulnar loops, a radial loop on the fourth finger, and a single distal crease of the fifth finger. An arch tibial or a small loop distal is the characteristic pattern of the hallucal area of the sole (Uchida and Soltan, 1963).

Lejeune *et al.* (1959) studied the dividing cells in cultures from nine patients affected with mongolism and found all of them to have 47 chromosomes, with the extra one a small acrocentric chromosome. In the

---

[9] Although lethal genes and other factors might play a role in the nonviability of other autosomal trisomies, it will be worthwhile to test the hypothesis of late DNA replication and gene expression in cases of unusual autosomal chromosome abnormalities.

Fig. 6. Metaphase plate of a blood cell from a patient with trisomy G_1. The cell was exposed to tritiated thymidine 6 hours and photographed before (left) and after (right) autoradiography. Note the presence of three G chromosomes late replicating over the long arms (G_1), and two G chromosomes late replicating only over the centromeric portion of the long arms and/or the short arms (G_2).

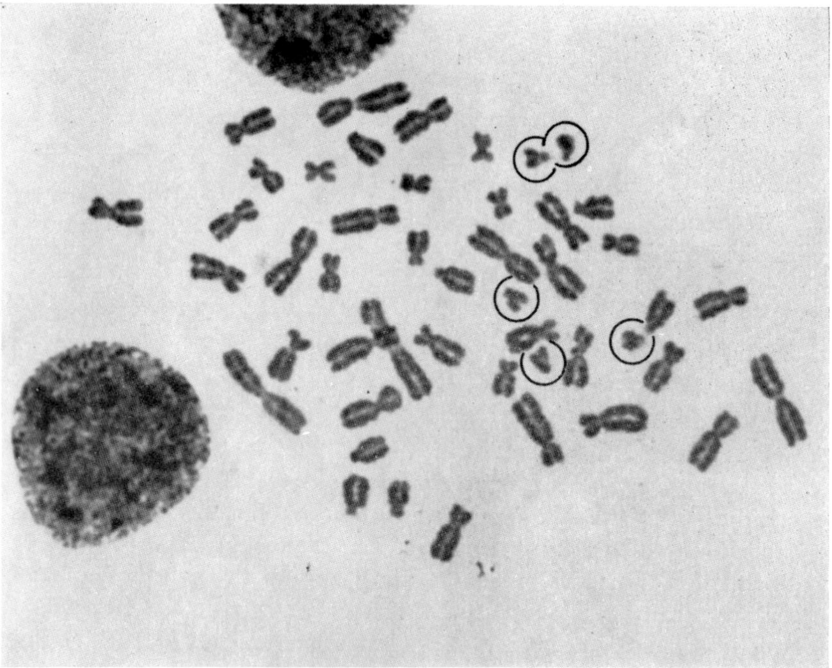

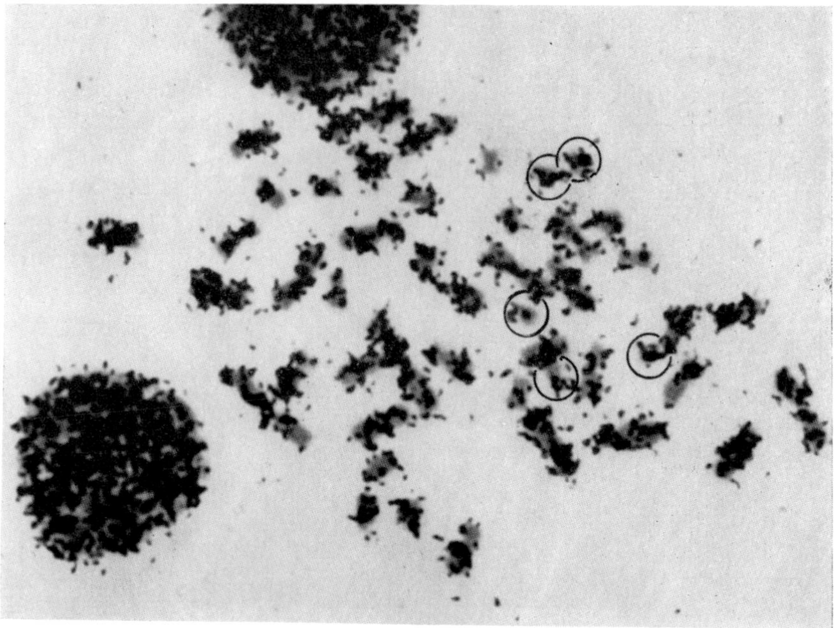

literature it has become customary to call the mongolism chromosome No. 21, but it is as yet uncertain whether the chromosome present in a trisomic state is a No. 21 or No. 22 (Fig. 6). Because of this, the term trisomy G_1 will be used in this section (Yunis *et al.*, 1965).

While mongolism has been most intensively studied in Caucasians, it has also been described in Orientals (Wagner, 1962) and Negroes (Luder and Musoke, 1955) and there is no reason to believe that it is restricted to just these races. In a review of the literature, Penrose (1961) found the incidence to be 1 per 636–776 Caucasian births. As many as 16% of institutionalized mental defectives are mongoloids (Faribault State Hospital, Minnesota, personal observation).

Considerable information has been accumulated in the last 5 years on the causes of mongolism. Approximately 80% of the mothers of mongoloid children have been over 35 years of age at the time of birth; most but not all the affected children have had the regular or primary nondisjunction[10] type of Down's syndrome. Among mongoloids born to younger parents (approximately 20% of cases), a variety of genotypes have been reported (Penrose, 1961; Collmann and Stoller, 1962), although the majority are also of the regular trisomy G_1 type.

1. Trisomy G_1 due to Primary Nondisjunction

It is now well established that the majority of cases of mongolism are sporadic or nonfamilial in nature. Because the incidence of sporadic mongolism increases in relation to the mother's age and since most cases are found among older women (over 35 years of age), it is generally accepted that with increased maternal age there is a greater rate of nondisjunction of the mongolism chromosome or G_1 (Penrose, 1961; Polani, 1963).

2. Association of Mongolism with Other Primary Nondisjunctions

Individuals with trisomy G_1 have been occasionally found to bear another extra chromosome (double primary nondisjunction). The most frequent association observed has been trisomy G_1 with an XXY sex complement (Ford *et al.*, 1959a; Hustinx *et al.*, 1961; Hamerton *et al.*, 1962), but a combined trisomy G_1 and XXX pattern has also recently been described (Day *et al.*, 1963b; Yunis *et al.*, 1964b). These patients

---

[10] When nondisjunction occurs in the gonads of normal individuals, it is called "primary nondisjunction."

appeared as typical mongols which is in accord with the mild and variable effect of the extra X chromosome.

An unusual patient bearing trisomy for chromosomes 18 and G_1 was reported by Gagnon et al. (1961). The patient showed much more severe phenotypic effects than those found in either single trisomy 18 or G_1, fulfilling the expectation of an additive effect in double autosomal trisomies.

3. Translocation Mongolism

Preliminary observations suggest that mongols born to young mothers as well as mongols with affected relatives often have the extra G_1 chromosome attached to another chromosome.

Many patients with translocation mongolism are familial,[11] and one of the parents shows 45 chromosomes instead of the normal number of 46. As expected, one of the small acrocentric chromosomes (a G_1 chromosome) is "missing," since it has been translocated to another chromosome. The parent carrying the translocation chromosome is usually the mother, and she is phenotypically normal, since no significant amount of genetic material is lost in the translocation process.

In most cases of translocation mongolism, the extra G_1 chromosome has been translocated into an acrocentric chromosome, either to a D or to another G chromosome. It is widely accepted that the short arms of the acrocentric chromosomes have nucleolar organizers and that these points are likely to break, producing a high frequency of structural chromosome aberrations (Ohno et al., 1961).

If the translocation is of the $G_1 \sim D$ type and the mother bears the translocation (Fig. 7), it has been observed that among the viable offspring in several reported pedigrees, approximately one third result in Mongols, one third in balanced translocation carriers, and one third in normal children (Fig. 8). However, for some unknown reason, very few mongoloid children are born to carrier fathers with the $G_1 \sim D$ translocation (MacIntyre et al., 1962; Forssman and Lehmann, 1962; Polani, 1963).

When a translocation occurs between two G chromosomes in a mongoloid patient, it is morphologically difficult to tell whether the trans-

---

[11] Translocation mongolism arising de novo in the affected child has been observed in some instances (Carter et al., 1960; Gustavson, 1962; Scherz, 1962; Penrose, 1963). Sergovich et al. (1964) recently found that only 2 out of 12 translocation mongols studied had a translocation carrier parent.

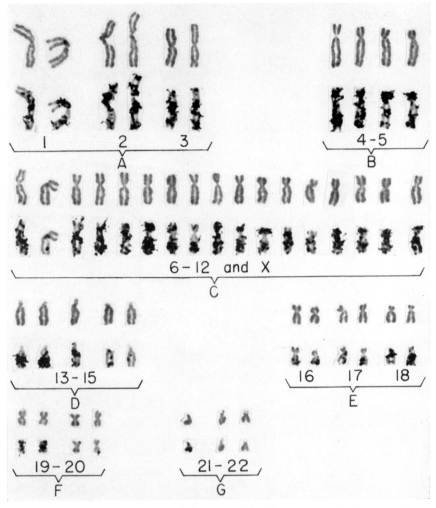

FIG. 7. Composite karyogram from a cell with a $G_1 \sim D_2$ translocation exposed to tritiated thymidine for $5\frac{1}{2}$ hours. In each chromosome group the upper and lower rows represent chromosomes before and after autoradiography. Note the presence of one G chromosome late replicating over the long arm (G_1), two earlier replicating G chromosomes (G_2), two D chromosomes late replicating over the lower half of the long arms (D_1), one D chromosome mostly late replicating over the centromeric portion of the long arm (D_2), and two earlier replicating D chromosomes (D_3). The $G_1 \sim D_2$ translocation chromosome could be either the 6th or 9th chromosome from the right end of group C. (From Yunis *et al.*, 1965.)

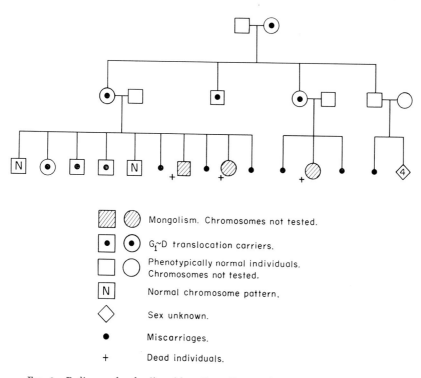

FIG. 8. Pedigree of a family with a $G_1 \sim D_2$ translocation chromosome. (From Yunis *et al.*, 1965.)

location is a $G_1 \sim G_1$ or a $G_1 \sim G_2$. At times the pedigree study is helpful because a $G_1 \sim G_1$ carrier, that is not a mosaic, would produce only trisomic G_1 (mongol) or monosomic G_1 (lethal) offspring. On the other hand, birth of normal individuals or of balanced translocation carriers to a parent with a $G_1 \sim G$ translocation would suggest that the translocation is $G_1 \sim G_2$. Other avenues of differentiation among the possible types of $G_1 \sim G$ translocations are the study of the chromosome pairing behavior during spermatogenesis (Penrose *et al.*, 1960) and the study of DNA replication of somatic cells, using tritiated thymidine.

Yunis *et al.* (1965) have studied the DNA replication pattern of two families showing a $G_1 \sim G_2$ translocation type. Discovery of the presence of balanced genomes (normal and translocation carriers) in their offspring (Fig. 9) and autoradiographic studies which showed one arm of the translocated chromosome to be late replicating and the other arm

Jorge J. Yunis

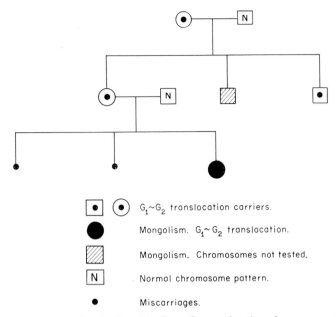

FIG. 9. Pedigree of a family with $G_1 \sim G_2$ translocation chromosome. (From Yunis *et al.,* 1965.)

early replicating (Fig. 10) led to the diagnosis of $G_1 \sim G_2$ translocation.

Penrose (1962) suggested that $G_1 \sim G_2$ translocation mongols are offspring of older fathers bearing the translocation. Although families favoring this mode of transmission were found at the time, Pfeiffer (1963), Shaw (1962), and Yunis *et al.* (1965) have shown that young mothers with a $G_1 \sim G_2$ translocation have also borne mongoloid children.

4. *Partially Deleted Extra G_1 Chromosome*

Ilbery *et al.* (1961) reported a boy with minimal features of mongolism in whom an extra small centric chromosome was present in a proportion of cells from bone marrow and blood cultures. The small chromosome

FIG. 10. Cultured leucocyte from a $G_1 \sim G_2$ balanced translocation female carrier. The cell was exposed to tritiated thymidine $5\frac{1}{2}$ hours and was photographed before and after autoradiography. One G chromosome is late replicating over the long arms (G_1) and one is late replicating over the short arm and centromere (G_2). The two "missing" G chromosomes formed a $G_1 \sim G_2$ translocation. (From Yunis *et al.,* 1965.)

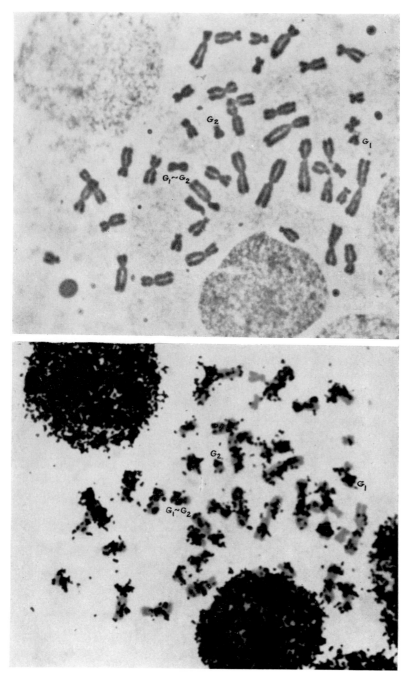

was thought to represent a portion of a chromosome G_1. Similarly, Dent et al. (1963) described a child with some mongoloid characteristics born to young parents. His cells had 46 apparently normal chromosomes and an extra tiny chromosome regarded as a deleted long arm of a G_1 chromosome.

5. Mosaicism

Patients showing two different cell populations, with one trisomic for chromosome G_1 and the other normal, have been reported. This condition is not rare and is usually suspected when the phenotypic expression of mongolism is not fully delineated or when the intelligence of the patient is higher than expected. In addition, they may have mongoloid children. Such individuals bearing a trisomy G_1 mosaicism have been found to vary from typical mongoloids to phenotypically normal individuals and have been born to both younger and older parents. Richards and Stewart (1962) found a typical mongoloid adult male with mosaicism; Blank et al. (1962) reported a patient with mild expression of mongolism but mentally retarded. Smith et al. (1962) described a trisomy G_1 mosaicism in a mother of two mongoloid children. The patient was a 19-year-old mother with a mongoloid dermatoglyphic pattern and an IQ of 82. Weinstein and Warkany (1963) described a 17-year-old patient who had been born to a 39-year-old mother and who bore trisomy G_1 mosaicism. Clinically the patient had no stigmata of mongolism, but gave birth to a typical mongoloid child with a trisomy G_1 karyotype.

Mosaicism involving more than two stem cell lines has also been described (Fitzgerald and Lycette, 1961; Gustavson and Ek, 1961; Lindsten et al., 1962; Valencia et al., 1963).

6. Mongolism due to Secondary Nondisjunction[12]

This group consists of mongoloid children born to mongoloid mothers. Polani (1963) reviewed the literature and found that ten mothers affected with Down's syndrome gave birth to twelve children, six of whom were mongols and six normal. At the time of the affected births, the mean age of the mongoloid mothers was 22.4 years, while that of their own mothers was 42.4 years. It is interesting to observe that half the children were affected, as might be expected from Mendelian laws.

---

12 Nondisjunction occurring "during meiosis in individuals who are already abnormal by virtue of a previous non-disjunctional event" is termed "secondary nondisjunction" (Harnden, 1962).

Rarely, mongolism of the usual trisomy G_1 type is associated with cases of mongolism in the same sibship or with other chromosomal and congenital anomalies. In one such family two phenotypically normal parents (aged 24 and 23) have given birth to three successive mongoloid children (personal observation) with the usual type of G_1 trisomy. Eighty metaphase plates from the blood and 21 from the skin of the mother and 47 metaphase plates from the father's leucocytes were apparently normal. In the absence of another explanation, this case might be interpreted as due to familial nondisjunction, but more extensive karyotyping is needed before mosaicism in one of the parents can be ruled out.

A probable case of familial tendency for nondisjunction has been described by Miller et al. (1961). In this family, there were two mongoloid females, one XXXXY male, and a leukemic male.

7. Mongolism without Detectable Chromosomal Abnormality

A very few cases of mongolism without apparent chromosomal abnormality have been found. Examples of this type have been reported by Schmid et al. (1961) and by Hall (1962). However, in the vast majority of cases, a trisomy G_1, or partial trisomy G_1 has been found. It seems quite reasonable, therefore, to conclude that the presence in triplicate of at least part of a G_1 chromosome is responsible for the syndrome.

8. Chromosome G_1

The chromosome G_1 is thought to have genes related to leukopoiesis and leukemogenesis in view of the following findings: (a) acute leukemia in mongols is at least three times more frequent than expected by chance alone (Krivit and Good, 1957); (b) chronic myelogenous leukemia is associated with deletion of part of the long arms of a chromosome tentatively identified as G_1 (Tough et al., 1961; Schmid, 1963); (c) alkaline phosphatase is generally increased in the leucocytes of mongoloid patients and decreased in chronic myelogenous leukemia (King et al., 1962).

B. TRISOMY 18 SYNDROME

In 1960, Edwards et al. and Patau et al. simultaneously described a new syndrome associated with the presence of an extra group E chromosome, here considered to be a No. 18 chromosome (see below). The most constant features of this syndrome are: failure to thrive, neurological retardation, malformed low set ears, small mandible, flexion deformities and overlapping of fingers, and hypertonicity. Other frequent findings include: umbilical and/or inguinal hernia, Meckel's diverticulum, heart defects (especially interventricular septal defects and patent ductus arteriosus), dorsiflexed short big toes, limited hip abduction, foot deformities, short sternum, urinary tract anomalies, small pelvis, eventration of the diaphragm, heterotopic pancreatic tissue, prominent occiput, and retarded osseous development (Rosenfield *et al.,* 1962; Smith, 1963).

The presence of more than six simple arches on the fingers is a characteristic dermatoglyphic pattern of these patients. In addition, single creases on the fifth finger, absent distal flexion creases on the other fingers, and simian creases in the palm have often been noted (Uchida and Soltan, 1963).

Affected individuals have a short life span and usually die in early infancy, although occasionally patients survive into early childhood. There is approximately a 3:1 female-to-male sex ratio (Hecht *et al.,* 1963b); this disparity may, in part, reflect increased intrauterine lethality in males. Estimates of the incidence of this syndrome range from as few as 0.23 per 1000 in a predominantly Caucasian group (Marden *et al.,* 1964) to as many as 1 per 500 in an apparently racially diverse population (Hecht *et al.,* 1963b). It is not yet known whether these differences are reflections of a sampling error in relatively small populations or are caused by significantly different racial incidence figures for the syndrome.

The mean paternal and maternal ages are elevated in this syndrome, but the mean maternal-paternal age difference is significantly reduced, suggesting that it is mainly elevated maternal age which is etiologically significant. As in mongolism, this has been interpreted as favoring the occurrence of primary nondisjunction during oogenesis as the usual cause of this syndrome (Hecht *et al.,* 1963b).

Although simple trisomy has been the most frequently observed pattern, a number of other genotypes have also been reported.

1. Double Trisomies

Double primary nondisjunction has been observed in which trisomy 18 has been combined in the same individual with mongolism or trisomy X. Gagnon *et al.* (1961) studied a patient who was trisomic for chromosomes 18 and 21. The extreme phenotypic expression of the patient can be interpreted as an additive effect of trisomy 18 and mongolism. Somewhat different is the clinical manifestation reported in two patients with combined trisomy 18 and trisomy X (Uchida *et al.,* 1962b; Ricci and Borgatti, 1963). As expected, in these two patients only the clinical expression of trisomy 18 was apparent.

2. *Translocation and Trisomy 18 Syndrome*

Translocation of an extra 18th chromosome piece to another chromosome has been observed in a few patients. These include one reported by Brodie and Dallaire (1962) who was phenotypically a classy trisomy 18. The patient's young mother proved to have a balanced translocation between part of a No. 18 and a D chromosome (forming a long-armed medium acrocentric chromosome) plus a small acentric chromosome fragment. The affected child had two 18 chromosomes plus the translocation chromosome and the small acentric fragment. Another typical case of trisomy 18, due to *de novo* translocation, was reported by Hecht *et al.* (1963a). The karyograms for the patient's cells showed only 46 chromosomes, with five D chromosomes, and a nearly mediocentric chromosome interpreted as being caused by the fusion of an extra long arm of an 18th chromosome to a "missing" D chromosome. The child's young parents had a normal chromosome complement. Another patient with trisomy for the long arms of the 18th chromosome was reported by Rohde *et al.* (1963). The patient had an 18 ∼ 18 chromosome translocation plus a normal 18th chromosome and a typical phenotypic expression peculiar to the trisomy 18 syndrome.

Wang *et al.* (1962) described a 5-month-old infant born to a 24-year-old mother who exhibited some but not all the usual features of trisomy 18. The karyogram showed 46 chromosomes with a longer than normal No. 3 chromosome interpreted as including an extra 18th chromosome piece. In addition, a ring D chromosome was noted. Another patient with only some stigmata of trisomy 18 was observed by Oikawa *et al.* (1963). Here the karyogram was reported as showing an 18 ∼ D translocation.

It is interesting to note that patients showing some of the cardinal features of trisomy 18, *without* chromosomal abnormality, have been found with a normal number of arches on their fingers. This is also true in patients with triplication of only part of an 18 chromosome. The absence of the usual heightened number of arches may become diagnostically significant because its absence would suggest a phenocopy or a partial trisomy 18.

3. *Mosaicism*

Koulischer *et al.* (1963) described a case of trisomy 18 mosaicism. The patient was a female child who died at 11 months of age and showed mental retardation, hypertonicity, failure to thrive, prominent occiput, low set ears, small mandible, short sternum, flexion of fingers, talus feet, and dorsiflexion of big toes.

4. *Trisomy 18 Syndrome without Detectable Chromosomal Abnormality*

A female infant who died at $4\frac{1}{2}$ months of age and who, clinically, closely resembled the patient described by Koulischer *et al.* (1963) and also had nine simple arches on the digits, was recently studied in our laboratory. The mother was 23 years old and the father 36 years old at the time of the proband's birth. The mother had a previous child who died 1 hour after birth and was said to resemble the proband. Extensive karyotyping in the parents' leucocytes and in 38 metaphase plates from blood and 23 from skin cells from the proband, failed to detect any chromosomal abnormality.

In cases such as this, occult mosaicism may be present, or there may be an extra No. 18 chromosome segment that escapes detection with our present techniques. When markers for the 18th chromosome have been identified, it may be possible to confirm such alternatives.

5. *The 18th Chromosome*

It should be noted that, because of technical difficulties, some workers have identified the extra chromosome in the syndrome as chromosome No. 17 (Edwards *et al.*, 1960; Gottlieb *et al.*, 1962), while others (Patau *et al.*, 1961a; Uchida *et al.*, 1962a) interpret it as a No. 18 chromosome. We have studied four cases affected with this syndrome and found that in three of them the extra chromosome was definitely a No. 18 chromosome. In the fourth case, we were unable to distinguish between chromosomes 17 and 18. Our material was stained with acetoorcein and observed under phase contrast microscopy. Patau (see his chapter, this volume) has observed that this difficulty is encountered if the chromosomes are not carefully identified under bright microscopy with Feulgen-stained preparations. Preliminary investigations utilizing tritiated thymidine suggest that the extra chromosome involved has the morphological and DNA replication characteristics of the 18th chromosome (Fig. 11) (Yunis *et al.*, 1964c).

C. Trisomy D_1 Syndrome

An autosomal disorder associated with an extra chromosome in the group D or 13–15 was recently reported by Patau *et al.* (1960). The most common clinical findings in this syndrome include: neurological

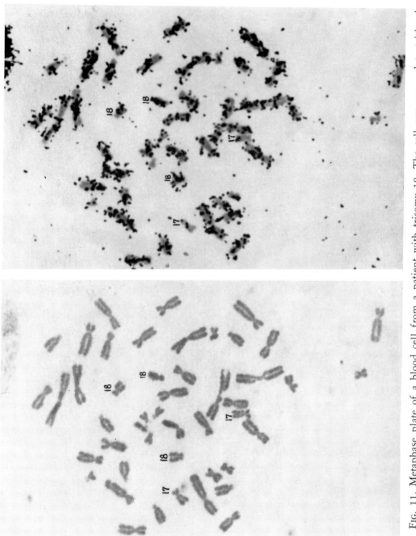

FIG. 11. Metaphase plate of a blood cell from a patient with trisomy 18. The cell was exposed to tritiated thymidine 5½ hours and photographed before (left) and after (right) autoradiography. Note three late-replicating No. 18 chromosomes and two earlier replicating No. 17 chromosomes. (From Yunis et al., 1964c.)

retardation, arhinencephaly, sloping forehead, eye defects ranging from anophthalmia to iridal colobomata, low set malformed ears, cleft palate and lip, polydactyly and/or syndactyly, heart defects (usually interventricular septal defects), and capillary hemangiomata. Other frequent findings are: deafness, seizures, hyperconvex narrow fingernails, flexed and overlapping fingers, rocker-bottom feet, abnormal calcification of skull, accessory spleens, retroflexible thumbs, urinary anomalies (especially hydronephrosis), large gallbladder, incomplete rotation of the colon, umbilical hernia, cryptoorchidism and abnormal scrotum in males, and partially bicornate uterus in females (Smith *et al.*, 1963; Rosenfield *et al.*, 1962). Dermatoglyphic studies have revealed a high incidence of horizontal palmar creases, a high axial triradius on the palms, and a characteristic arch fibular S or an arch fibular in the hallucal area on the sole (Uchida and Soltan, 1963). Recently, Huehns *et al.* (1964b) found specific neutrophil abnormalities in 6 patients with trisomy D_1 syndrome. The abnormalities consist of multiple projections and abnormal lobulation of most neutrophil nuclei.

Because chromosomes of the D group cannot at present be morphologically identified as pairs 13, 14, and 15, the presence of an extra chromosome D causing the syndrome described by Patau *et al.* (1960) will be referred to here as D_1 trisomy. With the introduction of DNA replication studies of chromosomes, it is now known that two of the D group chromosome pairs replicate later than the third (Morishima *et al.*, 1962; Schmid, 1963). Preliminary observations indicate that one of the two late-replicating pairs, and the extra chromosome involved in trisomy D_1 syndrome, have a characteristic late replication over the middle or lower half of the long arms (Yunis *et al.*, 1964d; see Fig. 12). Similarly, Therman *et al.* (1963), studying an iso D_1/telo D_1 mosaic observed that the isochromosome, the telocentric chromosome, and one of the normal D chromosomes "synthesize DNA late relative to at least one D pair and probably also somewhat later than another D pair."

As in mongolism and trisomy 18 syndrome, trisomy D_1 syndrome is generally produced by primary nondisjunction, and occasionally, by other mechanisms. The following are the genotypes so far observed.

1. Trisomy D_1 due to Primary Nondisjunction

Most of the known cases of D_1 trisomy have occurred sporadically in the population. The mean maternal age is elevated (although not as markedly as in mongolism or trisomy 18; Rosenfield *et al.*, 1962), and

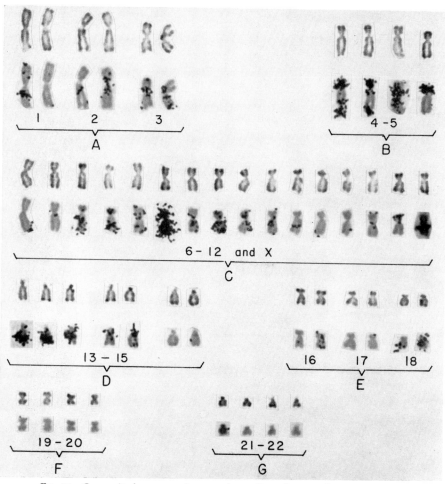

FIG. 12. Composite karyogram from a trisomy D_1 cell exposed to tritiated thymidine for 5 hours. In each chromosome group the upper and lower rows represent chromosomes before and after autoradiography, respectively. Note that 3 D chromosomes have a characteristic late replication over the middle or the lower half of the long arms (D_1), 2 are late replicating mostly over the centromere (D_2), and 2 are earlier replicating (D_3). (From Yunis *et al.*, 1964d.)

perhaps most cases are due to primary nondisjunction occurring during oogenesis. The incidence of D_1 trisomy has been reported as 0.45 per 1000 newborns (Marden *et al.*, 1964) and, as also noted in trisomy 18, there are significantly more affected females than males.

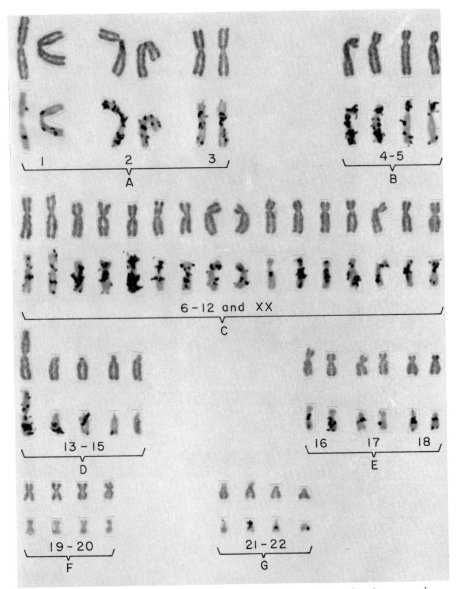

Fig. 13. Composite karyogram from a cell with a $D_1 \sim D_2$ translocation exposed to tritiated thymidine for 5 hours. In each chromosome group the upper and lower rows represent chromosomes before and after autoradiography, respectively. Note that one D chromosome is late replicating over the lower half of the long arm (D_1),

Cases of regular trisomy D_1 have been found associated with other chromosomal abnormalities in the same sibship. This relationship may be either a chance association or perhaps a consequence of a familial tendency to chromosomal aberrations. Examples of this situation are the association of D_1 trisomy and XO in the same sibship (Therman *et al.*, 1961) and the occurrence of a D trisomy and triploidy in twin fetuses (Carr, 1963).

2. Translocation D_1

A very interesting family showing individuals with partial trisomy D, D $\sim$ D balanced translocation, and partial loss of a D chromosome, has been described by Jacobsen *et al.* (1963). The partial loss of a D chromosome was observed in a fetus, and the boy carrying the partial trisomy D showed mental deficiency and some congenital anomalies usually observed in trisomy D_1 syndrome. A familial D $\sim$ D translocation resulting from centric fusion of the long arms of two D chromosomes has been reported in a few instances. In the families described by Walker and Harris (1962), Hamerton *et al.* (1963), and Yunis *et al.* (1964a), offspring of carriers were either normal individuals or D $\sim$ D translocation carriers. A high incidence of miscarriage was also noted. Because of the possibility of these carriers having a $D_1 \sim$ D translocation, Yunis *et al.* (1964a) studied the DNA replication of the abnormal chromosome in several members of one family and found it to be a $D_1 \sim D_2$ translocation chromosome (Fig. 13). Thus, carriers might produce trisomy D_1 offspring.

Jagiello (1963) also described a familial D $\sim$ D balanced translocation due to centric fusion of the long arms of two D chromosomes. In the first generation, a phenotypically normal male with three stemlines (balanced D $\sim$ D translocation, monosomy D, and translocation trisomy D) was observed. Two of his daughters demonstrated two stemlines (balanced D $\sim$ D translocation and translocation trisomy D), but again, the daughters were phenotypically normal.

3. Mosaicism

A patient bearing two cell populations, one normal and the other with 47 chromosomes and an extra D chromosome, was briefly reported by

---

one is late replicating over the long arm near the centromere (D_2), and two are earlier replicating (D_3). The two "missing" D chromosomes formed a D $\sim$ D translocating chromosome with the DNA replication pattern consistent with that of the long arms of a D_1 and a D_2 chromosome. (From Yunis *et al.*, 1964a.)

Conen and Erkman (1963). The patient was a 6-year-old child with bi-lateral anophthalmia, bilateral cleft lip and palate, rudimentary extra digit, and normal intelligence.

4. Isochromosome D_1

Suggestive evidence of isochromosome formation has been recently pre-sented by Therman *et al.* (1963). The patient was a 4-year-old mentally retarded girl with many of the anomalies usually seen in trisomy D_1 syn-drome. Cells from blood, bone marrow, and skin revealed two cell popu-lations: one cell population differed from the normal in having a telo-centric instead of a normal D chromosome. The other cell population consisted of 46 chromosomes with five D chromosomes and a chromosome interpreted as an isochromosome D_1.

5. Chromosome D_1

Huehns *et al.* (1964a) found persistence of Hb Gower[2] and an increased amount of Hb γ^4 in seven newborns with trisomy D_1. Three older children with D_1 trisomy had slightly elevated amounts of Hb F.

D. TRIPLOIDY

Triplication of the chromosome complement has been observed in two children and in a few fetuses. Both children observed (Böök and Santes-son, 1960, 1961; Ellis *et al.*, 1963) were mentally retarded, and in both cases the skin culture showed triploid and normal cells while the blood culture revealed only normal cells. Because no cases of full triploidy have been observed in human newborns, this condition is suspected to be lethal.

Patau (1963) suggested that triploidy can arise only at the time of fertilization. He refers to the experimental work of Fankhauser and God-win (1948) in which the authors, observing heat-treated newt eggs, noted retention of the second polar body. The presence of diploid (normal) and of triploid cells in the two patients reported may be due to a subsequent loss of a haploid set from triploid cells at an early stage of zygotic division.

It is now suspected that triploidy is not a rare cause of fetal loss. Indeed, several cases of triploid human fetuses have been recently ob-served (Delhanty *et al.*, 1961; Penrose and Delhanty, 1961; Carr, 1963; Patau, 1963).

It is of some interest to note that the cases of Ellis *et al.* (1963) and Patau (1963) have an XXX sex complement, while the rest had an XXY sex complement.

E. Tetraploidy and Octoploidy

Like triploidy, full tetraploidy or octoploidy is considered lethal in humans. Furthermore, it is well known that some normal tissues contain cells in which the chromosomal material has been duplicated or quadruplicated (i.e., some cells from liver and bone marrow). Evidence suggestive of a tetraploid human fetus has been recorded (Carr, 1963).

F. Other Autosomal Congenital Abnormalities

1. Partial Autosomal Trisomies

Since autosomal trisomies other than G_1, 18 and D_1 have not been found, it is presumed that they are not viable. Patau (1963b) suggested that this is related to the presence of lethal genes in these chromosomes, and Yunis (1964b) favors the idea that, contrary to other autosomes, G_1, 18, and D_1 chromosomes have a relatively small number of genes expressed and this makes their respective trisomic states not necessarily fatal. Despite the alternative hypotheses given, there is no reason why mosaicism or the presence in triplicate of part of an autosome other than G_1, 18, and D_1 will not be found. In fact, reports pointing in this direction already have appeared.

Two brothers with a probable partial trisomy for one of the C chromosomes have recently been described by Edwards et al. (1962). The father of the two affected children showed a balanced translocation between the short arms of a C chromosome and the long arms of a B chromosome. The two affected children had 45 normal chromosomes plus a $C \sim B$ translocation chromosome. Among the congenital anomalies present, the following were observed in both children: mental retardation, very narrow auditory canals, transverse flexion creases of palms, clubbed feet, broad halluces, webbing of second and third toes, and an unusual dermal ridge pattern.

Patau (1964) briefly described another case of partial trisomy for a C chromosome. The patient was a 5-year-old, severely mentally retarded girl "with few other anomalies." The chromosomes of the patient appear normal except for one of the B chromosomes that has an abnormal large long arm. Her mother and sister bear the same abnormal B chromosome and also show a C chromosome with deletion of a great portion of the long arms. At least three abortions are known in the offspring of the mother.

Shaw et al. (1964) have recently studied the familial transmission of a balanced reciprocal translocation between autosomes 4 and 5 found in four females in two generations. The offspring of one of the carriers was a male with multiple congenital anomalies, who died 60 hours after birth. His karyotype was consistent with partial trisomy for part of the long arm of a B chromosome.

2. Partial Loss of an Autosome

Because of the high number of genes normally expressed in each autosome, it is thought that human autosomal monosomies are lethal. Nevertheless, it is possible that a deletion of an autosome segment might not be fatal if it corresponds either to a heterochromatic segment or to a small euchromatic chromosome piece (Patau, 1963b). It is well known, for example, that the short arms of acrocentric chromosomes can be lost during a translocation process without appreciable loss of genetic material. Recently, Lejeune et al. (1963) described three unrelated patients showing a deletion of part of the short arm of a B chromosome, probably a No. 5.[13] All three children had mental retardation, microcephaly, hypertelorism, epicanthus, low set ears, and a peculiar "cat" cry. Patau et al. (1964) studied the DNA replication pattern of two patients affected with this syndrome and observed that the partial deletion corresponded to the short arm of a No. 5 chromosome, which is known to have late DNA replication (Schmid, 1963).

Several patients with missing short arm of one No. 18 chromosome have been recently reported (de Grouchy et al., 1963; Bühler et al., 1964; Van Dyke et al., 1964; Uchida et al., 1964). Since the number of patients reported is small and since they show mild and variable phenotypic expression, it is not known if they represent a partial deletion of a chromosome 18 or if the missing short arm of the 18 chromosome forms part of an undetected balanced translocation.

IV. CHROMOSOMES IN MALIGNANT DISEASES

It has been known for many years that abnormal cell divisions occur in malignant tumors and acute leukemias. With the advent of human cytogenetic techniques, it became firmly established that aberrations in the number and structure of chromosomes are frequently associated with

---

13 Lejeune et al. (1964) also reported a mother with two children affected with partial deletion of the short arm of the No. 5 chromosome and two more children affected with partial trisomy for the short arm of a No. 5 chromosome. She showed a balanced translocation between part of the short arm of a No. 5 chromosome and a D chromosome.

malignant diseases. Study of chromosomes in precancerous lesions and the very early stages of a malignant disease might lead to a better understanding of the significance of aneuploidy in cancer and leukemias.

Because many tumor cells do not grow advantageously in tissue culture and because cultures may produce mitotic abnormalities, the current trend is to study mitoses of malignant cells with direct techniques such as those of Lubs and Clark (1963) for solid tumors; Jacob (1961) and Ishihara *et al.* (1963) for pleural effusion cells; and Sandberg *et al.* (1962a) and Tjio and Whang (1962) for bone marrow cells.

A. MALIGNANT TUMORS AND ACUTE LEUKEMIAS

A high degree of chromosome pleomorphism has been observed in malignant tumors and acute leukemias. Malignant cell stemlines may vary in number (i.e., between 40 and 130), and generally some chromosomes of the set are morphologically different from those of normal tissue. This is due to the fact that chromosomes might undergo deletion, translocation, breakage, nondisjunction, endoreplication, inversion, abnormal fusion, etc. It is very interesting to note that chromosomal abnormalities of malignant cells are not characteristic for certain kinds of tissue; on the contrary, each individual tumor shows a unique trend which, once established, may be present throughout the course of the disease (Makino *et al.*, 1959). The malignant cells might disappear during remission and reappear during relapse with the same pretreatment pattern (Reisman and Zuelzer, 1963). Among unique features, specific chromosomes such as ring chromosomes, extra-large chromosomes, and chromosomes with several centromeres may be present and may serve as useful chromosome markers for special studies (Moorhead, 1962; Hsu, 1962). It has been suggested that, initially, several types of cell lines might appear in a particular tumor and, later on, one or two stem lines advantageously dominate the picture (Hauschka, 1961; Lubs and Clark, 1963) and might resist radiation and drug therapy (Sandberg *et al.*, 1962a; Tonomura, 1960). Other times, a progressive evolution of chromosome patterns toward a more stable one has been observed.

B. CHRONIC MYELOGENOUS LEUKEMIA

In 1960, Nowell and Hungerford found a deletion of part of the long arms of a G chromosome associated with chronic myelogenous leukemia (see Fig. 5 of Schmid's chapter). This unique structural abnormality, termed Philadelphia chromosome (Ph′), has been found in almost all patients with chronic myelogenous leukemia and has been conspicuously absent in patients with leukemoid reaction, atypical chronic myelogenous leukemia, and polycythemia vera (Nowell and Hungerford, 1960; Sandberg et al., 1962b; Yunis, 1962; Tough et al., 1963).

The Ph' chromosome is thought to be absent in lymphoid cells and present in neutrophil precursors, erythrocyte precursors, and probably in megakaryocytes of bone marrow (Trujillo and Ohno, 1962; Tough et al., 1963; Whang et al., 1963).

With the exception of 1 of 12 patients with chronic myelogenous leukemia reported by Fitzgerald et al. (1963), all other patients studied (Sandberg et al., 1962b; Tough et al., 1962; Whang et al., 1963) have revealed persistence of Ph' chromosomes in their marrows during treatment. This perhaps is related to the persistence of erythroid cells while the leukemic cells disappear. In peripheral blood, lowering of leucocyte count and specially the disappearance of immature cells, as observed sometimes during treatment, is accompanied with a disappearance of the cells with Ph' chromosome. The presence of Ph' chromosomes in the peripheral blood of untreated and some treated patients seems to be related to the presence of neutrophil myelocytes and promyelocytes (Baikie et al., 1960; Whang et al., 1963).

C. WALDENSTRÖM MACROGLOBULINEMIA

This disease was described by Waldenström (1944) and is characterized by intractable anemia and increased amounts of macroglobulin in serum, accompanied by fatigue, epistaxis, gingival hemorrhage, disturbances in vision, moderate lymphadenopathy, high sedimentation rate, and bone marrow lymphocytosis. The disease usually appears after age 40 and is more frequent in males. The relation of this disease to lymphosarcoma and leukemia is not clear but patients diagnosed as having the disease sometimes develop chronic lymphatic leukemia or lymphoma.

At least three different groups of workers have reported an extra chromosome to be present in some of the blood cells of these patients (Bottura et al., 1961; German et al., 1961; Benirschke et al., 1962). The extra chromosome is structurally different from normal chromosomes, has shown some variation among the patients studied, and perhaps originates from a No. 2 chromosome (Patau, 1961). We have studied cultured peripheral blood leucocytes from a patient with typical Waldenström macroglobulinemia and found a normal chromosome complement in 100 metaphase plates studied. Bone marrow material was not available for study.

V. DISEASES WITH A NORMAL CHROMOSOME COMPLEMENT

Along with the finding of chromosomal defects in some congenital malformations and malignant diseases, many other clinical entities have been studied for various reasons and found to be normal.

During 3 years of clinical service with the University of Minnesota Hospitals, our laboratory has gathered a list of diseases in which chromosomes from leucocytes have been studied and found to be normal (see Table I).

Reports of normal chromosome pattern in patients similar to those shown in the table and in a few others have appeared in the literature [Harnden, 1961; see also issues of *Human Chromosome Newsletters* (Edinburgh group, eds.) and *Mammalian Chromosome Newsletters* (T. C. Hsu, ed.); and data of Animal Cell Information Service (staff, Department of Biophysics, University of Colorado)].

Chromosomal abnormalities have been reported in patients with Marfan's syndrome (Kallen and Levan, 1962); Sturge-Weber syndrome (Patau *et al.*, 1961b); oral-facial-digital syndrome (Patau *et al.*, 1961c); and Stein Leventhal syndrome (Netter *et al.*, 1961; de Grouchy *et al.*, 1961; Leon *et al.*, 1963). We have been unable to confirm their findings (see Table I).

VI. CONCLUSION

Recent advances in human cytogenetics have established that certain congenital anomalies and most malignant diseases bear a chromosomal abnormality. The clinical usefulness of chromosome analyses became apparent when it was realized that approximately 1 of 200 Caucasian newborns bears a chromosome defect.

The study of human chromosomes is now contributing greatly to the diagnosis of specific clinical entities in patients with abnormal sex development, sterility, mental deficiency, and certain congenital anomalies. Furthermore, chromosome studies in relatives of individuals with autosomal chromosome abnormalities are quite useful to the genetic counselor in providing guidance for parents of affected children.

While new chromosomal abnormalities might be found in rare individuals and spontaneous abortions, the availability of autoradiography has provided a means of finding differences in the DNA replication patterns of normal and abnormal chromosomes. These studies are helpful clinically in the classification of chromosomal abnormalities and in attempting to reach a better understanding of chromosomal function.

TABLE I[a]

Clinical diagnosis	No. patients studied
Achondroplasia	2
Adrenogenital syndrome	3
Agammaglobulinemia	3
Albright's syndrome	2
Anophthalmia	1
Apert's syndrome (acrocephalosyndactyly)	2
Basal cell carcinomata, cysts of the jaw, and skeletal anomalies syndrome	4
Crouzon's disease	2
Chediak-Higashi syndrome	1
Del Castillo syndrome	2
Ectodermal dysplasia	2
Ectodermal nevus, pterygium of face and neck, and small anterior chamber of eyes	1
Epidermolysis bullosa dystrophica	1
Epiloia	1
Fabry's disease (angiokeratoma corporis diffusum syndrome)	1
Familial histiocytosis "X"	3
Familial nephritis and deafness	3
Familial seizures	6
Gaucher's disease	2
Hemifacial microsomia	1
Hemihypertrophy and hypogonadism	1
Hemochromatosis	2
Hurler's syndrome	3
Idiopathic hypercalcemia	3
Klippel-Feil deformity	2
Krabbe's disease	1
Laurence-Moon Biedl syndrome	2
Marfan's syndrome	3
Microcephaly	2
Ochronosis	1
Oculo-dental-digital (cleido cranial dysplasia) syndrome	1
Oral-facial-digital syndrome	4
Peut-Jegher syndrome	1
Phenylketonuria	2
Robin Pierre syndrome	2
Seizures, delayed bone age, syndactyly, micrognathia, low set ears, simian line	1
Seizures, mental retardation, cerebral malformations, capillary hemangiomata	1
Stein Leventhal syndrome	20
Sturge-Weber syndrome	2
Testicular feminization	3
Treacher-Collins syndrome	2
Turner's syndrome, male	4

[a] Diseases found to have a normal chromosome complement. On each patient, a minimum of 30 metaphase plates of cultured leukocytes was analyzed.

Preliminary attempts have been made to locate genes in certain chromosomes, such as deutan color blindness and the Xg^a antigen on the short arm of the X chromosome, and the enzyme alkaline phosphatase on the G_1 chromosome. It is expected that future availability of many more suitable gene markers and the study of chromosomal trisomies, monosomy, translocations, partial trisomies, and partial loss of a chromosome, will yield fruits in chromosome mapping.

During the last few years it has become known that in diploid human cells X chromosomes in excess of one are inactivated early in embryogenesis. This X inactivation is thought to appear as a random process and it would not be predictable which X remains active in each cell. Studies on the X chromosome that forms the sex chromatin body has provided an explanation for the dosage compensation effect operating between sexes. Furthermore, the randomness of the X inactivation would explain why X-linked heterozygote females may behave differently than the hemizygote males.

The availability of patients with chromosomal abnormalities and animal experimentation are providing important knowledge of chromosomal function, embryogenesis, and congenital diseases. These studies will help in the future to begin *in vitro* models of cell cultivation with abnormal chromosomes, in which it will be possible to find the biochemical factors involved in a particular entity.

Acknowledgments

The author wishes to thank Dean Robert B. Howard and Professor G. T. Evans for encouragement and support, and Drs. Paul Moorhead and Ernest Hook for reviewing the manuscript. This work was supported in part by a grant 1 GS-85 from the National Institutes of Health, U.S. Public Health Service.

References

Albright, F., Smith, P. H., and Fraser, R. (1942). *Am. J. Med. Sci.* **204**, 625.

Bahner, R., Schwarz, G., Harnden, D. G., Jacobs, P. A., Hienz, H. A., and Walter, K. (1960). *Lancet* ii, 100.

Baikie, A. G., CourtBrown, W. M., Buckton, K. E., Harnden, D. G., Jacobs, P. A., and Tough, I. M. (1960). *Nature* **188**, 1165.

Barr, M. L. (1961). *In* "Die Intersexualitat" (C. Overzier, ed.), p. 50. Thieme, Stuttgart.

Barr, M. L., Carr, D. H., Morishima, A., and Grumbach, M. M. (1962). *J. Mental Deficiency Res.* **6**, 65.

Bender, J. A., and Gooch, P. C. (1963). *Cytogenetics* **2**, 107.

Bender, M. A., and Gooch, P. C. (1961). *Lancet* ii, 463.

Benirschke, K., Brownhill, L., and Ebaugh, F. G. (1962). *Lancet* i, 594.

Blank, C. E., Gemmell, E., Casey, M. D., and Lord, M. (1962). *Brit. Med. J.* ii, 378,

Böök, J. A., and Santesson, B. (1960). *Lancet* **i**, 858.

Böök, J. A., and Santesson, B. (1961). *Lancet* **ii**, 318.

Bottura, C., Ferrari, I., and Veiga, A. A. (1961). *Lancet* **i**, 1170.

Boyer, S. H., Ferguson-Smith, M. A., and Grumbach, M. M. (1961). *Ann. Human Genet.* **25**, 215.

Bradbury, J. T., Bunge, R. G., and Boccabella, R. A. (1956). *J. Clin. Endocrinol. Metab.* **16**, 689.

Bray, P. F., and Josephine, A., (1963). *J. Am. Med. Assoc.* **184**, 179.

Brodie, H. R., and Dallaire, L. (1962). *Can. Med. Assoc. J.* **87**, 559.

Bühler, E. M., Bühler, U. K., and Stalder, G. R. (1964). *Lancet* **i**, 170.

Carr, D. H. (1963). *Lancet* **ii**, 603.

Carr, D. H., Barr, M. L., and Plunkett, E. R. (1961). *Can. Med. Assoc. J.* **84**, 873.

Carter, C. O., Hamerton, J. L., Polani, P. E., Gunalp, A., and Weller, S. D. V. (1960). *Lancet* **ii**, 678.

Chèvremont, M. (1961). *Pathol. Biol.* **9**, 973.

Close, H. G. (1963). *Lancet* **ii**, 1358.

Collmann, R. D., and Stoller, A. (1962). *New Zealand Med. J.* **61**, 24.

Conen, P. E., Bailey, J. D., Allemang, W. H., Thompson, D. W., and Ezrin, C. (1961). *Lancet* **ii**, 294.

Conen, P. E., and Erkman, B. (1963). *Abstr. Am. Assoc. Pathol. Bacteriol., Cincinnati, April 28.* p. 28.

Cooper, H. L., Kupperman, H. S., Rendon, O. R., and Hirschhorn, K. (1962). *New Engl. J. Med.* **266**, 699.

Crawfurd, M. d'A. (1961). *Ann. Human Genet.* **25**, 153.

Day, R. W., Larson, W., and Wright, S. W. (1963a). *J. Pediat.* **64**, 24.

Day, R. W., Wright, S. W., Koons, A., and Quigly, M. (1963b). *Lancet* **ii**, 154.

de Assis, L. M., Epps, D. R., and Bottura, C. (1960). *Lancet* **ii**, 129.

de Grouchy, J., Cottin, S., Lamy, M., Netter, A., Netter-Lambert, A., Trevoux, R., and Delzant, G. (1960). *Rev. Franc. Etudes Clin. Biol.* **5**, 377.

de Grouchy, J., Lamy, M., Theffry, S., Arthuris, M., and Salmon, C. (1963). *Compt. Rend.* **256**, 1028.

de Grouchy, J., Lamy, M., Yaneva, H., Salomon, Y., and Netter, A. (1961). *Lancet* **ii**, 777.

de la Chapelle, A., (1962). *Acta Endocrinol. Suppl.* **65**, 9.

de la Chapelle, A., and Hortling, H. (1963). *Acta Endocrinol.* **44**, 65.

de la Chapelle, A., Hortling, H., Edgren, J., and Kääriäinen, R. (1963). *Hereditas* **50**, 351.

del Castillo, E. B., Trebucco, A., and de la Balze, F. A. (1947). *J. Clin. Endocrinol. Metab.* **7**, 493.

Delhanty, J. D. A., Ellis, J. R., and Rowley, P. T. (1961). *Lancet* **i**, 1286.

Dent, T., Edwards, J. H., and Delhanty, J. D. A. (1963). *Lancet* **ii**, 484.

Edwards, J. H., Harnden, D. G., Cameron, A. H., Crosse, V. M, and Wolff, O. H. (1960). *Lancet* **i**, 787.

Edwards, J. H., Fraccaro, M., Davies, P., and Young, R. B. (1962). *Ann. Human Genet.* **26**, 163.

Ellis, J. R., Marshall, R., Normand, K. S., and Penrose, L. S. (1963). *Nature* **198**, 411.

Fankhauser, G., and Godwin, D. (1948). *Proc. Natl. Acad. Sci. U.S.* **34**, 544.

Ferguson-Smith, M. A. (1958). *Lancet* **i**, 928.

Ferguson-Smith, M. A. (1959). *Lancet* **i**, 219.

Ferguson-Smith, M. A., and Johnston, A. W. (1960). *Ann. Internal Med.* **53**, 359.

Ferguson-Smith, M. A., Lennox, B., Mack, W. S., and Stewart, J. S. S. (1957). *Lancet* **ii**, 167.

Ferguson-Smith, M. A., Johnston, A. W., and Weinberg, A. N. (1960a). *Lancet* **ii**, 126.

Ferguson-Smith, M. A., Lennox, B., Stewart, J. S. S., and Mack, W. S. (1960b). *Mem. Soc. Endocrin.* No. 7, 173.

Ferguson-Smith, M. A., Mack, W. S., Ellis, P. M., and Dickson, M. (1963). *Lancet* **ii**, 1121.

Ferguson-Smith, M. A., Mack, W. S., Ellis, P. M., Dickson, M., Sanger, R., and Race, R. R. (1964). *Lancet* **i**, 46.

Ferrier, P., Gartler, S. M., Sorrell, H., Waxman, M. D., and Shepard, T. H. (1962). *Pediatrics* **29**, 703.

Fitzgerald, P. H., and Lycette, R. R. (1961). *Heredity* **16**, 509.

Fitzgerald, P. H., Adams, A., and Gunz, F. W. (1963). *Blood* **21**, 183.

Ford, C. E. (1960). *Am. J. Human Genet.* **12**, 104.

Ford, C. E., Jones, K. W., Miller, O. J., Mittwock, U., Penrose, L. S., Ridler, M., and Shapiro, A. (1959a). *Lancet* **i**, 709.

Ford, C. E., Jones, K. W., Polani, P. E., de Almeida, J. C., and Briggs, J. H. (1959b). *Lancet* **i**, 711.

Ford, C. E., Polani, P. E., Briggs, J. H., and Bishop, P. M. F. (1959c). *Nature* **183**, 1030.

Forssman, H., and Lehmann, O. (1962). *Acta Paediat.* **51**, 180.

Fraccaro, M., Kaijser, K., and Lindsten, J. (1960a). *Lancet* **ii**, 899.

Fraccaro, M., Gemzell, C. A., and Lindsten, J. (1960b). *Acta Endocrinol.* **34**, 496.

Fraccaro, M., Taylor, A. I., Bodian, M., and Newns, G. H. (1962). *Cytogenetics* **1**, 104.

Fraser, J. H., Campbell, J., MacGillivray, R. C., Boyd, E., and Lennox, B. (1960). *Lancet* **ii**, 626.

Frøland, A., Johnsen, S. G., Andresen, P., Dein, E., Sanger, R., and Race, R. R. (1963). *Lancet* **ii**, 1121.

Gagnon, J., Katyk-Longtin, N., de Groot, J. A., and Barbeau, A. (1961). *Union Med. Canada* **90**, 1220.

Gartler, S. M., Waxman, S. H., and Giblett, E. (1962). *Proc. Natl. Acad. Sci. U.S.* **48**, 332.

German, J. L. (1962). *Trans. N.Y. Acad. Sci.* **24**, 395.

German, J. L., Biro, C. E., and Bearn, A. G. (1961) *Lancet* **ii**, 48.

German, J. L., Bearn, A. G., and McGovern, J. H. (1962). *Am. J. Med.* **33**, 83.

Gilbert-Dreyfus, P., Sebaoun-Zugman, M., Sebaoun,-J., Delzant, G., and Schaison, F. (1963). *Pathol. Biol.* **2**, 1244.

Gottlieb, M. I., Hirschorn, K., Cooper, H. L., Lusskin, N., Moloshok, R. E., and Hodes, H. L. (1962). *Am. J. Med.* **33**, 763.

Greenblatt, R. B. (1958). *J. Clin. Endocrinol. Metab.* **18**, 227.

Grumbach, M. M. (1961). *Recent Progr. Hormone Res.* **17**, 91.

Grumbach, M. M., and Barr, M. L. (1958). *Recent Progr. Hormone Res.* **14**, 255.

Grumbach, M. M., Morishima, A., and Taylor, J. H. (1963). *Proc. Natl. Acad. Sci. U. S.* **49**, 581.

Gustavson, K. H. (1962). *Acta Paediat.* **51**, 337.

Gustavson, K. H., and Ek, J. I. (1961). *Lancet* **ii**, 319.

Hall, B. (1962). *Lancet* **ii**, 1026.

Hamerton, J. L., Lagiello, G. M., and Kirman, B. H. (1962). *Brit. Med. J.* **i**, 220.

Hamerton, J. L., Giannelli, F., and Carter, C. O. (1963). *Cytogenetics* **2**, 194.

Harnden, D. G. (1961). *In* "Human Chromosomal Abnormalities" (W. M. Davidson and D. Robertson Smith, eds.), p. 123. Thomas, Springfield, Illinois.

Harnden, D. G. (1962). *In* "Chromosomes in Medicine" (J. L. Hamerton, ed.), p. 17. Heinemann, London.

Harnden, D. G. (1964). Personal communication.

Harnden, D. G., and Armstrong, L. N. (1959). *Brit. Med. J.* **ii**, 1287.

Harnden, D. G., and Stewart, J. S. S. (1959) *Brit Med. J.* **ii**, 1285.

Hauschka, T. S. (1961). *Cancer Res.* **21**, 957.

Hayward, M. D. (1960). *Heredity* **15**, 235.

Hecht, F., Bryant, J., Arakaki, D., Kaplan, E., and Gentile, G. (1963a). *Lancet* **i**, 114.

Hecht, F., Bryant, J. S., Motulsky, A. G., and Giblett, E. R. (1963b). *J. Pediat.* **63**, 605.

Hirschhorn, K., Decker, W. H., and Cooper, H. L. (1960). *New Engl. J. Med.* **263**, 1044.

Hsu, T. C. (1962). *Intern. Rev. Cytol.* **8**, 69.

Huehns, E. R., Hecht, F., Keil, J. V., and Motulsky, A. G. (1964a). *Proc. Natl. Acad. Sci.* **51**, 89.

Huehns, E. R., Lutzner, M., and Hecht, F. (1964b). *Lancet* **i**, 589.

Hungerford, D. A., Donnelly, A. J., Nowell, P. C., and Beck, S. (1959). *Am. J. Human Genet.* **11**, 215.

Hustinx, T. W. J., Eberle, P., Geerts, S. J., ten Brink, J., and Woltring, L. M. (1961). *Ann. Human. Genet.* **25**, 111.

Ilbery, P. L. T., Lee, C. W. G., and Winn, S. M. (1961). *Med. J. Australia* **48**, 182.

Ishihara, T., Yasumoto, K., and Sandberg, A. A. (1963). *J. Natl. Cancer Inst.* **30**, 1303.

Jacob, G. F. (1961). *Lancet* **ii**, 724.

Jacobs, P. A., and Strong, J. A. (1959). *Nature* **183**, 302.

Jacobs, P. A., Baikie, A. G., Court Brown, W. M., MacGregor, T. N., Maclean, N., and Harnden, D. G. (1959). *Lancet* **ii**, 423.

Jacobs, P. A., Harnden, D. G., CourtBrown, W. M., Goldstein, J., Close, H. G., MacGregor, T. N., Maclean, N., and Strong, J. A. (1960). *Lancet* **i**, 1213.

Jacobs, P. A., Harnden, D. G., Buckton, K. E., CourtBrown, W. M., King, M. J., McBride, J. A., MacGregor, T. N., and Maclean, N. (1961). *Lancet* **i**, 1183.

Jacobsen, P., Dupont, A., and Mikkelsen, M. (1963). *Lancet* **ii**, 584.

Johnston, A. W., Ferguson-Smith, M. A., Handmaker, S. D., Jones, H. W., and Jones, G. S. (1961). *Brit. Med. J.* **ii**, 1046.

Jones, H. W., Ferguson-Smith, M. A., and Heller, R. H. (1963). *Am. J. Obstet. Gynecol.* **87**, 578.

Jost, A. (1958). *In* "Hermaphroditism, Genital Anomalies and Related Endocrine Disorders" (H. W. Jones and W. W. Scott, eds.), p. 15. Williams & Wilkins, Baltimore, Maryland.

Judge, D. L. C., Thompson, J. S., Wilson, D. R., and Thompson, M. W. (1962). *Lancet* ii, 407.

Kallen, B., and Levan, A. (1962). *Cytogenetics* 1, 5.

Kaplan, N. M. (1961). *Lancet* ii, 1455.

Kesaree, N., and Woolley, P. V. (1963). *J. Pediatrics* 63, 1099.

King, M. J., Gillis, E. M., and Baikie, A. G. (1962). *Lancet* ii, 1302.

Klevit, H. D., Mellman, W. J., and Eberlein, W. R. (1963). *J. Pediatrics* 63, 713 (abstr.).

Klinefelter, H. F., Reifenstein, E. C., and Albright, F. (1942). *J. Clin. Endocrinol. Metab.* 2, 615.

Koulischer, L., Pel, C. S., and Périer, O. (1963). *Lancet* ii, 945.

Krivit, W., and Good, R. A. (1957). *Am. J. Diseases Children* 94, 289.

Langdon-Down, J. (1866). *London Hosp. Clin. Lect. Rept.* 3, 259.

Lejeune, J., Gautier, M., and Turpin, R. (1959). *Compt. Rend.* 248, 1721.

Lejeune, J., Lafourcade, J., Berger, R., and Turpin, R. (1964). *Compt. Rend.* 258, 5767.

Lejeune, J., Lafourcade, J., Berger, R., Vialatte, J., Boeswillwald, M., Seringe, P., and Turpin, R. (1963). *Compt. Rend.* 257, 3098.

Lemli, L., and Smith, D. W. (1963). *J. Pediatrics* 63, 577.

Lennox, B. (1961). *Brit. Med. Bull.* 17, 196.

Leon, N., Beçak, W., Beçak, M. L., and Dorfman, R. I. (1963). *Acta Genet.* 13, 252.

Lindsten, J. (1963). "The Nature and Origin of X Chromosome Aberrations in Turner's Syndrome. A Cytogenetical and Clinical Study of 57 Patients." Almqvist & Wiksell, Uppsala.

Lindsten, J., and Tillinger, K. C. (1962). *Lancet* i, 593.

Lindsten, J., Alvin, A., Gustavson, K. H., and Fraccaro, M. (1962). *Cytogenetics* 1, 20.

Lubs, H. A., and Clark, R. (1963). *New Engl. J. Med.* 268, 907.

Luder, J., and Musoke, L. K. (1955). *Arch. Disease Childhood* 30, 310.

Lyon, M. F. (1962). *Am. J. Human Genet.* 14, 135.

MacIntyre, M. N., Staples, W. I., Steinberg, A. G., and Hample, J. M. (1962). *Am. J. Hum. Genet.* 14, 335.

Maclean, N., Mitchell, J. M., Harnden, D. G., Williams, J., Jacobs, P. A., Buckton, K. E., Baikie, A. G., CourtBrown, W. M., McBride, J. A., Strong, J. A., Close, H. G., and Jones, D. C. (1962). *Lancet* i, 293.

Maclean, N., Harnden, D. G., CourtBrown, W. M., Bond, J., and Mantle, D. J. (1964). *Lancet* i, 286.

Makino, S., Ishihara, T., and Tonomura, A. (1959). *Z. Krebsforsch.* 63, 184.

Marden, P. M., Smith, D. W., and McDonald, M. J. (1964). *J. Pediatrics* 64, 357.

Miller, O. J., Breg, W. R., Schmickel, R. D., and Reher, W. (1961). *Lancet* ii, 78.

Moorhead, P. S. (1962). *Univ. Mich. Med. Bull.* 28, 294.

Morishima, A., Grumbach, M. M., and Taylor, J. H. (1962). *Proc. Natl. Acad. Sci. U. S.* 48, 756.

Netter, A., Block-Michel, H., Salomon, Y., Thervet, F., de Grouchy, J., and Lamy, M. (1961). *Ann. Endocrinol.* **22**, 841.

Nowakowski, H., Lenz, W., and Parada, J. (1959). *Acta Endocrinol.* **30**, 296.

Nowell, P. C., and Hungerford, D. A. (1960). *J. Natl. Cancer Inst.* **28**, 85.

Ohno, S., and Makino, S. (1961). *Lancet* **i**, 78.

Ohno, S., Trujillo, J. M., Kaplan, W. D., and Kinosita, R. (1961). *Lancet* **ii**, 123.

Oikawa, K., Kochen, J. A., Scharr, J. B., and Hirschhorn, K. (1963). *J. Pediatrics* **63**, 715.

Overzier, C. (1963). "Intersexuality." Academic Press, New York.

Patau, K. (1961). *Lancet* **ii**, 600.

Patau, K. (1963). *Pathol. Biol.* **2**, 1163.

Patau, K. (1964). Congenital Malformations. International Med. Congr. Ltd. New York, p. 52.

Patau, K., Smith, D. W., Therman, E., Inhorn, S. L., and Wagner, H. P. (1960). *Lancet* **i**, 790.

Patau, K., Therman, E., and Inhorn, S. L. (1964). *Am. Soc. Hum. Genet., Boulder* (abstr.), p. 20.

Patau, K., Therman, E., Smith, D. W., and DeMars, R. (1961a). *Chromosoma* **12**, 280.

Patau, K., Therman, E., Smith, D. W., Inhorn, S. L., and Picken, B. F. (1961b). *Am. J. Human Genet.* **13**, 287.

Patau, K., Therman, E., Inhorn, S. L., Smith, D. W., and Ruess, A. L. (1961c). *Chromosoma* **12**, 573.

Peer, L. A. (1958). *Transplant. Bull.* **5**, 404.

Penrose, L. S. (1961). *Brit. Med. Bull.* **17**, 184.

Penrose, L. S. (1962). *Lancet* **i**, 1101.

Penrose, L. S. (1963). *Nature* **197**, 933.

Penrose, L. S., and Delhanty, J. D. A. (1961). *Lancet* **i**, 1261.

Penrose, L. S., Ellis, J. R., and Delhanty, J. D. A. (1960). *Lancet* **ii**, 409.

Pfeiffer, R. A. (1963). *Lancet* **i**, 1163.

Plunkett, E. R., and Barr, M. L. (1956). *Lancet* **ii**, 853.

Polani, P. E. (1961). *Brit. Med. Bull.* **17**, 200.

Polani, P. E. (1962). *In* "Chromosomes in Medicine" (J. L. Hamerton, ed.), p. 73. Heinemann, London.

Polani, P. E. (1963). *Pediat. Clin. North Am.* **10**, 423.

Polani, P. E., Hunter, W. F., and Lennox, B. (1954). *Lancet* **ii**, 120.

Raphael, T., and Shaw, M. W. (1963). *J. Am. Med. Assoc.* **183**, 1022.

Raynaud, A., and Frilley, M. (1947). *Ann. Endocrinol.* **8**, 400.

Reisman, L. E., and Zuelzer, W. W. (1963). *Blood* **22**, 818.

Ricci, N., and Borgatti, L. (1963). *Lancet* **ii**, 1276.

Richards, B. W., and Stewart, A. (1962). *Lancet* **i**, 275.

Rohde, R. A., Amos, L., and Sapin, S. (1963). *Lancet* **ii**, 1309.

Rosenberg, H. S., Clayton, G. W., and Hsu, T. C. (1963). *J. Clin. Endocrinol. Metab.* **23**, 203.

Rosenfield, R. L., Breibart, S., Isaacs, H., Klevit, H. D., and Mellman, W. J. (1962). *Am. J. Med. Sci.* **244**, 763.

Sandberg, A. A. (1961). *Recent Progr. Hormone Res.* **17**, 90.

Sandberg, A. A., Koepf, C. F., Ishihara, T., and Hauschka, T. S. (1961). *Lancet* **ii**, 488.

Sandberg, A. A., Ishihara, T., Crosswhite, L. H., and Hauschka, T. S. (1962a). *Cancer Res.* **22**, 748.

Sandberg, A. A., Ishihara, T., Crosswhite, L. H., and Hauschka, T. S. (1962b). *Blood* **20**, 393.

Sasaki, M., and Makino, S. (1960). *Texas Rept. Biol. Med.* **18**, 493.

Scherz, R. G. (1962). *Lancet* **ii**, 882.

Scherz, R. G., and Roeckel, I. E. (1963). *J. Pediatrics* **63**, 1093.

Schmid, W. (1963). *Cytogenetics* **2**, 175.

Schmid, W., Lee, C. H., and Smith, P. M. (1961). *Am. J. Mental Deficiency* **66**, 449.

Segal, S. J., and Nelson, W. L. (1957). *J. Clin. Endocrinol. Metab.* **17**, 676.

Sergovich, F. R., Soltan, H. C., and Carr, D. H. (1964). *Cytogenetics* **3**, 34.

Shaw, M. W. (1962). *Cytogenetics* **1**, 141.

Shaw, M. W., Cohen, M. M., and Hildebrandt, H. M. (1964). *Am. Soc. Hum. Genet., Boulder* (abstr.), p. 22.

Smith, D. W. (1963). *Pediat. Clin. North Am.* **10**, 389.

Smith, D. W., Therman, E., Patau, K., and Inhorn, S. L. (1962). *Am. J. Diseases Children* **104**, 534.

Smith, D. W., Patau, K., Therman, E., Inhorn, S. L., and DeMars, R. I. (1963). *J. Pediatrics* **62**, 326.

Solomon, I. L., and Green, O. C. (1963). *J. Pediatrics* **63**, 333.

Stewart, J. S. S., and Sanderson, A. R. (1960). *Lancet* **ii**, 21.

Stewart, J. S. S., Mack, W. S., Govan, A. D. T., Ferguson-Smith, M. A., and Lennox, B. (1959). *Quart. J. Med.* **28**, 561.

Therman, E., Patau, K., Smith, D. W., and DeMars, R. I. (1961). *Am. J. Human Genet.* **13**, 193.

Therman, E., Patau, K., DeMars, R. I., Smith, D. W., and Inhorn, S. L. (1963). *Port. Acta Biol. Ser. A* **7**, 211.

Tjio, J. H., and Levan, A. (1956). *Hereditas* **42**, 1.

Tjio, J. H., and Whang, J. (1962). *Stain Technol.* **37**, 17.

Tonomura, A. (1960). *Gann* **51**, 47.

Tough, I. M., CourtBrown, W. M., Baikie, A. G., Buckton, K. E., Harnden, D. G., Jacobs, P. A, King, M. J., and McBride, J. A. (1961). *Lancet* **i**, 411.

Tough, I. M., CourtBrown, W. M., Baikie, A. G., Buckton, K. E., Harnden, D. G., Jacobs, P. A., and Williams, J. A. (1962). *Lancet* **ii**, 115.

Tough, I. M., Jacobs, P. A., CourtBrown, W. M., Baikie, A. G., and Williamson, E. R. D. (1963). *Lancet* **i**, 844.

Trujillo, J. M., and Ohno, S. (1962). *Congr. Intern. Soc. Hematol. 9th Mexico City 1962.* Vol. 1, p. 305. Publ. by Universidad National Autonoma de Mexico.

Turner, H. H. (1938). *Endocrinology* **23**, 566.

Turpin, R., Lejeune, J., and Breton, A. (1962). *Compt. Rend.* **255**, 3088.

Uchida, I. A., and Bowman, J. M. (1961). *Lancet* **ii**, 1094.

Uchida, I. A., and Soltan, H. C. (1963). *Pediat. Clin. North Am.* **10**, 409.

Uchida, I. A., Bowman, J. M., and Wang, H. C. (1962a). *New Engl. J. Med.* **266**, 1198.

Uchida. I. A., Lewis, A. J., Bowman, J. M., and Wang, H. C. (1962b). *J. Pediatrics* **60**, 498.

Uchida, I. A., Wang, H. C., and Mcrae, K. N. (1964). *Am. Soc. Hum. Genet., Boulder* (abstr.), p. 22.

Vaharu, T., Patton, R. G., Voorhess, M. L., Gardner, L. I. (1961). *Lancet* **i**, 1351.

Valencia, J. I., Delozzio, C. B., and DeCoriat, L. F. (1963). *Lancet* **ii**, 488.

Van Dyke, H. E., Valdmanis, A., and Mann, J. D. (1964). *Am. J. Hum. Gen.* **16**, 364.

Von Anders, G., Prader, A., Hauschteck, E., Scharer, K., Siebenmann, R. E., and Heller, R. (1960). *Helv. Paediat. Acta* **15**, 515.

Wagner, H. R. (1962). *Am. J. Diseases Children* **103**, 706.

Waldenström, J. (1944). *Acta. Med. Scand.* **17**, 216.

Walker, S., and Harris, R. (1962). *Ann. Human Genet.* **26**, 151.

Wang, H. C., Melnik, J., McDonald, L. T., and Uchida, I. A. (1962). *Nature* **195**, 733.

Warburg, E. (1963). *Acta Endocrinol.* **43**, 12.

Weinstein, E. D., and Warkany, J. (1963). *J. Pediatrics* **63**, 599.

Wells, L. J., and Fralick, R. L. (1951). *Am. J. Anat.* **89**, 63.

Whang, J., Frei, E., III, Tjio, J. H., Carbone, P. P., and Brecher, G. (1963). *Blood* **22**, 664.

Wilkins, L., and Fleischmann, W. (1944). *J. Clin. Endocrinol. Metab.* **4**, 357.

Wilkins, L., Grumbach, M. M., and Van Wyk, J. J. (1954). *J. Clin. Endocrinol. Metab.* **14**, 1270.

Woodruff, M. F. A., and Lennox, B. (1959). *Lancet* **ii**, 476.

Yunis, J. J. (1962). *Univ. Minn. Med. Bull.* **34**, 69.

Yunis, J. J. (1964a). Personal observation.

Yunis, J. J. (1964b). *Am. Soc. Hum. Genet. Boulder* (abstr.), p. 20.

Yunis, J. J. (1965). *Nature* **205**, 311.

Yunis, J. J., and Gorlin, R. A. (1963). *Chromosoma* **14**, 140.

Yunis, J. J., and Hook, E. B. (1965). In press.

Yunis, J. J., Alter, M., Hook, E. B., and Mayer, M. (1964a). *New Engl. J. Med.* **271**, 1133.

Yunis, J. J., Hook, E. B., and Alter, M. (1964b). *Lancet* **i**, 437.

Yunis, J. J., Hook, E. B., and Mayer, M. (1965). *Am. J. Human Genet.* In press.

Yunis, J. J., Hook, E. B., and Mayer, M (1964c). *Lancet* **ii**, 286.

Yunis, J. J., Hook, E. B., and Mayer, M. (1964d). *Lancet* **ii**, 935.

Zuelzer, W. W., Beattie, K. M., and Reisman, L. E. (1964). *Am. J. Human Genet.* **16**, 38.

Author Index

Numbers in italics indicate the pages on which the complete references are listed.

Abbe, E., 115, 116, *127*
Adams, A., 232, *237*
Albright, F., 189, 194, *235, 239*
Allemang, W. H., 209, *236*
Alter, M., 182, *186,* 206, 212, 227, *242*
Alvin, A., 218, *239*
Ambrose, C. T., 38, *46*
Amos, L., 221, *240*
Anderson, T. F., 53, *56*
Andresen, P., 192, *237*
Arakaki, D., 27, 29, *46,* 221, *238*
Armstrong, L. N., 203, *238*
Arthuris, M., 230, *236*
Ashley, D. J. B., 2, *20*
Atkin, N. B., 79, *90*

Bach, F., 33, 34, 36, *47*
Bahner, R., 195, 197, *235*
Baikie, A. G., 190, 193, 205, 219, 232, *235, 238, 239, 241*
Bailey, J. D., 209, *236*
Ballas, A., 34, *46*
Barbeau, A., 213, 220, *237*
Barer, R., *128*
Barkhan, P., 23, 34, *46, 47*
Barnicot, N. A., 184, *185*
Barr, M. L., 2, 3, 4, 10, 13, 14, *16, 17, 18, 19,* 188, 189, 193, 194, 203, 205, 207, 208, *235, 236, 238, 240*
Basset, D. L., 125, *128*
Battips, D. M., 22, 28, *48,* 57, 73
Beams, H. W., 9, *17*
Bearu, A. G., 203, 232, *237*
Beattie, K. M., 204, *242*
Beçak, M. L., 234, *239*
Beçak, W., 234, *239*
Beck, S., 22, *48,* 203, *238*
Beck, W. S., 28, 29, *49*
Beckman, L., 36, *46*
Bender, J. A., 189, 209, *235*
Bender, M. A., 28, 41, *46, 47,* 95, *109*

Benirschke, K., 232, *235*
Bennett, A. H., *128*
Berger, R., 177, *185,* 230, *239*
Berman, L., 41, *47*
Bertram, E. G., 2, 13, *16*
Bertram, L. F., 4, *16*
Beutler, E., 2, *16*
Bianchi, N. O., *109*
Biro, C. E., 232, *237*
Bishop, P. M. F., 3, *17,* 193, 204, *237*
Blank, C. E., 218, *235*
Block-Michel, H., 234, *240*
Bloom, W., 22, *47*
Boccabella, R. A., 2, 3, *16, 18,* 188, 189, *236*
Bodian, M., 203, 204, 208, *237*
Böök, J. A., 228, *236*
Boeswillwald, M., 177, *185,* 230, *239*
Bohle, A., 2, *16*
Bond, J., 188, 190, 194, 195, 205, *239*
Bond, V. P., 33, *47*
Borgatti, L., 206, 220, *240*
Boschann, H. W., 13, *17*
Bottura, C., 51, *56,* 203, 232, *236*
Bowman, J. M., 205, 206, 220, 222, *241, 242*
Boyd, E., 205, *237*
Boyer, S. H., 196, *236*
Boyes, J. W., 180, *185*
Bradbury, J. T., 3, *16,* 188, 189, *236*
Bray, P. F., 208, *236*
Brecher, G., 26, 33, 34, *48, 49,* 51, *56,* 232, *242*
Breg, W. R., 193, 219, *239*
Breibart, S., 220, 224, *240*
Breton, A., 204, *241*
Briggs, J. H., 3, *17,* 188, 193, 194, 204, *237*
Brodie, H. R., 221, *236*
Brooke, J. H., 41, *48*

243

Brownhill, L., 232, *235*
Bryant, J. C., 58, *73*
Bryant, J. S., 220, 221, *238*
Buckton, K. E., 190, 193, 199, 200, 205, 208, 219, 232, *235, 238, 239, 241*
Bühler, E. M., 230, *236*
Bühler, U. K., 230, *236*
Bunge, R. G., 3, *16*, 188, 189, *236*

Cameron, A. H., 14, *18*, 219, 222, *236*
Campbell, J., 205, *237*
Carbone, P. P., 51, *56*, 232, *242*
Carpentier, P. J., 12, *17*
Carr, D. H., 6, 13, *16, 17,* 193, 194, 207, 208, 213, 227, 228, 229, *235, 236, 241*
Carstairs, K., 23, 26, *47*
Carter, C. O., 213, 227, *236, 238*
Carter, T. C., 89, *90*
Casey, M. D., 218, *235*
Caspersson, T., 118, 119, *127*
Casselman, W. G. B., 8, *19*
Chèvremont, M., 189, *236*
Childs, B., 58, 67, 68, *73*
Chrustschoff, G. K., 22, *47*
Cieciura, S. J., 68, 71, *73*
Clark, R., 231, *239*
Clayton, G. W., 203, *240*
Close, H. G., 190, 193, 199, 205, *236, 238, 239*
Cohen, M. M., 66, *73*, 229, *241*
Cohen, P. E., 209, 228, *236*
Collmann, R. D., 212, *236*
Conger, A. D., 101, *109*
Conrady, A. E., *128*
Coons, A. H., 38, *46*
Cooper, E. H., 23, *47*
Cooper, H. L., 30, 32, *47,* 166, *185,* 200, 208, 222, *236, 237, 238*
Cottin, S., 200, *236*
Court Brown, W. M., 188, 190, 193, 194, 195, 199, 200, 205, 208, 219, 232, *235, 238, 239, 241*
Craig, A. P., 67, *73*
Crawfurd, M. d'A., 193, *236*
Cronkite, E. P., 33, *47*

Crosse, V. M., 219, 222, *236*
Crosswhite, L. H., 51, *56*, 232, *241*

Dallaire, L., 221, *236*
Davidson, R. G., 58, 67, 68, *73*
Davidson, W. M., 2, 11, 12, *17*
Davies, P., 229, *236*
Davis, M., 41, *49*
Day, R. W., 205, 206, 212, *236*
de Almeida, J. C., 3, *17,* 188, 194, *237*
de Assis, L. M., 203, *236*
Decker, W. H., 200, *238*
De Coriat, L. F., 218, *241*
Defendi, V., 92, 95, *110*
de Groot, J. A., 213, 220, *237*
de Grouchy, J., 200, 230, 234, *236, 239*
Dein, E., 192, *237*
de la Balze, F. A., 194, *236*
del Castillo, E. B., 194, *236*
de la Chapelle, A., 179, *185,* 196, 200, 209, *236*
Delhanty, J. D. A., 215, 218, 228, *236, 240*
Delozzio, C. B., 218, *241*
Delzant, G., 193, 200, *236, 237*
DeMars, R. I., 10, *17,* 68, *73,* 176, *186,* 222, 224, 227, 228, *240, 241*
Dempsey, E. W., 125, *128*
Dent, T., 218, *236*
Dickson, M., 192, 194, *237*
Dobbelaar, M. J., 12, *17*
Donnelly, A. J., 22, *48,* 203, *238*
Dorfman, R. I., 234, *239*
Dudley, B., *153*
Dupont, A., 227, *238*

Eagle, H., 31, *47,* 68, *73*
Earle, W. R., 58, *73*
Ebaugh, F. G., 31, 33, *48,* 232, *235*
Eberle, P., 212, *238*
Eberlein, W. R., 209, *239*
Edgren, J., 209, *236*
Edwards, J. H., 27, 29, 46, *47,* 67, *73,* 218, 219, 222, 229, *236*
Edwards, R. G., *90*
Eggen, R. R., 14, *17*
Eisenbrand, J., 125, *128*

Ek, J. I., 218, *238*
Ellis, J. R., 184, *185*, 215, 228, *236*, *240*
Ellis, P. M., 192, 194, *237*
Elves, M. W., 41, *47*
Epps, D. R., 203, *236*
Epstein, L. B., 26, *49*
Erkman, B., 228, *236*
Eskelund, V., 6, *17*
Ezrin, C., 209, *236*

Fairbanks, V. F., 2, *16*
Fairchild, L. F., 101, *109*
Fankhauser, G., 228, *237*
Ferguson-Smith, M. A., 14, *17*, 190, 192, 194, 196, 200, 203, 205, *236*, *237*, *238*, *239*, *241*
Ferrari, I., 51, *56*, 232, *236*
Ferrier, P., 200, *237*
Ficq, A., 92, *109*
Firschein, I. L., 33, 34, 36, *47*
Fitzgerald, P. H., 36, *48*, 218, 232, *237*
Fleischmann, W., 194, *242*
Fliedner, T. M., 33, *47*
Ford, C. E., 3, 14, *17*, 22, 38, *47*, 51, *56*, *90*, 184, *185*, 188, 193, 194, 196, 204, 212, *237*
Forssman, H., 213, *237*
Fowler, J. F., 2, *17*
Fraccaro, M., 92, *110*, 193, 196, 203, 204, 208, 218, 229, *236*, *237*, *239*
Fralick, R. L., 204, *242*
Fraser, J. H., 205, *237*
Fraser, R., 194, *235*
Freedman, S., 30, *47*
Frei, E., III, 51, *56*, 232, *242*
Frilley, M., 204, *240*
Frøland, A., 46, *47*, 71, 73, 192, *237*
Gagnon, J., 213, 220, *237*
Gardner, L. I., 209, *241*
Gartler, S. M., 200, 203, *237*
Gatenby, J. B., 9, *17*
Gautier, M., 68, 69, 71, 73, 187, 210, *239*
Gavaudan, N., 38, *47*
Gavaudan, P., 38, *47*
Geerts, S. J., 212, *238*

Geitler, L., 2, *17*
Gemmell, E., 218, *235*
Gemzell, C. A., 196, *237*
Gentile, G., 221, *238*
German, J. L., III, 14, *17*, 92, *110*, 179, *185*, 192, 203, 232, *237*
Giannelli, F., 92, *110*, 182, *185*, 227, *238*
Giblett, E. R., 203, 220, *237*, *238*
Gibson, B. H., *90*
Gierlach, Z. S., 125, *128*
Gilbert, C. W., 14, *17*, 92, *110*, 179, *185*
Gilbert-Dreyfus, P., 193, *237*
Gillis, E. M., 219, *239*
Godwin, D., 228, *237*
Goldstein, J., 199, *238*
Gooch, P. C., 41, *46*, 189, 209, *235*
Good, R. A., 219, *239*
Goodman, H. C., 125, *128*
Gorlin, R. A., 206, *242*
Gottlieb, M. I., 222, *237*
Govan, A. D. T., 194, *241*
Graham, M. A., 2, 3, 4, *17*, *19*
Green, O. C., 203, *241*
Greenblatt, R. B., 195, *237*
Grumbach, M. M., 2, 3, 13, 14, *16*, *17*, *19*, 92, *110*, 179, *185*, 188, 192, 193, 194, 196, 203, 207, 224, *235*, *236*, *237*, *238*, *239*, *242*
Guard, H. R., 6, *18*
Gunalp, A., 213, *236*
Gunz, F. W., 232, *237*
Gurr, E., 9, *18*, *153*
Gustavson, K. H., 213, 218, *238*, *239*

Haitinger, M., 125, *128*
Hale, A. J., 23, *47*
Hall, B., 219, *238*
Hamerton, J. L., 22, 38, *47*, *90*, 184, *185*, 212, 213, 227, *236*, *238*
Hample, J. M., 213, *239*
Handmaker, S. D., 205, *238*
Harnden, D. G., 14, *18*, 68, 71, 73, 188, 190, 193, 194, 195, 196, 197, 199, 200, 203, 205, 208, 218, 219, 222, 232, 234, *235*, *236*, *238*, *239*, *241*

Harris, R., 227, *242*
Hashem, N., 33, 34, 36, *47*
Hastings, J., 30, *47*
Hauschka, T. S., 3, 13, *19,* 51, *56,* 207, 231, 232, *238, 241*
Hauschteck, E., 26, *47,* 193, *242*
Hayflick, L., 70, *73*
Haywood, M. D., 14, *18,* 204, *238*
Hecht, F., 220, 221, 224, 228, *238*
Heller, R., 193, *242*
Heller, R. H., 200, *239*
Henney, K., *153*
Hienz, H. A., 195, 197, *235*
Higgins, G. C., *153*
Hildebrandt, H. M., 229, *241*
Hirschhorn, K., 30, 32, 33, 34, 36, *47,* 166, *185,* 200, 208, 221, 222, *236, 237, 238, 240*
Hitzig, W. H., 26, *47*
Hodes, H. L., 222, *237*
Hook, E. B., 182, *186,* 206, 212, 214, 215, 216, 222, 223, 224, 225, 227, *242*
Hortling, H., 200, 209, *236*
Hsu, T. C., 39, *47,* 68, 71, *73,* 93, 95, *110,* 155, *185,* 203, 231, *238, 240*
Huehns, E. R., 224, 228, *238*
Hughes, W. L., 91, *110*
Hungerford, D. A., 22, 28, 32, 38, 39, *48,* 57, *73,* 175, *185,* 203, 231, 232, *238, 240*
Hunter, W. F., 2, 3, *18, 19,* 188, 194, *240*
Hustinx, T. W. J., 212, *238*
Hyrniuk, W., 2, *19*

Ilbery, P. L. T., 216, *238*
Inhorn, S. L., 170, 171, 177, *185, 186,* 219, 222, 224, 228, 230, 234, *240, 241*
Isaacs, H., 220, 224, *240*
Ishihara, T., 51, *56,* 207, 231, 232, *238, 239, 241*
Israëls, M. C. G., 41, *47*

Jackson, J. F., 41, *48*
Jacob, G. F., 231, *238*

Jacobs, P. A., 3, 14, *18,* 22, *47,* 51, *56,* 188, 190, 193, 195, 197, 199, 200, 205, 208, 219, 232, *235, 238, 239, 241*
Jacobsen, P., 227, *238*
Jagiello, G. M., 227, *238*
James, T. H., *153*
Jensen, F., 58, 68, *73*
Johnsen, S. G., 192, *237*
Johnston, A. W., 196, 203, 205, *237, 238*
Jones, D. C., 190, 193, 205, *239*
Jones, G. S., 205, *238*
Jones, H. W., 200, 205, *238, 239*
Jones, K. W., 3, *17,* 188, 194, 212, *237*
Josephine, A., 208, *236*
Jost, A., 200, 204, *239*
Judge, D. L. C., 200, *239*
Jupnik, H., *128*

Kaback, M. M., 26, *48,* 166, *185*
Kääriäinen, R., 209, *236*
Kaijser, K., 92, *110,* 193, *237*
Kallen, B., 234, *239*
Kaplan, E., 221, *238*
Kaplan, N. M., 190, *239*
Kaplan, W. D., 13, *19, 90,* 213, *240*
Katyk-Longtin, N., 213, 220, *237*
Keil, J. V., 228, *238*
Kellogg, D. S., 68, 71, *73*
Kesaree, N., 207, *239*
King, M. J., 199, 200, 208, 219, *238, 239, 241*
Kinosita, R., 13, *19, 90,* 213, *240*
Kirman, B. H., 212, *238*
Klevit, H. D., 27, 37, 42, *48,* 209, 220, 224, *239, 240*
Klinefelter, H. F., 189, *239*
Klinger, H. P., 5, 9, *18,* 79, *90*
Kochen, J. A., 221, *240*
Köhler, A., 116, *127*
Koepf, C. F., 207, *241*
Kolodny, R., 33, 34, 36, *47*
Koons, A., 206, 212, *236*
Kopriwa, B. M., 102, *110*
Koprowski, H., 58, 68, *73*

Kosenow, W., 12, *18*, 125, 126, *128*
Koulischer, L., 221, 222, *239*
Krebs, A. T., 125, *128*
Krippaehne, M. L., 22, 31, *48*
Krivit, W., 219, *239*
Krooth, R. S., 125, *128*
Kupperman, H. S., 208, *236*
Kruse, P. F., 98, *110*

La Cour, L. F., 51, 52, *56*
Lafourcade, J., 177, *185*, 230, *239*
Lagiello, G. M., 212, *238*
Lajtha, L. G., 14, *17*, 22, 47, 51, *56*, 92, *110*, 179, *185*
Lamy, M., 200, 230, 234, *236, 240*
Langdon-Down, J., 210, *239*
Langeron, M., 116, *127*
Larson, W., 205, *236*
Leblond, C. P., 102, *110*
Lee, C. H., 219, *241*
Lee, C. W. G., 216, *238*
Lehmann, O., 213, *237*
Lejeune, J., 39, *48*, 68, 69, 71, 73, 160, 161, 177, *185*, 187, 204, 210, 230, *239, 241*
Lemli, L., 195, *239*
Lennox, B., 1, 2, 3, 9, *18, 19*, 20, 188, 189, 190, 194, 196, 205, *237, 239, 240, 241, 242*
Lenz, W., 192, *240*
Leon, N., 234, *239*
Lester, H. M., *153*
Lettre, H., 125, *128*
Levan, A., 22, 29, 38, *48, 49*, 155, *185*, 187, 234, *239, 241*
Lewis, A. J., 205, 220, *242*
Lima-de-Faria, A., 91, *110*
Lindahl-Kiessling, K., 41, *48*
Lindsay, H. A., 4, *16*
Lindstein, J., 92, *110*, 189, 193, 195, 196, 197, 199, 218, *237, 239*
Lischner, H., 26, *48*
Loftus, J., 46, *48*
Longmore, T. A., *153*
Loos, W., *127*
Lord, M., 218, *235*
Lubs, H. A., 231, *239*

Lucia, S. P., 41, *49*
Luder, J., 212, *239*
Ludwig, K. S., 5, 9, *18*
Lüers, T., 13, *17*
Lusskin, N., 222, *237*
Lutzner, M., 224, *238*
Lycette, R. R., 36, *48*, 218, *237*
Lyon, M. F., 2, 3, 14, *18*, 89, *90*, 188, 189, 199, *239*

McBride, J. A., 190, 193, 199, 200, 205, 208, 219, *238, 239, 241*
McCoy, T. A., 98, *110*
McDonald, L. T., 221, *242*
McDonald, M. J., 8, *19*, 188, 190, 194, 220, 225, *239*
MacDuffee, R. C., 53, *56*
MacGillivray, R. C., 205, *237*
McGovern, J. H., 203, *237*
MacGregor, T. N., 199, 200, 205, 208, *238*
MacIntyre, M. N., 213, *239*
McIntyre, O. R., 31, 33, *48*
Mack, J. E., *153*
Mack, W. S., 190, 192, 194, *237, 241*
MacKinney, A. A., 26, 33, 34, *48*
McKusick, V. A., 14, *18*
Maclean, N., 12, 13, *18*, 188, 190, 193, 194, 195, 199, 200, 205, 208, *238, 239*
Mcrae, K. N., 230, *242*
Makino, S., 3, 13, *19*, 75, *90*, 94, *110*, 168, 182, 183, *186*, 203, 207, 231, *239, 240, 241*
Mann, J. D., 230, *242*
Mantle, D. J., 188, 190, 194, 195, 205, *239*
Marberger, E., 2, *18*
Marden, P. M., 8, *19*, 190, 194, 220, 225, *239*
Marshall, R., 228, *236*
Marshall, W. H., 23, *48*
Martin, J. J., *153*
Martin, L. C., 116, *127*
Maxwell, M., 98, *110*
Mayer, M., 182, *186*, 212, 214, 215, 216, 222, 223, 224, 225, 227, *242*

Meighan, S. S., 51, *56*
Mellman, W. J., 22, 27, 28, 32, 35, 37, *48, 49,* 57, 73, 166, *185,* 209, 220, 224, *239, 240*
Melnick, J., 221, *242*
Metzgar, D. P., 38, *48*
Meyer, D. L., 30, 46, *49*
Michel, K., 137, *153*
Mikkelsen, M., 227, *238*
Miles, C. P., 10, 14, *18*
Miller, O. J., 193, 212, 219, *237, 239*
Mitchell, J. M., 190, 193, 205, *239*
Mittwock, U., 212, *237*
Moloshok, R. E., 222, *237*
Moore, K. L., 2, 4, 10, 14, *18, 19*
Moorhead, P. S., 22, 27, 28, 30, 37, 40, 41, *48, 49,* 57, 58, 68, 70, 73, 92, 94, 95, *110,* 168, 169, 179, 182, 183, *186,* 189, 231, *239*
Morgan, J. F., 68, 73
Morishima, A., 2, 13, 14, *16, 17, 19,* 92, *110,* 179, *185,* 188, 193, 194, 207, 224, *235, 238, 239*
Morton, H. J., 68, 73
Moskowitz, M., 38, *48*
Mostofi, F. K., 2, *20*
Motulsky, A. G., 220, 228, *238*
Muldal, S., 14, *17,* 92, *110,* 179, *185*
Musoke, L. K., 212, *239*
Myers, L. M., 2, *19*

Neblette, C. B., *153*
Nelson, W. L., 194, *241*
Nelson, W. O., 2, *18*
Netter, A., 200, 234, *236, 240*
Netter-Lambert, A., 200, *236*
Newns, G. H., 203, 204, 208, *237*
Newton, A. A., 70, 73
Nichols, W. W., 29, *48*
Nishimura, I., 75, *90*
Nitowsky, H. M., 58, 67, 68, 73
Normand, K. S., 228, *236*
Nowakowski, H., 192, *240*
Nowell, P. C., 22, 28, 32, 33, 34, 38, 39, 41, *48,* 57, 73, 203, 231, 232, *238, 240*

Ohno, S., 2, 3, 13, *19,* 79, 85, *90,* 207, 213, 232, *240, 241*
Oikawa, K., 221, *240*
Opitz, J. M., 169, *186*
Osgood, E. E., 22, 31, 33, 41, *48, 49*
Osterberg, H., *128*
Overzier, C., 203, *240*

Parada, J., 192, *240*
Park, W. W., 14, *19*
Parker, R. C., 66, 68, 73
Patau, K., 155, 156, 158, 159, 160, 167, 170, 171, 172, 173, 174, 176, 177, 178, 179, 181, *185, 186,* 188, 196, 205, 219, 222, 224, 227, 228, 229, 230, 232, 234, *240, 241*
Patton, R. G., 209, *242*
Paul, J., 59, 66, 73
Pavan, C., 92, *109*
Pearce, L. C., 12, *19*
Pearmain, G., 36, *48*
Peer, L. A., 1, *19,* 189, *240*
Pel, C. S., 221, 222, *239*
Penrose, L. S., 184, *185,* 212, 213, 215, 216, 228, *236, 237, 240*
Peppers, E. V., 58, 73
Périer, O., 221, 222, *239*
Petrakis, N. L., 27, 41, *49*
Pfeiffer, R. A., 216, *240*
Phillips, R. J. S., 89, *90*
Picken, B. F., 234, *240*
Piez, K., 31, *47*
Plunkett, E. R., 3, *19,* 188, 189, 207, 208, *236, 240*
Polani, P. E., 3, 14, *17, 19,* 188, 193, 194, 195, 199, 203, 204, 212, 213, 218, *236, 237, 240*
Politis, G., 27, *49*
Pomriaskinsky-Kobozieff, N., 38, *47*
Ponten, J. A., 58, 68, 73
Prader, A., 193, *242*
Prescott, D. M., 28, 41, *47,* 95, *109*
Price, G., 125, *128*
Puck, T. T., 68, 71, 73
Punnett, H. H., 33, *49*
Punnett, T., 33, *49*

Quigly, M., 206, 212, *236*

Race, R. R., 192, *237*
Raphael, T., 205, *240*
Ravdin, R. G., 58, 68, 73
Rawnsley, H., 35, *49*
Raynaud, A., 204, *240*
Reher, W., 193, 219, *239*
Reifenstein, E. C., 189, *239*
Reisman, L. E., 204, 231, *240, 242*
Rendon, O. R., 30, *47,* 208, *236*
Ricci, N., 206, 220, *240*
Richards, B. W., 118, *127, 128,* 218, *240*
Ridler, M., 212, *237*
Rigas, D. A., 33, *49*
Roath, S., 41, *47*
Roberts, K. B., 23, *48*
Robertson Smith, D., 2, 11, 12, *17*
Robinson, A., 14, *19,* 68, 71, *73*
Roeckel, I. E., 193, *241*
Rohde, R. A., 221, *240*
Romeis, B., 116, *127*
Rosenberg, H. S., 203, *240*
Rosenfield, R. L., 220, 224, *240*
Rothfels, K. H., 22, *49,* 52, *56,* 155, *186*
Rowley, J., 14, *17,* 92, *110,* 179, *185*
Rowley, P. T., 228, *236*
Ruess, A. L., 170, *186,* 234, *240*

Sachs, L., 79, *90*
Saksela, E., 40, *49,* 58, 68, 70, *73,* 94, *110,* 166, 168, 169, 179, 182, 183, *185, 186*
Salmon, C., 230, *236*
Salomon, Y., 234, *236, 240*
Salonius, A. L., 169, *186*
Sandberg, A. A., 51, *56,* 193, 194, 207, 231, 232, *238, 240, 241*
Sanderson, A. R., 6, *19,* 205, *241*
Sanger, R., 192, *237*
Santesson, B., 228, *236*
Sapin, S., 221, *240*
Sasaki, M., 94, *110,* 167, 168, 182, 183, *186,* 203, *241*

Scandlyn, B. J., *90*
Schaison, F., 193, *237*
Scharer, K., 193, *242*
Scharr, J. B., 221, *240*
Scherz, R. G., 193, 213, *241*
Schmickel, R. D., 193, 219, *239*
Schmid, W., 93, 94, *110,* 177, 178, 179, *186,* 192, 207, 219, 224, 230, *241*
Schork, P., 33, *47*
Schultz, J., 53, *56*
Schultze, K. W., 2, *19*
Schwartz, S., 125, *128*
Schwarz, G., 195, 198, *235*
Sebaoun, - J., 193, *237*
Sebaoun-Zugman, M., 193, *237*
Segal, S. J., 194, *241*
Sergovich, F. R., 213, *241*
Seringe, P., 177, *185,* 230, *239*
Serr, D. M., 2, *19*
Shapiro, A., 212, *237*
Shaw, M. W., 67, *73,* 205, 216, 229, *240, 241*
Shepard, T. H., 200, *237*
Shillaber, C. P., 131, 133, *153*
Siebenmann, R. E., 193, *242*
Siminovitch, L., 22, *49,* 52, *56,* 155, *186*
Skoog, W. A., 28, 29, *49*
Smith, D. R., 2, *17*
Smith, D. W., 8, *19,* 176, *186,* 188, 190, 194, 195, 219, 220, 222, 224, 225, 227, 228, 234, *239, 240, 241*
Smith, G., 30, 46, *49*
Smith, P. H., 194, *235*
Smith, P. M., 219, *241*
Sohval, A. R., 8, 14, *19*
Solish, G., 2, *19*
Solomon, I. L., 203, *241*
Soltan, H. C., 210, 213, 220, 224, *241*
Sorrell, H., 200, *237*
Sparkes, R. S., 27, 29, *46*
Speckhard, M., 8, *19*
Spina, J., 32, 46, *48, 49*
Spitta, E. J., 116, *127*
Stalder, G. R., 230, *236*
Staples, W. I., 213, *239*

Steinberg, A. G., 213, *239*
Stewart, A., 218, *240*
Stewart, J. S. S., 190, 194, 200, 205, *237, 238, 241*
Stich, H., 51, *56,* 125, *128*
Stohlman, F., 26, 33, 34, *48, 49*
Stoll, P., 2, *16*
Stoller, A., 212, *236*
Stolte, L. A. M., 17, *17*
Strong, J. A., 3, *18,* 188, 190, 193, 199, 205, *238, 239*
Strugger, S. P., 125, *128*
Stubblefield, E., 93, 95, 99, 100, *110*
Stulberg, C. S., 41, *47*

Tanaka, Y., 26, *49*
Tavares, A. S., 2, *20*
Taylor, A. I., 8, *20,* 203, 204, 208, *237*
Taylor, G., 41, *47*
Taylor, J. H., 14, 16, *17, 19,* 91, 92, *110,* 179, *185,* 188, 207, 224, *238, 239*
ten Brink, J., 212, *238*
Theffry, S., 230, *236*
Theiss, E. A., 2, *20*
Therman, E., 170, 171, 176, 177, *185, 186,* 219, 222, 224, 227, 228, 230, 234, *240, 241*
Thervet, F., 234, *240*
Thompson, D. W., 209, *236*
Thompson, J. S., 200, *239*
Thompson, M. W., 202, *239*
Tillinger, K. C., 195, 199, *239*
Tips, R. L., 30, 46, *49*
Tjio, J. H., 22, 38, *49,* 51, *56,* 57, 73, 125, *128,* 187, 231, 232, *241, 242*
Tobie, J. E., 125, *128*
Tonomura, A., 231, *239, 241*
Tough, I. M., 219, 232, *241*
Trebucco, A., 194, *236*
Trevoux, R., 200, *236*
Tricomi, V., 2, *19*
Trujillo, J. M., 213, 232, *240, 241*
Turner, H. H., 194, *241*
Turpin, R., 68, 69, 71, *73,* 177, *185,* 187, 204, 210, 230, *239, 241*

Uchida, I. A., 205, 206, 210, 220, 221, 222, 224, 230, *241, 242*
Ushijima, R. N., 30, 46, *49*

Vaharu, T., 209, *242*
Valdmanis, A., 230, *242*
Valencia, J. I., 218, *241*
Van Dyke, H. E., 230, *242*
Van Wyk, J. J., 3, *17,* 188, 194, *242*
Veiga, A. A., 232, *236*
Vialatte, J., 177, *185,* 230, *239*
Von Anders, G., 193, *242*
Voorhess, M. L., 209, *242*
Vosgerau, H., 2, *16*

Wagner, D., 2, *20*
Wagner, H. P., 219, 222, *240*
Wagner, H. R., 212, *242*
Waldenström, 232, *242*
Walford, R. I., 26, *49*
Walker, J. E., 6, *17*
Walker, S., 227, *242*
Walter, K., 195, 197, *235*
Wang, H. C., 205, 220, 221, 222, 230, *241, 242*
Warburg, E., 190, *242*
Warkany, J., 218, *242*
Waxman, M. D., 200, *237*
Waxman, S. H., 203, *237*
Weinberg, A. N., 203, *237*
Weinstein, E. D., 218, *242*
Weller, S. D. V., 213, *236*
Wells, L. J., 204, *242*
Welshons, W. J., 90
Werth, G., 125, *128*
Whang, J., 51, *56,* 57, 73, 231, 232, *241, 242*
Wildy, P., 70, *73*
Wilkins, L., 3, *17,* 188, 194, *242*
Williams, J. A., 190, 193, 205, 232, *239, 241*
Williamson, E. R. D., 232, *241*
Wilson, D. R., 200, *239*
Wimber, D. E., 92, *110*
Winn, S. M., 216, *238*
Wolff, O. H., 14, *18,* 219, 222, *236*
Woltring, L. M., 212, *238*

Woodruff, M. F. A., 1, *20,* 189, *242*
Woods, P. S., 91, *110*
Woolley, P. V., 207, *239*
Wredden, J. H., *128*
Wright, S. W., 205, 206, 212, *236*

Yaneva, H., 234, *236*
Yasumoto, K., 231, *238*

Yeh, M., 2, *16*
Young, R. B., 229, *236*
Yunis, J. J., 182, *186,* 200, 203, 206,
209, 212, 214, 215, 216, 222, 223,
224, 225, 227, 229, 232, *242*

Zernike, F., 123, *127*
Zuelzer, W. W., 204, 231, *240, 241*

Subject Index

Abbe's theory, 115-116
Achromats, 118
Agglutinating agents, for erythrocytes, 22, 28, 29, 33-36, 38
Air dried technique, 40, 44, 53, 102
Alkaline phosphatase, 219
Aneuploidy, 187-235
Antibiotics, 38, 61-62, 66
Apochromats, 119
Asynchronous DNA replication, 91-94, 100, 171
Autoradiography of chromosomes, 91-110, *see also* DNA replication
  air dried preparation, 102
  developers, 104-105
  equipment for, 108-109
  liquid emulsion, 102
  removal of emulsion, 107-108
  squash preparation, 100-102
  stripping film, 102-104
  techniques, 98-109
Autosomal anomalies, 209-230
  deletions, 177, 227, 230, 231-232
  translocations, 213-217, 221, 227
  trisomies, *see also* Trisomy
    partial, 216, 218, 221, 227, 229-230

Basic salt solution, *see* Hank's solution
Bicarbonate, sodium, 61
Blood culture, *see* Leukocyte culture
Bone marrow direct preparation, 51-55
  air dried preparation, 53
  in leukemia, 51
  squash preparation, 52-53
Bright field microscopy, 111-123
  of chromosomes, 121, 125, 130-131, 156, 158, 163-164
  depth of focus, visual, 116-117
  image formation, 115-116
  lens aberration, 113-114

lens properties, 117-123
linear magnification, 112-113
magnification, 113
numerical aperture, *see* Numerical aperture
resolving power, 115-116, 120
total magnification, 113
Buccal smear, 4-8, 12-13

Camera-microscope, alignment of, 131-132
Camera types, 133-137
Carbolfuchsin stain, 6-7
Cat cry syndrome, 230
Cell cycle, 95-97
Chicken embryo extract, 58-59
Chicken plasma, 58
Chromatid breaks, due to radiation, 99
Chromocenter, 6, 7
Chromosome
  abnormalities, 187-242
    in Klinefelter's syndrome, 190-194
    in malignant diseases, 230-232
    in mongolism, 212-218
    in true hermaphroditism, 203-204
    in Turner's syndrome, 195-199
  arm ratio, 155, 157
  C', 166, 168, 169, 170, 178-179
  centromere region, 156
  contraction, 156, 162
  D_1, 171, 172, 176, 181-182, 224, 225, 226, 227, 228
  D_2, 214, 225, 226, 227
  D_3, 214, 225, 226
  DNA content, 156, 162-163, 165
  DNA replication, 91-94, 158-159, 171-173
  G_1, 171-173, 176, 184, 210-212, 213-217, 219
  G_2, 210, 214-217, 227

group A (1-3), 177
group B (4-5), 158-160, 165, 177-178
group C (6-12 and X), 160, 178-181
group D (13-15), 181-182
group E (16-18), 163-164, 182
group F (19-20), 182
group G (21-22 and Y), 182-184
identification, 155-186
length variation, 155, 156, 158, 159, 160
mapping, 192, 196, 199, 219, 224, 227, 228
measurements, 156, 158-159
mosaics, see Mosaicism
nomenclature, 173-184
normal complement in various diseases, 233-234
no. 4; 172, 177-178
no. 5; 177-178, 230
no. 16; 182-184
no. 18; 22, 163-164, 182, 222, 223
number of human, 187
pairing off method, 158-160, 181
phase microscopy, 123, 124-125, 163-164
Philadelphia, 55, 106, 219, 231-232
satellites, 166, 175
secondary constrictions, 166-170, 178-179, 182, 183
X, 160, 168-169, 172, 179-181, 192, 198-199, 206, 207, 209
Y, 172, 182-183, 192, 201, 207-209
Colchicine, 38-39, 62, 96-97
Color blindness studies, 192, 196, 199
Condensers, 120-122, 124, 126
alignment, 132
depth of focus, 121
iris diaphragm, 120-121
numerical aperture, 120-121
working distance, 120
Continuous labeling technique, 96-97, 99-100
Cover slip thickness, influence of, 117-118
Culture medium, 36-37, 60, 63, 98

Darkroom for autoradiography, 103-105
for photographic procedures, 148-152
Del Castillo's syndrome, 194, 234
Deletion of chromosome, partial
autosomal, 55, 106, 219, 227, 230, 231-232
X, 169, 198-199
Y, 183, 209
Denver report, 173
Depth of focus
photographic, 137, 139
visual, 116-117
Dextran, 29
Dictyate oocytes, 79
DNA replication, see also Autoradiography of chromosomes
autosomes, 92-94
early, 96-97
late, see Late replicating chromosomes
lymphocytes, 33, 41
methodology, 94-97
period of, 95-97
Philadelphia chromosome, 106
techniques, 97-109
X chromosome, see Late replicating chromosomes
Y chromosome, see Late replicating chromosomes
Down's syndrome, see Mongolism

Eagle's medium, 60
Exposure time, determination, 139-140
Eyepieces, 118-119

Feulgen stain, 162
Fibrinogen, 29
Film processing, 149-150
Films (BW), 142, 147
color sensitivity, 143
contrast, 144
developers, 148-149
film grain, 144
fixing bath, 149
high contrast, 146, 158
resolving power, 144
speed, 143
types, 145-147

Films, color, 146-147
Filters, *see* Light filters
Fixation of chromosomes, 6, 8-9, 39-40,
    43-44, 76
Fixatives, photographic, 149
Fluorescence microscopy, 125-127
    excitation illumination, 126-127
    filter selection, 126-127
    fluorescence intensity, 125
    light sources, 126-127
Fluorites, 118

Germ cells, direct handling of, 75-90
    fixation, 76
    pre-treatment, 77-85
    squashes, 76-77
    stain, 77
Giemsa stain, 44-45, 105-106
Glare, control, 132, 139
Gonadal cell techniques, *see* Germ cells,
    direct handling of
Gonadal dysgenesis, *see* Turner's syn-
    drome *and* Pure gonadal dysgenesis

Hank's solution, 60-61
Hemoglobin
    fetal, 227, 228
    γ^4, 228
    Gower^2, 228
Heparin, 26-27
Hermaphrodite, *see also* True hermaph-
    roditism
    male pseudo, 204
Heterochromatin, 183
    heterochromatic X, 2, 3, 13-14, 79, 83
    heterochromatic Y, 77, 79, 83
Human complement, chromosomes, 177-
    184
Hypotonic treatment, 39, 79, 83

Identification of chromosomes, 155-186
    in the absence of special markers, 155-
        165
    by DNA replication pattern, 170-173,
        177-184
    nomenclature, 173-184
    by satellites, 166

by secondary constrictions, 166-170,
    178-179, 182, 183
Image magnification, microscopic, 112-
    113
    photomicrographic, 132-137
Immersion systems, 117
Insertion, 86-89
Interphase nuclei
    of definitive oogonia, 79
    sexual dimorphism of, 2, 3, 13
Isochromosome
    D_1, 171, 224, 228
    X, 198
    Y, 209

Klinefelter's syndrome, 189-194
    association with Down's syndrome,
        212
    chromatin negative, 194
    frequency of, 190
    maternal age effect, 192
    mental deficiency, 190, 193
    mosaicism in, 193-194
    phenotype, 189-190
    sex chromatin in, 189-190
    sterility, 190, 192
    testicular histology, 192
    XXY sex chromosome complement
        in, 190
    XXXY sex chromosome complement
        in, 192-193
    XXXXY sex chromosome comple-
        ment in, 192-193
Koehler's illumination, 115, 122, 124,
    131-132

Late replicating chromosomes, 96-97,
    106
    D_1, 171, 172, 181-182, 224, 225,
        226, 227
    G_1, 171-173, 184, 211, 213-217
    and gene inactivation, 209-210
    no. 4; 172, 178
    no. 5; 172, 178, 230
    no. 18; 182, 222
    X, 168-169, 172, 179-180, 192, 198,
        206, 207, 209
    Y, 106, 172, 192, 201, 209

Lens aberrations, 113-114
  chromatic, 113
  spherical, 113
Lens properties, 117-123
Leukemia
  acute, 231
  association with mongolism, 219
  atypical chronic myelogenous leuke-
    mia, 231-232
  chronic myeloid, 231-232
Leukocyte culture, 21-46
  applications of, 41-42
  cell inoculum size, 30-32
  collection and storage of leukocytes,
    26-27
  effect of cell concentration, 31-32
  life span of, 40-41
  lymphocytes in, 23-26
  macromethods of, 42-45
  micromethods of, 45-46
  mitotic cells, 23-26
  polymorphonuclears in, 26, 30
  separation of leukocytes, 27-30
Leukocyte techniques, see Leukocyte cul-
    ture
Light filters, 140-142
Light sources, microscopic, 122-123, 126-
    127
London report, 173, 176
Lyon hypothesis, 14, 198-199, 209, 235

Malignant tumors, chromosomes in, 230-
    231
Marfan's syndrome, chromosomes in,
    233-234
Maternal age
  effect on Klinefelter's syndrome, 192
    on mongolism, 212, 213, 216, 218
    on trisomy D_1 syndrome, 224
    on trisomy 18 syndrome, 220
    on Turner's syndrome, 196
Meiosis
  metaphase, first and second meiotic,
    81-85
  non-disjunction, frequency, 85
  prophase, first meiotic, 79-81
  translocation analysis, 86-89

Microscopy, 111-128
Microtechnique, leukocyte culture, 45-46
Mitogenic agents, 22, 28, 33-36, 38
Mitosis
  anaphase, germ cells, 79
  fetal ovary, 77
  of leukocytes
    initiation, 33-36
    secondary, 40-41
  metaphase, germ cells, 79
  prophase, germ cells, 77-79
  telophase, germ cells, 77-79
Mongolism, 210-219
  association with leukemia, 219
    with other primary non-disjunc-
      tions, 212-213
  dermatoglyphics, 210
  familial, 219
  frequency in institutions, 212
  G/D translocation, 86-88, 213
  G/G translocation, 171, 173, 213-217
  identification of the mongolism chro-
    mosome, 171-173, 175-176, 184,
    210-212
  maternal age effect, 212
  mosaicism, 218
  newborn incidence, 212
  non-disjunction
    primary, 212
    secondary, 218
  normal chromosomes, 219
  partial trisomy G_1, 216, 218
  phenotype, 210
  regular, 210-213
Monochromatic light, 124-125, 140-142
Monochromats, 118
Monosomy, see Turner's syndrome
Mosaicism
  in Klinefelter's syndrome, 193-194
  in mongolism, 218
  in triploidy, 228
  in trisomy D_1 syndrome, 227-228
  in trisomy 18 syndrome, 221-222
  in true hermaphroditism, 203-204
  in Turner's syndrome, 196-198
  in XO/XY, 200, 204

Neutrophils, *see also* Leukocyte
  alkaline phosphatase, 219
  drumstick incidence, 12
  in mosaicism of sex chromosomes, 12-
    13
  techniques for sex detection, 11-13
  in trisomy D_1, 224, 227
Non-disjunction
  effect of maternal age, *see* Maternal
    age
  meiotic, frequency of, 85
  primary, 192, 193, 212, 220, 224
  secondary, 218
Nuclear sex, *see* Sex chromatin
Nucleolar organizers, 77-79, 213
Numerical aperture, 113, 115-116, 118-
    119, 120-121, 126, 137, 139

Objectives, 117-119, 123, 124
Octoploidy, 229
Oral-facial-digital syndrome, 233-234
Orcein stain, 63, 162

Papers, photographic, 147-148
  developers, 148-149
  fixing bath, 149
  paper grades, 147, 148
Partial trisomies, 198-199, 205-206, 216,
    218, 221, 227, 229-230
Pentasomy X, 207
pH, 31, 37-38, 67
Phase contrast microscopy, 123-125
  bright, 124
  of chromosomes, 123, 124-125, 163-
    164
  condensers, 124
  dark, 124
  image formation in, 123
  objectives, 123, 124
Phenol red, 61
Philadelphia chromosome, 55, 106, 219,
    231-232
Photographic chemicals, 148-149
Photomicrography of chromosomes, 129-
    153, 156, 158, 163-164
Phytohemagglutinin, 22, 28, 33-36, 38
  life span of stimulated cultures, 40-41

Polycythemia vera, 231-232
Polymorphism of
  D chromosomes, 181
  G chromosomes, 166, 183-184
  no. 16 chromosomes, 182
  X chromosomes, 180-181
  Y chromosomes, 183
Primordial germ cells, 79
Print, positive, 150-151
    contact printing, 150
    photographic enlarging, 150-151
    print developing, 151
Pulse labeling technique, 96, 99-100
Pure gonadal dysgenesis, 199-200

Quadrivalent, 86, 87, 89

Resolving power, 115-116, 120
  influence of light color upon, 116
Ring chromosomes
  D chromosome, 221
  X chromosome, 199

Satellites, 166, 175
Secondary constrictions of chromosomes,
    93-94, 166-170
  techniques, 166-170
Serum, 37, 59
Sex chromatin, 1-16
  in buccal smears, 4-8, 12-13
  correlation with sex chromosomes, 1,
    3, 13-16
  dimorphism, 2, 3, 13
  in germ cells, 79
  hypotonic solution effect on, 10-11
  importance of, 1
  incidence, 4, 7, 10, 12, 15-16
  in Klinefelter's syndrome, 15, 189-190
  morphology, 3-5, 12
  in mosaicism of sex chromosomes, 12-
    13
  multiple masses in females, 15-16, 207
    in males, 15-16, 192
  negative, 14, 79, 194, 196
  in neutrophils, 11-13, 207
  in newborns, 8
  in opossum, 3

origin, 2, 13-14
patterns, 14-16
positive, 14, 79, 189-190, 196, 198, 203
size, 5
techniques, 5-13
in true hermaphrodites, 203
in Turner's syndrome, 15, 194-199
in XXX syndrome, 15
Sex chromosomal abnormalities, 14-16, 188, 189-209
Sex chromosomes, correlation with sex chromatin, 1, 3, 13-16
Skin culture technique, 57-71
   biopsy, 63, 67-68
   maintenance, 64
   materials, 58-63
   medium, 60, 63
   preparation of slides, 65-66, 70-71
   primary cultures, 63-64, 68-69
   subcultures, 64-65, 69-70
   uses of, 57-58
Stains, 6-7, 9-11, 44-45, 63, 77, 105, 107, 162
Stein-Leventhal syndrome, chromosomes in, 233-234
Sturge-Weber syndrome, chromosomes in, 233-234
Squash technique, 52-53, 75-77, 100-102

Temperature, 38
Testicular feminization, 234
Testes
   differentiation, 207
   histology in Klinefelter's syndrome, 192
Tetraploidy, 229
Tetrasomy X, 207
Thymidine, 94
   tritiated, 94-95, 99
Translocation
   meiotic, analysis of, 86-89
   in mongolism, 213-217
   in partial trisomy B, 229-230
   in partial trisomy C, 229
   reciprocal, 86-89

in trisomy D_1 syndrome, 227
in trisomy 18 syndrome, 221
Triploidy, 228
Trisomy, double, 206, 220
Trisomy D_1 syndrome, 222-228
   dermatoglyphics, 224, 227
   hemoglobins in, 227, 228
   isochromosome D_1, 171, 224, 228
   maternal age effect, 224
   mosaicism, 227-228
   neutrophil abnormalities, 224, 227
   newborn incidence, 225
   partial trisomy, 227
   phenotype, 222, 224
   telocentric D_1, 171, 224, 228
   translocation carrier, 86, 88, 226-227
   trisomy D_1, regular, 224-225, 227
Trisomy 18 syndrome, 219-222
   dermatoglyphics, 220
   double trisomies, 220
   maternal age effect, 220
   mosaicism, 221-222
   newborn incidence, 220
   with normal karyotype, 222
   partial trisomy, 221
   phenotype, 219-220
   translocation, 221
   trisomy 18, regular, 219, 222
Trisomy G_1 syndrome, see Mongolism
Trisomy syndromes, 204-206, 210-228
Trisomy 21 syndrome, see Mongolism
Trisomy X syndrome, 204-206
   double trisomies, 206
   mosaicism, 205
   newborn incidence, 205
   offspring, 205
   partial trisomy X, 198-199, 205-206
   phenotype, 205
Trivalent, 86, 88
True hermaphroditism, 200-204
   XX, 203
   XX/XY, 203-204
   XX/XXY, 204
   XX/XXY/XXYYY, 204
Trypsin, 61, 81
Tuberculin, 36

Turner's syndrome, 194-199
  chromatin negative, 194-196
  chromatin positive, 196-199
  chromosome anomalies in, 195-199
  chromosome mosaicism in, 196-198
  fertility in, 198
  gonadal dysgenesis, 195
  gonadal histology, 195
  incidence of, 195
  isochromosome in, 198-199
  male, 234
  mosaicism in, 196-198
  in neonates, 195
  nomenclature, 194-195
  partial deletion of X chromosome,
      169, 198-199
  phenotype, 194-196
  XO group, 195-196

Ullrich's syndrome, 199

Waldenström macroglobulinemia, 232

X chromosome, see Chromosome and
    Late replicating chromosome

X monosomy, origin of, 196, see also
    Turner's syndrome
Xg^a antigen, 192, 196, 199
XO/XY mosaicism, 200-202, 204
XXX sex chromosome complement, 205
XXXX sex chromosome complement,
    207
XXXXX sex chromosome complement,
    207
XXXXY sex chromosome complement,
    192-193
XXXY sex chromosome complement,
    192-193
XXYY sex chromosome complement,
    207-208
XYY sex chromosome complement, 207

Y chromosome, see also Chromosome
  abnormalities, 207-209
  function, 207
  late replication, see Late replicating
      chromosomes
  mosaicism, 200-202, 204, 209
  numerical anomalies, 207-208
  partial deletion, 183, 209
  structural anomalies, 208-209